This book is a must-read if you want to...

- uncover the REAL Miss Bluebell with new insight and information never published before
- explore the fascinating story of her troupe, the Bluebell Girls, who captivated audiences for decades
- gain exclusive access to the personal stories and experiences of the main players, as told to a trusted Fleet Street journalist
- discover Miss Bluebell's own journey of hard graft, empowerment, ambition, and resilience in occupied France
- relive some of the milestones in the Bluebell Girls' history, and learn how they took the world by storm
- learn how the Bluebell Girls have influenced the dancing world
- immerse yourself in the glamour and decadence of Paris in the 1930s and 1940s
- delve into the fascinating history of the Folies Bergère – the entrepreneurs, musicians and performers who made it a global phenomenon.
- explore behind the scenes at the Lido in the heart of Paris, and how it became the home of the Bluebell Girls.

The Bluebell Story

A Tale of
Grit and Glamour

Sylvia Disley

First published in Great Britain in 2025
by Book Brilliance Publishing
265A Fir Tree Road, Epsom, Surrey, KT17 3LF
+44 (0)20 8641 5090
www.bookbrilliancepublishing.com
admin@bookbrilliancepublishing.com

© Copyright Sylvia Disley 2025

Photographs from Sylvia Disley's private collection.

The moral right of Sylvia Disley to be identified as
the author of this work has been asserted in accordance
with the Copyright, Designs and Patents Acts 1988.

All rights reserved. No part of this publication may be reproduced, stored in a retrieval system, or transmitted, in any form or by any means without the prior written permission of the publisher, nor be otherwise circulated in any form of binding or cover than that in which it is published and without similar condition being imposed on the subsequent purchaser.

A CIP catalogue record for this book is
available at the British Library.

ISBN 978-1-913770-95-2

This book is an unauthorised biography.
It reflects the author's present recollections of experiences over time, including interviews and research conducted by the author. Some names and characteristics have been changed, some events have been compressed, and some dialogue has been recreated.

Every effort has been made to trace copyright holders and to obtain their permission for the use of copyright material. The publisher apologises for any errors or omissions and would be grateful for notification of any corrections that should be incorporated in future reprints or editions of this book.

Dedicated to the Lido: Le plus célèbre cabaret du monde.

In the hope of its resurrection someday.

CONTENTS

Foreword 1
Introduction 3
The Lido 9
Unto Us 17
Vine Street Dancing Classes 35
The Hot Jocks 47
The Jackson Girls 61
The Folies Bergère 105
Marcel 121
The Bluebell Girls 141
Mistinguett 163
Red Stars, Beautiful Ladies and Paramount Girls 179
The Threat of War 197
Bluebell's Incarceration 225
Marcel's Flight 243
Bluebell Alone 253
Marcel Interned 267
Paris Again 275
Epilogue 311
Postscript 313
About the Author 315
Acknowledgements 317

FOREWORD

MARGARET 'BLUEBELL' Kelly's life is a story of vision, tenacity and sheer brilliance – a story that deserves to be known, shared and celebrated by everyone in the entertainment industry. As the founder of the world-renowned Bluebell Girls, Bluebell broke new ground and left an indelible mark on cabaret, creating a legacy that continues to inspire dancers, choreographers and performers to this day.

Her journey began in Dublin, but her influence quickly spread worldwide, especially in Paris, where the Bluebell Girls became the epitome of glamour and elegance at the Lido de Paris. Bluebell was not just a choreographer or a troupe manager; she was a trailblazer in every sense of the word. She took the idea of a showgirl – a role often overlooked – and elevated it into a celebrated art form, marked by precision, beauty and impeccable showmanship.

In an era when entertainment was largely controlled by men, Bluebell forged her path with unwavering determination. She hand-picked dancers not only for their grace and beauty, but for their discipline and work ethic, assembling a troupe that redefined the standards of stage performance. The Bluebell Girls became more than just a dance group – they became an institution, admired for their ability to blend artistry and spectacle in a way that had never been seen before.

The Bluebell Story captures the essence of Bluebell's remarkable life, not just the public persona of Miss Bluebell, but the woman behind the scenes who battled obstacles, faced challenges head-on, and stayed true to her vision of what performance could be. Her story is more than just the history of a troupe; it's a narrative of persistence, creativity and leadership that resonates with anyone striving to carve out their own space in the entertainment world.

Bluebell didn't just create opportunities for herself; she created a legacy that has opened doors for countless dancers and performers over the decades. Her work has inspired so many, including myself, and her life offers invaluable lessons about what it means to be a creator, a leader and an artist in the truest sense.

It's an honour to introduce this book, and I encourage every reader – whether you're a dancer, a performer or simply someone who loves stories of trailblazers – to fully immerse yourself in the extraordinary journey of Margaret 'Blubell' Kelly. Her life and legacy are a reminder that with passion, dedication and vision, one person can truly change the face of an entire industry.

Eddie Slattery
Choreographer, Dance Educator, and Performer

INTRODUCTION

How I Came To Write *The Bluebell Story*

THE SEED WAS PLANTED in 1959 when two women chose to take a ski holiday together in Switzerland. The younger woman, in her mid-twenties, was Eleanor Landreau, an up-and-coming fashion model in Paris. Her companion was Margaret Kelly, in her mid-forties, known as Miss Bluebell, choreographer and director of the Bluebell Girls at the Lido in Paris, the most celebrated cabaret in the world.

Socially, they were equals. Eleanor, a former Bluebell Girl herself, had married Jean-Pierre Landreau, the musical director of the Lido. Miss Bluebell had married Marcel Leibovici, the musical director of the Folies Bergère in which she had danced and where she had formed her first dance troupe.

As on all ski holidays, there were plenty of après-ski opportunities and the two women found themselves reminiscing about their shared time at the Lido over the odd glühwein or coffee provided in the resort. After one such occasion, Eleanor remarked on what an interesting life Miss Bluebell had led and suggested that someone should write her biography.

'I shall ask my sister, Sylvia, to write it,' she said. 'She's a journalist in Fleet Street but I am sure I can persuade her to come over to write it.'

So it was that I gave up my job in Fleet Street where I had worked successfully for fourteen years as a news reporter and feature writer on several national newspapers, to embark on her fascinating life story. Before I set off for to France, I called on George Greenfield, leading literary agent and good friend to John Le Carré and director of the Enid Blyton company, to see if he would represent me, to which he agreed. As I was leaving his office, he suggested I draw up a contract with Miss Bluebell. I regarded her as a friend and replied saying that a contract would not be required…

My first task was to invest in a portable tape recorder, still a relatively new invention in those days. Previous machines could hardly be lifted off the ground but, by 1960, I was able to purchase a Telefunken – a German model weighing in at a lightweight 21lbs! On top of that, I carried my trusty Olympia typewriter, a bag containing type paper, the manuscript as it grew, and personal baggage. And all by surface public transport to minimise costs. Needless to say, despite the 'modern' technology, by the time I had completed the final chapter, I had to go into hospital to have an operation to repair the damage to my hand due to carrying around such a heavy weight on six return trips to Paris!

I would stay six weeks at a time, in a commercial travellers' hotel in the cheapest district available. Every evening, I would cross Paris by Metro and bus to interview Miss Bluebell for two hours in her apartment. After our first two interviews, I stopped off at my sister Eleanor's flat to play the tape back to her.

'My word!' she said. 'You're having a hard time of it, aren't you?'

'It's like digging a field with a dinner fork!' I replied.

However, it soon became easier as Miss Bluebell's memories began to surface and things progressed smoothly for a while. It would take me most of the next day to type up the previous evening's interview, living on coffee and biscuits, before journeying back to interview her the following evening. However, one evening, her husband Marcel answered the door.

'Bluebell must rest!' he told me and so I retreated to my hotel.

The next night, he reiterated, 'Bluebell must rest!' and proceeded to pick up my tape recorder to hand it back to me. On feeling its weight, his expression changed.

'You poor girl!' he exclaimed, before continuing, 'Come in, I'll talk to you instead!'

There followed the first of several interviews with Marcel which were quite remarkable. In all my years in Fleet Street, I had never interviewed anyone with such a long and precise memory as his. Marcel was able to remember exact dates, events and even dialogue that were long forgotten by Miss Bluebell.

With his help, I was now able to piece together the many fascinating facts that made up her life and, moreover, their extraordinary wartime adventures together.

Further interviews followed with Paul Derval, director of the Folies Bergère, and Pierre-Louis Guérin, manager of the

Lido. During my many trips to Paris, I had the opportunity to watch the Lido show on several occasions. It was a spectacle that you could see many times without tiring.

On one occasion, Bluebell invited me to go with her and Marcel to their holiday home in the countryside about an hour's drive from Paris. The children were already there as it was half-term holiday. It was then that I discovered how fast Marcel drove but while I was sitting in the back seat not exactly enjoying a white-knuckle ride, Bluebell, being a non-driver, seemed quite relaxed and even said how well the car was going, unaware of the danger she was in. If Marcel had spent a few years in either Britain or America, his need for speed would have been cured. No police force in these countries would have allowed such excessive speed. A lot of speeding fines and even the loss of a driving licence might have cured Marcel.

Before leaving Paris, Miss Bluebell pointed me in the direction of a former Bluebell girl whom she thought might help me with my research. However, this woman refused outright to help me with the biography, having had a very different memory from Miss Bluebell's.

'I desperately needed help from Miss Bluebell once and she refused. So, no, I won't help you with her biography,' she told me. I didn't realise at the time, but she told me more about Miss Bluebell in five minutes than anyone else did.

I travelled to Liverpool to interview a dozen or so of the original Jackson Girls who were a cheerful and helpful bunch. They thoroughly enjoyed the chance to reunite and to remember their former dancing days, as well as to share their recollections of 'The Duchess,' as they nicknamed Miss Bluebell.

Introduction

Finally, I interviewed Alfred Jackson, another lively and cheerful character, at his home in Devon. The interview was so successful and Alfred enjoyed reminiscing about his former life so much that he and his wife, a former Jackson girl herself, invited me to stay the night. In the morning, I was awakened by Mrs Jackson carrying in a cup of tea, followed by Alfred playing the ukulele such was his happiness in remembering his show business life!

All of these valuable contributions were to create a multitude of transcripts which had to be carefully written up. Each event had to be dovetailed into the main story, literally cutting and pinning as I went along, as computers were still a long way from being invented. The whole project from start to finish took me two years. Further interviews were required for the final chapter and, keen to prompt any further memories, I sent the manuscript ahead of me for Miss Bluebell to read.

However, I was surprised to hear that Miss Bluebell said that she did not want this to be the story of M and Mme Leibovici. And for reasons I will never know, she refused to authorise this biography. Of course, without authorisation, publishers were reluctant to take on her story.

After Bluebell had received my completed manuscript and refused to authorise it despite how much it praised her achievements, she was approached by another author who asked if he could write her biography. Not only did she agree, but she gave him my manuscript.

I then had to act fast. I approached London's leading literary lawyer who not only wrote to her, but even went to Paris to reason with her. He demanded that she should return the manuscript to me but it was to no avail.

Bluebell then sent my manuscript to her agent in London, and said that I could collect it from his address. I went to his home at the appointed time, knocked on his door and rang the bell – no answer. I then went to the nearest telephone box and phoned him.

When he answered, he was furious that I had caught him out. I responded in like manner and threatened to call the police if he did not return my property to me. This seemed to work, as I finally received my manuscript from him.

Had he managed to copy any of it? I will never know.

On 30th July 2022, over twenty years after her death, the Lido finally closed its doors seventy-seven years since it first opened in 1946. Now, the truth behind this remarkable lady and the man she loved is yours to read.

Sylvia Disley

THE LIDO

THE LAST FEW COUPLES drift back to their tables. Waiters deftly lever corks from Champagne bottles and spill the vaporous wine into glasses, then silently steal away into red plush unobtrusiveness. A silent darkness falls over the *salle*[1] and even old regulars at the bar glance expectantly at their watches. The time, a few seconds before 11:25 pm. All heads turn to the black marble stage and darkened velvet curtains.

The orchestra of Paris' Lido Cabaret, *le plus célèbre cabaret du monde*[2], explodes into life rather than strikes up. Some say the sound is too great for the limited space. But then the same could be said of the spectacle seen there. *Multum in parvo*[3]. During the next hour or so, so much happens that the uninitiated mind boggles. Rain falls, an ice rink slides forward over the stage, a swimming pool is suddenly revealed, fountains play, ponies trot, seals bark, nudes laugh on swings over the

---
[1] French: room
[2] French: the most famous cabaret show in the world
[3] Latin: a great deal in a small space

audience or parade on glass catwalks above upturned faces, a vast waterfall cascades deafening water in its thousands of gallons, and one's senses are swamped by the rushing torrent, the music and black-lighting, while seemingly exotic girls from faraway places, dressed in fluorescent leaves, sway by.

The overture reaches its expected climax and the male singer in midnight blue walks on stage. Sixteen long-legged girls, with smooth chignons and high heels topping six feet tall, wait in the wings, wearing flame and yellow costumes. Their make-up is surprisingly discreet. For cabaret work, when the girls dance close to the audience, ordinary stage make-up is too bizarre. As the singer disappears to applause, another silence falls.

'Et maintenant, mesdames et messieurs, voici les Bluebell Girls!' [4]

Usually any show, especially a cabaret show, is built around one act, for which the audience generally has to wait until after the intermission. But at the Lido the acts are all equal in entertainment value, and the speciality is the Bluebell Girls. And they make their first appearance fast. The curtains part, revealing sixteen coloured panels. At a given moment in the music, they flick open and shut alternately, like greyhound traps, letting loose the girls hidden behind. At the end of the fast routine – the opening music is invariably fast – there is an organised scramble for the dressing room; a two-and-a-half-minute change (during the rehearsals, the girls were convinced they would never make it!) and they are back on stage again, although the first tableau is still in progress. Glamorous nudes and singers have filled the gap.

A stranger wandering backstage would not notice a forty-nine-year-old woman, fair-haired, quite slim and youthful in

---

[4] French: and now, ladies and gentlemen, here are the Bluebell Girls!

Interior of the Lido

build, standing in the wings behind a curtain, peering critically at the stage through a mesh window set at face-height in a drape of the curtain. From time to time, girls tear past her on their way to the stage or a dressing room. A nude pauses to ask her a question in French, to which the woman answers in French. One of the tall, blonde and beautiful Kessler Twins makes a remark to her in German, and the woman replies in German. She dresses like a Frenchwoman – a well-paid French businesswoman. Her clothes are expensively unpretentious, her hair is far too casually perfect to be home-set, and the dry flavour of her perfume is discreet. The interested observer might begin to wonder what nationality she is, for she speaks French with little attempt at a French accent, but eventually a tall, blonde and very 'soignée' dancer stops and speaks to her in English incongruously larded with a heavy Lancashire accent, and is answered by the woman in English with an Irish-Liverpool intonation.

When the first full-length act, an American comedian, comes on, the woman moves away and walks back to the dressing rooms. She moves like a dancer, or a duchess. Nobody ever sees her run. She passes by several dressing rooms, mostly with wide open doors. In a fast-moving cabaret, there is little time to close doors when the male and female dancers, nudes, soloists and acts are all trying to keep up with a tight schedule. It's the same with the stagehands: they have to be rehearsed with their split-second schedules quite as much as the performers when a new show is being prepared.

The woman walks into one of the dressing rooms.

'Well, what happened to you, Valerie? In the second number?'

Nobody else had noticed it.

'I'm sorry, Miss Bluebell,' the blonde replies. 'I had a blank for half a second.'

'Well, don't let it happen again. Get here early for tomorrow's rehearsal and I'll put you through it alone.'

The reminder of the following day's weekly rehearsal is met with groans in the room. They don't stop work until 2 am and some of them are usually asleep until three in the afternoon.

Ignoring the groans, Miss Bluebell turns to another girl, a newcomer who has come over from London the previous week. 'Your make-up is much better. Last week you looked like a Picasso painting.' And with this quip, she walks out and goes to her own private dressing room.

The show spins on. Each time the girls come on, Bluebell watches like a hawk from her hidden vantage point. During the evening, she goes forward to sit with a journalist in the auditorium. But she is soon back at her post. Every single artist who goes on to the Lido stage is under Miss Bluebell's direction, for she is backstage director, ballet mistress, manager and proprietor of the famous Bluebell Girls.

At the end of the second show, when the auditorium and dressing rooms have emptied, she walks alone once more along the corridor, across the shining black stage, up a spiral staircase flanked by white tiled walls, and out into the Lido Arcade which opens into the Champs Élysées. It takes her only a few minutes to cross the road to Rue Marbeuf, where she lives in a nine-roomed apartment on the fourth floor.

She lets herself in and within a few minutes is in bed, thinking over the work she has to do the following day: a rehearsal at nine o'clock with the new troupe leaving for Tokyo in a week's time, and remember to make sure she gets her own passport back from the Japanese Embassy… and mustn't forget her hair appointment at lunchtime… an hour with her secretary… when? Sometime. See two of her girls in her office after lunch about their contracts… oh and make sure Patrick meets the two new Lido girls at Le Bourget… leave for the Lido at 2:30 pm for the weekly rehearsal. However many hundreds of times a show plays, it can become untidy without rehearsals – like Valerie's blank tonight. What else? Oh yes, remember to contact Radio Television Française about Thursday's TV programme. What was it that reporter had said tonight?

'I am sure, Miss Bluebell, that you must have been born into a show business family. You can't keep going at such a pace if you hadn't.'

How wrong can you be?!

Like many others, she had built herself up into somebody quite different from the person she might have been. Where had it all started, and who was she anyway? Even she did not know. Nobody knew. It had all started a long time ago in a very untheatrical setting, far removed from the spotlights, Champagne bubbles, blare of dance orchestra and distinctive smell of greasepaint from the cabaret. Instead, it had begun in a darkened cathedral, with its lighted candles, thoughtful silence and smell of incense, when she was only two weeks old. Before that is a mystery. She would never know. Nobody would ever know.

UNTO US

FEW NEWBORN INFANTS could have caused more ructions in people's lives than did Margaret Kelly. Two weeks after her birth, on 24th June 1910, she was handed over by her teenage, red-haired Irish mother, also named Margaret Kelly, to a priest at Dublin's Roman Catholic Pro-Cathedral. The priest, Father Fricker, had arranged the fostering of the child by a spinster called Mary Murphy.

Mary Murphy had until then lived with her two sisters, Josephine and Agnes, and her brother Peadar, all unmarried. The arrival of the newborn baby into the home split up the Murphy family. In 1910, there was little enough to eat in most Irish homes; bringing in an extra mouth to feed when it wasn't one of your own was sheer foolhardiness. Peadar complained to Father Fricker, but Mary clung to the baby desperately.

Peadar subsequently left home and Mary, fearful that the baby's mother might change her mind and reclaim the child, had persuaded her sisters to emigrate to England. They agreed, and although Mary had not legally adopted the child, she and her two sisters took her away to live in Liverpool. Here the three women took all kinds of employment, from dressmaking to charring. Life was hard and there were far too many Irish immigrants trying for too few jobs on the mainland. After three months, Josephine and Mary decided to return to Dublin with the baby, leaving behind Agnes, who, during her short sojourn in Liverpool, had met and married a fellow Irish exile named George Kelly.

But life back in Dublin became just as difficult for the two remaining sisters. Without Peadar's income, which they had previously relied upon, they both had to go out to work, paying a neighbour to look after the four-month-old child, who in turn added to their troubles by becoming ill as a result of the inadequate diet she experienced in Liverpool. Apart from malnutrition, the child was suffering from German measles.

But it was not only an accurate diagnosis or correct prescription that their old family physician, Dr O'Connell, who had brought the entire Murphy family into the world, left with the baby that day in the tiny Dublin home. With his usual cheerful smile, the well-built and rosy-cheeked doctor strode into the little bedroom, took his first look at the baby, and said in his thick Irish brogue, 'Why, to be sure, if I had a little girl with those enormous blue eyes, I'd not be callin' her Margaret. I'd name her Bluebell.'

So it was that Margaret Kelly became Bluebell. It was typical of Mary Murphy's whimsical character that she should have taken up a suggestion like that. Bluebell herself never thought it odd. It was only later in life, when she met Americans called Earl, Duke, Chuck or Babe, they would say, 'Bluebell! My God, that's a funny name!'

Her illness at three months made life still harder for Mary and Jo. Mary stayed at home with her while Jo tried to be the breadwinner. But it did not work. Money was short and Mary was still afraid she might meet the baby's mother again. Eventually they returned to Liverpool. Agnes had written to say they could stay with her and George in their new home there.

Mary was grateful to have the promise of a secure home to go to at last, but her optimism was short-lived. When they reached the familiar docks, they scanned the crowds for a sign of either George or Agnes, but there was none. Puzzled, they went to their address, in Bridgeford Avenue, in the West Derby area of Liverpool. As they arrived, they saw men carrying furniture out of the house. George had lost his job and they had not been able to keep up the payments on the house and furniture. The bailiffs would only leave one table and one chair.

That night they all slept on the floor and as Mary settled herself down beside the child, oblivious of the tribulation around it, she said, 'Sure, you're a babe of doom, y'are.'

It was a struggle for all of them at first. The three sisters pulled together and found jobs – dressmaking, domestic work, anything they could get – until George found employment.

Bluebell was an additional burden. As time went by and other children of her age in the street were first crawling and then toddling about, it became clear she could not walk. A bone deficiency kept her chair-ridden. She sat in a chair or cot all day and had to be wheeled in a pushchair when they took her out.

She was still an invalid when once again the family split up, when she was two years old. By this time, Agnes had a baby boy of her own and was expecting another. It was not only the lack of space in their small terrace house but the shortage of money to feed the extra mouths that worried George. Mary, Jo and Bluebell had to go, and so, shortly after Bluebell's second birthday, Mary and the child moved into 48 Deysbrook Lane, West Derby, for which Mary paid four shillings and sixpence a week.

Soon after, Jo married an Irishman named James Kelly, who ran the smithy in the Dog and Gun area of Croxteth and they settled down in a small rented house nearby. Half the Murphys had now become Kellys, a name the baby had first introduced into the family.

Deysbrook Lane had more than one saving grace which prevented it from taking on the appearance of most of the poor areas or slums of Liverpool. It consisted of only one row of houses opposite a large field, the sports ground of St Francis Xavier's College for Boys. From upstairs, one could look right over the fields for miles. The terrace houses were about 200 years old, with bricks weathered almost black, and a distinct antique style of their own, unlike the red brick Liverpool tenements.

The terrace was comprised mainly of self-contained half-houses, four of which were grouped around an 'entry', a cobbled tunnel about ten yards long, burrowing straight through the building, so that people living in the rear could have their own separate entrance doors at the back. This tunnel, which perhaps to some of the district's more sensitive inhabitants seemed the epitome of the depressive nature of a slum, had many uses. Children played in it when it rained and it enabled coalmen to deliver coal through to the common backyard, which housed the washing lines, dustbins, maybe a patch of grass, the occasional discarded tin bath full of earth and imaginatively planted with a few flowers and, of course, the privy, the kind that had to be taken away from time to time and emptied.

There was no sanitation nor sewerage system in Deysbrook Lane, nor was there any form of gas or electricity. The house was lit by oil lamps, and cooking was done on a range or on the open grate. Water was brought in from an outside tap, to be heated on the fire or range to wash in, and for one's ablutions, a tin bowl was used. There was, of course, no bath, and throughout her childhood, Bluebell was taken to the public baths two or three times a week by the fastidious Mary. The home in which she lived throughout her early life had but one room downstairs with a small kitchen at the back and one bedroom upstairs, which she always shared with Aunt Mary, a lighted candle and a figurine of the Blessed Virgin.

They did not have much to do with the people in the other half of the house. All their neighbours were friendly enough, but it was such a hard-working district that nobody had time to be very sociable, except, of course, in times of hardship. Then, like the typical working-class northerners they were, all the neighbours would be willing to lend a helping hand. Many of the other housewives went out to work. When they all reached home in the evening, they would only just have time to clean their homes, get supper and go to bed early enough to wake first thing in the morning to go to work again. Life was a cycle of drudgery.

Mary had to join this cycle. There was little she was trained for, but she had some nursing experience, though she was unqualified. She found herself a job as a hospital help at the newly opened military medical facility, Alder Hey Hospital in West Derby. Here she kept the wards clean, helped the sisters take temperatures, sterilised equipment, and assisted patients to the bathroom and lavatory. Life was full, helping the patients by day and an invalid child at night. The hours were long, but with the child permanently chair-ridden, she could easily find a neighbour who would be willing, for a consideration, to look after her while she was out – she was less bother than a 'normal' child.

It seemed at times that it would be only through sheer luck that Bluebell would survive infancy. Much of her childhood was to be spent in hospitals. She was still unable to walk at the age of three and a half, when she was taken seriously ill with scarlet fever. Ultimately, she became too sick for Mary or any of the neighbours to nurse. Mary appealed to the church, who managed to gain admission for her at the Freshfield Sanatorium, a hospital for children, staffed by a nursing order of nuns, which had its premises in a large house near the coast. Here Bluebell remained for a whole year. Her resistance was so low by this time that the scarlet fever was soon followed by measles, whooping cough, and several other childhood ailments. But her year in hospital proved to be a blessing in disguise and probably the most crucial of her whole life. One nun, Sister Ursula, was devoted to her, and it was she who encouraged the child to take her first faltering steps. Neither at Agnes Kelly's house nor at Deysbrook Lane had anybody seriously tried to help her to walk. She herself had not made the effort, and the busy family had simply accepted it. There were not the clinics, as there would later be in Welfare State Britain, to take such a child.

Sister Ursula had infinite patience, because at times it seemed that Bluebell would never walk, and often the child cried because of the exertion. Standing, unaided, was as hard at first as walking. As soon as she had mastered the art of standing, walking followed suit. Eventually, she was able to haul herself around the ward holding the iron bars at the end of one bed and then tottering across to the next one, sometimes falling in between.

At the end of the year in the hospital, Bluebell could just walk, but after so many illnesses she was still very weak and had to be pushed in the same pushchair Mary had previously used when she took her home. Before she left the hospital, she caught a ringworm so all her golden ringlets were shaved off. Now she was being taken home wearing a bonnet over her shaved head, being pushed in a pushchair, and with a dummy in her mouth, although she was over four years old.

As they turned the corner of Deysbrook Lane, a neighbour stopped Mary, looked down at the child and said, 'Oh, I see you've a new baby. And how's young Bluebell? Is she out of hospital yet?'

The tears streamed down Mary's face when she had to admit 'This *is* Bluebell.'

From then on, the young Bluebell experienced a tough routine, which she was to remember for the rest of her life. In many ways, she felt it shaped her character and turned her into a hard and dogged fighter later on. Every morning Mary would get her up at half past six, give her a breakfast of tea with bread and butter, then sit her in a chair and go off to work at the hospital.

At half past eight, an older girl attending the Leyfield Convent School would call to take her to school, about fifteen minutes' walk away. The same girl brought her back from school, and Bluebell would eat her solitary lunch – a glass of milk, left covered with a saucer, and a slice of bread and butter, left between two plates. She would be collected again for afternoon school and returned home at half past four, where she would have to sit waiting, often in the cold, for Mary to return at half past seven. In the evening, they would have two boiled eggs and probably bread and butter and tea again. These were the days of the 1914–1918 war, but the only difference this made to their already meagre diet was that in addition to a lack of almost everything else, there was a total lack of jam. They only had meat once a week, on Sundays.

After Mary had done her housework, the day would end with a ritual fine-tooth-combing and curling up in rags of Bluebell's already naturally curly hair, joint prayers said aloud before the Blessed Virgin above the permanently-lit candle, and, at half past nine or ten, both would climb wearily into their beds, Bluebell having graduated from the iron-sided cot which she had occupied during her early invalid infancy.

Throughout the whole of her childhood, she had very few toys; now and then a ball to play with, but no dolls. Considering herself a 'tomboy', she envied children in the neighbourhood who had bicycles and especially those from the better-off districts who trotted by on ponies. She never craved such things for herself but would have loved to have the chance to have a ride on one.

The near-starvation diet, together with the long hours of hard work she had to do at the hospital, not earning anything like the wages the nurses received because she was unqualified, had their effect on Mary, and when Spanish influenza swept through an exhausted Britain after the war, Mary was among the first to succumb to it. It was one of the most frightening experiences of her childhood when Bluebell came home to find Mary lying ill in bed, for she had never seen her resilient aunt sick before. Their closest neighbour, Mrs Humphries, the widow who lived on the other side of their communal entry, was there with her, and as soon as Bluebell arrived, she was told to run to the doctor's as fast as she could. She rushed outside, then skidded to a standstill on the path.

Suddenly she realised what might happen to her if she lost Aunt Mary. Mary had often threatened, when she was naughty, to send her back to her mother in Ireland, to the church, to a convent, or an orphanage. Although she did not know it at the time, these were mere empty threats, used to enforce discipline. In her Irish temper, Mary had used the fact that Bluebell was adopted whenever she needed to discipline her, and it had worked.

Bluebell sat on the front step and cried bitterly, not daring to leave her aunt even to go to the doctor's. For her compassion, she received only a scolding from Mrs Humphries when she looked out of the door some minutes later to see if the doctor was coming, only to find Bluebell still crying there.

The thought of being sent back to her real mother genuinely terrified her. She had one recurrent dream – that her own parents had come to fetch her and that she did not want to go with them. In every dream her mother was a tall, good-looking woman with red hair, for that was how she had been described to her.

Bluebell never missed having a real mother or anyone to call mother, and the lack of a father never even occurred to her. But she would have liked to have had a brother to look after her, and later envied girl friends who went off to their first dance escorted by their brothers.

Later on in life she learnt that had Mary really wished to be rid of her, she had ample opportunities. As a toddler, Bluebell was pretty, and several couples had offered to adopt her. But Mary would never let her go, though often Agnes, George and Josephine urged her to do so, pointing out to her the advantages the child would have, the security and the better chances in life.

After her five-week illness, Mary never again attained her former wiry fitness and, although she was only in her late thirties, her blonde hair turned dead white.

Bluebell's foster mother was considered by many locals to be the most outlandish person in the district and yet also a woman with such an innate humility that any pleasures she experienced had to be selfless ones. Certainly, Mary was tougher than her family thought she was. Housekeeping for four adults back in Dublin could not have been easy, in addition to her voluntary work with the church. She was a woman who liked nothing better than to feel people depended on her for their physical comfort. Perhaps there was a nagging fear that her family in Dublin, who depended on her so much, might disintegrate one day. This might have made her precipitate the event by readily accepting a baby who caused that very disintegration, but who would repay her by being dependent on her for years to come.

A child without the ties of marriage was Mary's idea of bliss, for in her outlook, she was quite sexless. There were no men and women in Mary's life. They were all 'people'. She once said, 'There has to be someone like me or else there would not be anyone to take other people's children to school or look after them when their parents are sick.'

Perhaps it was the recognition of this quality in Mary which prompted Fr Fricker to give the baby to her in the first place, as much to gratify her needs as the child's. How often he must have had cause to bless the Mary Murphys of this world; their whole existence one of giving and serving and never asking for any more in return than the right to do so.

Yet like so many humble people, her personality, such as it was, broke out in certain obvious ways. The flashpoint of her temper was very low. She often threw things at Bluebell when she was naughty and she could be the very devil for causing trouble among the family. The colour of her Irish personality revolted at her drab existence, displaying its mutiny in the clothes she wore – children's sandals; brilliant red, blue or green ankle socks; her skirt, coat and gloves always in different and often clashing colours.

In the privacy of her bedroom she wore bright red or green pyjamas, and everything in her home, even the brass bedsteads, was painted pale blue. She wore her white hair straight with a fringe and the whole family knew that the blue-tinted spectacles she wore were for effect, rather than for any clinical reasons. With her childlike spirit, Mary Murphy never aged in forty years.

Now that she could walk and even run, Bluebell enjoyed a childhood that developed along more normal lines, as far as her life with Aunt Mary could ever be called normal. She was never without scrapes on her knees from racing through the fields and leaping ditches, climbing trees, jumping over ropes and playing hopscotch with other local kids, and many were the times they were caught orchard-scrumping by irate landowners and led smartly out of forbidden territory by the ear. She preferred playing with the local boys, climbing trees, playing football or rounders at the West Derby Recreation Ground in Mill Lane, or teasing the ducks on the farm pond near Aunt Jo's place.

Frequently, the frilly and inevitably blue dresses Mary made for her were torn. Most of her tomboyish escapades happened after she had been taken home from school at half past four to await Mary to return home from the hospital at half past seven. Three hours can hold much adventure for an active child left on her own.

She adored her cousins George and Cyril, her aunt Agnes' two boys, and they often used to play football and cricket in the street together until the police came to disperse them. From the time they used to make the twelve-mile train journey out to the Freshfield Hospital with their mother, Agnes, to visit Bluebell when she could not walk, they were her closest playmates. Many were the times they had to be hurried away from the hospital for 'over-exciting' her.

Now it was she who led them in many of their vagaries, ganging up with other kids, fighting over and sharing out among themselves rare treasures such as the few pairs of roller skates that came their way. With one on at a time, they would have to content themselves with three-legged skating races. Pushing with one leg and skating on the other, they would travel at top speed down Whitby Street where her cousins lived, then tear into Simms Road, at the end of which was a tunnel leading to the Tuebrook Packing Case Company. Straight into the tunnel they would go, and the watchman spent half his life chasing them out again.

Bluebell was always 'one of the boys' and whenever the Kellys came to visit, Uncle George, the two boys and Bluebell frequently ended up in the tiny backyard playing cricket, with Uncle George bowling diagonally across the yard which was so small that more often than not the ball would be batted over the high brick wall into the foundry beyond, and Cyril or George Junior would have to fight Bluebell to decide who was to have the honour of climbing the wall to get it. If she won, she invariably tore her frilly dress and frothy knickers on the high rough red brick wall before Aunt Mary could rush out to stop her.

Sometimes, at Mary's behest, Bluebell would play with the children from the better homes in the district, to 'elevate your social status, dear'. But Bluebell preferred the kids from the poorer homes because they were more fun, and, to her, more real, more adult and in closer contact with real life. Anyway, the girls from the better homes were too much like little ladies for her and never climbed trees.

But however much Bluebell became 'one of the kids,' Mary Murphy always tried to set her apart from the rest. The frilly clothes she made for her brought her criticism from the nuns at school. Often, they would make her stand up in class and say, 'Now look at Margaret Kelly. Her dresses are far too short,' and she would wish fervently that Mary did not always make her appear so different from the other children. Her silk and fine lawn dresses belied their living conditions at home and their diet of bread and butter and tea. Food which one ate in the privacy of one's home could not be seen, clothes could, was the maxim by which Mary lived.

Nor would Mary let her do any housework. Bluebell must always be a 'little lady'. Such things were 'beneath' her. Mary seemed to have the idea that Bluebell was well-born and should be brought up accordingly, whatever their means. As an excuse to prevent her from helping in the house, Mary would say she wanted her to keep her hands 'nice' to be a dancer, and should never let them be soiled by housework.

'Like', said Josephine drily, 'the poor Chinese classes binding their daughters' feet and growing their nails in the hope they'll marry well.'

Often, when Mary was out, Bluebell got out the cleaning rags. She loved cleaning the letterbox and knocker with metal polish, and washing down the surrounding paintwork afterwards which was inevitably smeared with polish. She would whiten the steps going down to the small front garden, and redden the top step, and black-lead the range. But Mary was always unhappy when she came home and found out, and sometimes became so angry with her when she persisted that eventually Bluebell gave up attempting to help. So Mary came home each day from a hard day's work and did all the housework, because Bluebell knew she would not have it any other way.

For the rest of her life, apart from the war years, Bluebell never did any housework. She never learnt to cook, and never cleaned a room. In that respect only did her childhood compare with her later life, and her hands remained as perfect and youthful as they were when she first started to dance.

In many other ways Bluebell found herself different from the other children, always due to Mary's eccentricities. The very name Bluebell which Mary, with her special Irish character and humour, had accepted with such alacrity from Dr O'Connell, regularly caused ructions at Leyfield Convent. One teacher, especially, would bang her desk and shout, 'No pet names, PLEASE!' whenever she heard another child call her Bluebell.

At school she had to be Margaret, but as soon as they ran out into the playground the kids would all yell outrageous nicknames at each other, with the others frequently calling out to her 'Bluebell Kelly, with the India-rubber belly', a cross which most Liverpool children called Kelly had to bear.

Like most Catholics, she was confirmed early. But here again she found herself set apart from the other children, once more due to Mary. Every year she would take part in the festivals of certain saints, walking in the processions of children all dressed in white, and sometimes leading the other children in these rituals in West Derby. She was confirmed, along with a number of other girls, on the Feast of St Veronica. Appropriately, all the other girls had chosen Veronica as their new saint's name. The Archbishop of Liverpool, Frederick William Keating, a rather austere and impressive man, came to St Paul's in West Derby to confirm the children. Bluebell knelt with all the other girls before him. Monotonously he began to read out the chosen names of the girls in the first row, nodding at them as he did so.

'Veronica, Veronica, Veronica, Veronica, Veronica, Veronica, Veronica, Veronica, Ver…' – a pause.

He adjusted his spectacles and looked again at his papers. Then, glaring at Bluebell, he said loudly, 'Sylvia Ursula'.

There was a rustle of white silk and titters. She closed her eyes hard, her face a blazing contrast to her white silk dress. *Trust Mary to make me different from everyone else again*, she thought. There were, however, good reasons for the names; Ursula was, of course, the name of the gentle nun who had first helped Bluebell to walk. And Sylvia was, quite simply, Mary's favourite name.

Life was to become still harder for Aunt Mary. James Kelly, Jo's husband, had died soon after the First World War as a result of his war experiences in France. Jo had lived a tough life since her marriage, working as a grave digger in the local cemetery during the war years, and soon she became subject to epileptic fits. She died soon after her husband and after the funeral, Bluebell found she had a little 'sister'.

Eagerly, Mary had taken in her orphaned niece, Kathleen, Jo's daughter, who was still only a toddler. Bluebell enjoyed having a small companion, for it made the home more like a family, and Aunt Mary soon began cutting up Bluebell's old clothes and making similar pretty dresses for Kathleen.

But another child to feed was too much for Mary. She had hardly enough money to feed herself and Bluebell. Kathleen brought them down to less than starvation level. After two months, Mary had to seek help again from the church, finding through the priest, just as Bluebell's own mother had done, a Catholic family to take in Kathleen. The adoption caused uproar in Mary's family.

'How could you have your own flesh and blood adopted by a stranger, while you keep an unrelated child in the house?' Mary was asked more than once by the rest of the family.

But Mary closed her mind to the happiness another little girl could have brought her, if only she had more money, just as she closed her mind also to frequent reminders that she could have had Bluebell adopted for the same good reasons and with equal facility earlier on.

Since so much of her childhood was spent in hospital, Bluebell's schooling was erratic, at best. As she had been 'smuggled' from Dublin, and was not officially adopted, she was never on an official register in England. In fact, she could have stayed away from school all the time simply because, officially, she did not exist. The school board in the district was quite strict with the other children. Frequently, other parents could be heard on the doorsteps of Deysbrook Lane complaining: *Why does Bluebell Kelly stay away from school without trouble while my boy's been away for only two days and here you are, always at my door? Answer me that.*

It was a question the school attendance officers found hard to answer and sometimes, as a result of neighbours' complaints, representatives of the school board would call on Mary Murphy, who always gave the stock answer: 'She hasn't been well, but she's going back tomorrow.'

And back tomorrow Bluebell would go, with a bunch of flowers for the teacher from their small front garden, and sometimes from somebody else's!

But now there was another reason for her frequent absences from school, where she was always bottom of the class, and in which, with monotonous regularity, she came last in the annual examinations for promotion to the next form. For Mary kept true to her promise to the doctor at the children's hospital, who had recommended, as a result of Bluebell's bone weakness, that she should take up some form of exercise. She decided that Bluebell should learn to dance, a most unusual thing for any West Derby child to do. She would have to travel to Liverpool for her instruction.

Young Margaret 'Bluebell' Kelly

VINE STREET DANCING CLASSES

SO IT WAS THAT SHE began the only training that was to bring a future livelihood, not only to her, but to Mary and to thousands of others. The school she attended was in Vine Street, Liverpool, owned and run by Madame Lilian Cummings (in private life, Mrs Fothergill, wife of a Liverpool policeman). As regularly as Bluebell was at the bottom of the class at the convent, so was she at the top of the class at the dance school.

She thought the world of Madame Cummings, a handsome, sporty type of woman of about thirty, with an open face. She was tall, with a very good figure; short dark hair and dark eyes. She always wore black for her classes: black tights and a black leotard. The standard of instruction was not as high as it would be at a leading London school, but Madame Cummings believed in providing a broad and varied background and tried to introduce her pupils to every type of dance. If there were any pupils who did not work hard, she would merely suggest to their mothers that they should be removed from the school. She had tremendous authority with children, in a very likeable way, and was never known to punish any of them. All her regular pupils gladly worked hard for her.

Although it was considered quite a big thing for Bluebell, a kid from Deysbrook Lane, West Derby, to be attending a Liverpool dancing school, the establishment was by no means grand. It was definitely one of the poorer districts, with its long lines of red brick terrace houses spilling their steps straight down on to the pavements which swarmed with dirty kids who played around the iron railings which shielded the basements in which so many of them lived.

But to Bluebell, the small hall which Madame Cummings hired for her school could have been the Covent Garden Opera House. Excitement built up in her every time she approached it. In fact, it was only twelve paces by eighteen, with four darkened oak beams in the vaulted ceiling. A stage was at one end, but the classes were held in the 'auditorium'. There were dressing rooms backstage, for all the world like a real theatre. The grubby cream walls were decorated only with gas lamps, which lit the hall in wintertime and ventilators near the floor made of parquetry provided the one incongruously elegant touch to the otherwise dingy décor, *rather like a tramp wearing spats*, Bluebell thought.

Bluebell soon became an exhibition pupil and was frequently called upon to demonstrate to new pupils who had been brought for auditions by their often sumptuously dressed mothers. Once fired with an enthusiasm for dancing, her capacity to work tremendously hard, compared with even the other industrious northern children at the school, served her well.

At last she had found her calling and was completely dedicated to it from the start. She seemed to have all the natural attributes necessary for a dancer – a sense of rhythm, timing, good lungs, and, in spite of a life-long meagre diet, a surprisingly good and sturdy build, which improved the more she danced. She was neither overweight nor skinny but had good strong muscles with no surplus fat on them at all.

To begin with, her one physical fault was a lack of strength in the ankles, the last remaining legacy from her invalid infancy. Eventually, practice eradicated this deficiency too, and the only remaining weakness from her early days, which turned out to be a great attribute to her dancing, was an almost freakish elasticity not normally associated with strong bones.

She was a good kicker and could do the splits, even front splits (while other children had to be taught by sliding into position with their feet on trays!), and she could hold her leg high above her head. She adored any form of acrobatics, chiefly because it all came so easily to her. This did not prevent her, sometimes, from aching in every limb after a hard lesson. With each new movement, another muscle was born, or so it seemed, and it was all she could do at times to climb on to the tram afterwards to go home.

Everyone at the convent, including the staff, took her absences for dancing classes for granted, as they had for her illnesses, which were now becoming less frequent, and soon she was organising her own little troupe among her school friends, teaching them what she knew about dancing, and running her own small concerts for charity at the convent or at the Alder Hey Hospital. From the age of eight she became a troupe leader and loved to make up little dances with balloons or fans as props, with Mary acting as her more-than-willing stage manager.

Despite her Catholic background, which could have made her disapprove of girls going on stage, Mary's greatest desire was to see Bluebell in the theatre. But neither she nor Bluebell believed that it was possible. Like most poor people, they thought all good things, even work that one enjoyed, was forbidden to them, believing that people needed to be rich to get on the stage in the first place. They used to go to the theatre in Liverpool, sit in the gallery admiring famous dancers and actors, and wish desperately that they were wealthy enough for Bluebell to work in such a place. Such stars, they assumed, must have started off by being very rich, and taken up stage work in the same way people took up some costly sport they liked doing, such as big game hunting.

As they lived from hand to mouth all the time, Bluebell never did the things she would have liked to do. Had there been the money, her ambition would have been to go to a ballet school and then, if possible, into a ballet company, like Sadler's Wells. Her ultimate height, just over 5ft 4½ inches, would have been a good height for a ballet dancer, neither too short nor too tall, and the hard work of a serious ballet school would not have deterred her.

Eventually she became a scholarship pupil at Vine Street Dancing School, which meant that, in addition to her ordinary classes, she was given free private tuition. Even so, the 12/6d a term for class tuition made quite a hole in the salary Mary earned, not to mention the provision of dancing shoes. On top of this, Mary would have to make Bluebell's practice dresses too.

Now the small living room in Deysbrook Lane, which served in turn as dining room, living room and kitchen, also became a practice and work room. A table or chair was used as a barre for exercises, while Mary machined away at new dance outfits. Mary delighted in the new steps Bluebell learnt, each of which were shown to her to the accompaniment of the gramophone. Often Mary rushed round to the Kellys to tell them all about it, sometimes hitching up her skirts to demonstrate the steps herself, only to be told, 'For goodness' sake, act your age, Mary!'

At all the displays, Mary was by far the most enthusiastic mother present, though she hid her pride from Bluebell. Afterwards, she would often say, 'Wasn't little Diane good?' or 'Susan was lovely, wasn't she?' Bluebell often wondered, *What does she think of me?* Mary did it to spur her on, though privately she bragged to all the neighbours about her child. Her tactics had the desired effect. Bluebell worked harder still, in the hope of gaining a word of praise from Mary, which never came.

Dance classes in the city made Bluebell notice one thing about Mary which had not been obvious to her in West Derby. The dance school was a half-hour tram journey plus a quarter of an hour's walk away, and Mary usually came to fetch Bluebell after lessons. Bluebell was one of the smartest little girls in the school, always wearing a red riding hood over her frilly dress for the journey to Liverpool.

In her childishness, she could not understand why Mary herself looked so different from the other mothers, who wore fur coats, heavy make-up and chunky jewellery when they drove in their cars to pick up their little girls. By contrast, Mary's thin figure was always pathetically and shabbily dressed more like an underpaid nanny collecting somebody else's well-off daughter.

And although Bluebell did not worry about not driving home in a car, she often asked her aunt why she did not have a fur coat like the other mothers. Because they looked so different, she tried to persuade Mary not to come to collect her, but Mary, undaunted, not only came, but would make herself painfully obvious by climbing onto a chair and peering through a glass panel above the door to see what the class was doing.

Every six months the school gave a concert, which involved rehearsals and more time off from the convent. Although Bluebell had now managed to become one of their best dancers and often had to perform solos, Mary's money did not run to the extravagant and sometimes flamboyant costumes the other little girls wore for such occasions. Some had fairy lights, lit by a small battery concealed in their dresses, sprinkled among their frilly skirts. A few mothers even dyed their child's hair blonde and red to make them stand out. Mary would sit up into the night machining and sewing costumes for the many items in each concert – ranging from Irish jigs to Spanish flamencos to classical ballet and to tap routines.

Bluebell's solos varied from singing 'Oh! What a Difference The Navy's Made to Me!' to dancing a hornpipe to Spanish and Eastern dances. The Vine Street Dancing School concerts were held in Liverpool's Crane Hall (now known as the Epstein Hall). Their productions were not unlike those given by thousands of other small schools throughout the country – the result of months of hard work, not a few tears, and plenty of stage nerves.

Working life comes early to the poorer classes with the rent man knocking regularly on the door and food going up in price. There were not many things that Bluebell had not tried to do to put more money into Mary's purse. She had done her share of rising at 5 am to walk five miles to a farm where she would be paid 3/6d for a day's potato pulling, a back-breaking job if ever there was one. In addition, for several years she was the most popular and inefficient caddy at the prestigious West Derby Golf Club, which was ten minutes, three ditches and several fields away from Deysbrook Lane.

Mary did not approve, but she could hardly object, for sometimes Bluebell would earn five shillings in an evening – two shillings a game and a sixpence or even a nine-pence tip on top for each game. She gave it all to Mary, who needed the money more than ever now because she had removed Bluebell from the convent, not without some ignominy, and was sending her to a private school. Bluebell had been accused by a teacher at the convent of talking during class. Bluebell, who, even as a child, had never told a lie, insisted that she had not. The teacher had lost her temper and thrown a book at her, hitting Bluebell in the eye. Consequently, Mary had swept into the Mother Superior's study and taken her child away for good.

Bluebell felt out of place at the select private school, among children from the better-off districts of West Derby, and her Deysbrook Lane Bolshevism came to the fore when, one day, a rather pompous little girl called Carol came to school and proudly showed off her new panama hat.

'Three guineas it cost!' she announced. 'Three whole guineas!'

Seeing that the other children were all feigning disinterest, she added, 'And you can do anything with it. Absolutely anything!'

'Give it to me, then,' Bluebell said, and took the hat.

She grasped it in both hands and pulled it in opposite directions as hard as she could until the material gave. Then she scrunched it up in her fists. Finally, she thrust the now dilapidated hat on a chair and bounced on it.

Why had she done this? Was it a revolt against her own drab existence, she wondered? She picked up the remains and realised the enormity of what she had done. Silently she handed back the hat to the equally amazed and silent

Carol. Then she turned and fled, running blindly and crying brokenly all the way home. She confessed immediately to Mary, who boxed her ears, but when Carol's mother called, she was surprisingly cheerful.

'You've done what I couldn't do!' she told Bluebell. 'Carol's always boasting about her clothes, but this seems to have cured her.'

And she did not claim the three guineas, which was just as well as it would have taken a month's wages for Mary to pay it back.

Only on one occasion, as a child, did Bluebell decide that silence, instead of the bare-faced truth, would be the better policy, and it wasn't.

One Sunday, having overslept, she missed Mass. Wishing to avoid the penalty of having to say her rosary as penance, she decided not to mention this at her confession the following Saturday. As she had no other sins to declare that week, she was only given three Hail Marys to say, but while she was saying them, she was called back into the confessional. There she received a long lecture for not confessing her omitted sin and was given two rosaries to say. Dutifully, she went out and said them, even though the priest was not watching, for surely, he was blessed with omniscience, just like God. On the way home, she decided to tell Mary about this miracle.

'Well of course he knew,' Mary replied briskly. 'I told him in my confession. I'm responsible for you, so it was my fault you didn't go to Mass.'

The truth will out. It was a lesson Bluebell was never to forget.

To the average child, Christmas and holidays are the two highlights of the year. But to many working-class children in those days, the first was a toy-less and sometimes even joyless festival and the second non-existent. Bluebell had no holidays, though on rare occasions she and Mary would go for the afternoon to New Brighton on the Wirral, the nearest seaside resort to Liverpool. It meant taking the fifteen-minute walk to West Derby village to catch the tram which never seemed to come. They would hop from one foot to the other impatiently while waiting in the centre of the village square by the old village stocks and the drinking fountain, constructed defiantly opposite The Sefton Arms and The Hare and Hounds and inscribed 'Water is Best. The Gift of Richard Robert Meade-King, 1894.'

Eventually the tram would come clanging along by the courthouse and W. Brooks & Co., the grocers where Aunt Mary always shopped because it was the respectable place to do so, whereupon it would stop with a screech and turn around. Then would follow a three-quarter of an hour ride to the pier head, a twenty-minute boat trip to New Brighton, where they would stay on the sands, eat their packed sandwiches and have a hot or cold drink, before the time came, all too soon, to get the boat back. A trip to New Brighton was regarded with such excitement that they would talk about it for weeks beforehand and weeks after the great day.

So it was with an excitement amounting almost to fever pitch that they heard one day that as one of Madame Cummings' six best pupils, Bluebell was picked to play a month's pantomime season in Torquay and Newquay on the south coast. The girls would be called The Little Darlings, and included Effie, a plump girl of fourteen who would turn out to be very influential in Bluebell's life.

Mary was delighted. Her Bluebell travelling all the way to the far south-west and dancing with a professional company!

What would the neighbours say? Especially those who had made it plain that in Mary's circumstances dance classes had been a downright extravagance. Here was the career Mary had imagined for her child. She was even going to get paid for it – five shillings a week, and all expenses found!

Uncle George disapproved but gruffly took the child to the local Co-op store and bought her shoes and an overcoat. Eventually, the big day came and they were all seen off at the station, where Bluebell had to duck down as she passed the ticket office because, although the youngest in the troupe, she was also the tallest and had to make herself look smaller so as not to attract attention. The trip was made on a shoestring and all the girls travelled half-fare.

The theatres they played in Torquay and Newquay were very small, more like church or civic reception halls, but for Bluebell, who had long dreamed of being 'on the boards', and always thought it an impossibility, this was the real thing. She watched the principals from the side of the stage at every spare moment during each show and thought how wonderful it was to see true professionals at work. The troupe stayed in genuine theatrical digs and used real theatrical dressing rooms. She picked up a great many tips in those two little theatres, and between shows and rehearsals enjoyed her first stay at a seaside resort, playing rounders on the sands with the other children and hide-and-seek in the coves as if it were midsummer instead of midwinter.

Mary wrote every day, and out of her five shillings a week Bluebell sent home two and sixpence by postal order. With the money she had left over at the end of the first week, she kept a pledge she had made to herself from the time she had been a little girl – that with her first week's wages, she would buy herself a whole tin of evaporated milk, the kind of which, as a small child, she had sneaked sips from Aunt Mary's pantry when she was hungry. Proudly, she bore her tin home and drank the lot. She never craved it again as it quenched her childhood thirst.

It seemed almost an anti-climax to go back to her private school in West Derby after this first taste of professional life. But she had to resign herself to the fact that perhaps it would be the only such experience she would have. Bluebell listened with envy to Effie, as she announced that she had landed a job with a regular touring company.

THE HOT JOCKS

AT THE END OF 1924, aged fourteen, Bluebell left school. A week later, she was practising alone at the barre in the dancing school and dismally wondering what she should do. Should she try child nursing, for which she felt totally unsuited, or should she be a hospital help, like Aunt Mary?

She had to get a job quickly, within a matter of days if possible. The cost of living seemed always a little higher than Mary's pay. Their rent had gone up to six shillings a week and she felt she could no longer be dependent on her aunt.

Oh well, she thought, *when one door closes, another door always opens...*

The door burst open. It was Effie! But not the plump fourteen-year-old from a few months ago who had danced with Bluebell in Torquay. This was an adult Effie, a complete theatrical, even wearing lipstick.

'Well, Bluebell! And what are you doing these days?'

'Nothing,' Bluebell responded, and told her gloomily about her position. 'I left school last week. I have to get a job, but I'm not any good at anything.'

Effie laughed.

'You're joking, of course. Well, consider this your red-letter day. You're going to join the Hot Jocks and come on tour with me.'

Effie explained that the Hot Jocks were a Scottish touring party she had joined. While Bluebell changed, Effie perched herself on the narrow form against the wall of the dressing room and, leaning her back against the cushion of the children's overcoats, which hung there eternally, she explained.

'There's a vacancy in the chorus. They need somebody quite urgently. All I'd have to say is that you are from the Vine Street Dancing School, and one of their best-ever pupils at that, and tell them what you're like, and you're in. They'd take you without an audition, too, because they're on tour right now and won't be able to come here to see you. I'm on a week's holiday at present, but I can write to them and fix it up if you're willing. What d'you think?'

'It's Aunt Mary,' Bluebell said, pulling on her frilly dress and ankle socks. 'If she says yes, I'm all for it – you know that.'

'Done!' said Effie, standing up and going to the door. 'Oh, just one thing. If you wear those clothes, they'll think you're still a juvenile and not take you. Better get some more grown-up things – and stockings too. Are you here tomorrow? Let me know what your aunt says, and I'll write immediately. Oh and bring a photograph of yourself that I can send them too.'

Aunt Mary's yes came almost before Bluebell had finished telling her about it, and the next day she arranged time off from work so that she could go to the dance school with Bluebell to meet Effie. Final details were arranged, and Mary was reluctantly convinced that Bluebell's dresses must be lengthened. By the following weekend, Bluebell went to the Vine Street Dancing School to be told by a triumphant Effie that she was to leave for Scotland with her within three days.

Bluebell realised her dancing school days were now at an end and her years of learning just beginning. With almost a feeling of nostalgia, she had her final private lesson with Madame Cummings, who had, without too much show of it, returned the mutual feeling of respect. Theirs had been a worthwhile alliance. Bluebell had started at her school while still a physically disabled infant, and although their friendship had never transcended the normal teacher-pupil relationship, Madame Cummings was understandably proud of Bluebell's metamorphosis from sickly child to qualified dancer. She was to see very little of Madame Cummings after that lesson. The tall, handsome and statuesque dance teacher, who had been devoted to her husband and dance school, and who had never had a family, died in childbirth not many months later.

From the day Effie first broached the idea of Bluebell joining the Hot Jocks touring company, life in Deysbrook Lane was hectic. Bluebell met Effie regularly and lapped up any instructions the more experienced girl could give her before she left.

After one of these meetings, Bluebell barged into Mary's kitchen and said, 'I have to buy some make-up. Effie says so.'

'What'll you need?' asked Mary.

Up until then, the only cosmetic she had provided for her appearances in the Crane Hall concerts was an occasional lipstick, which she bought for threepence from Woolworths.

'I'll need at least two greasepaints – 5 and 9,' she added, referring to the numbers of two greasepaints all stage folk had at the time.

'Five and ninepence!' exclaimed Mary. 'That's an awful lot of money to spend on your face!'

Within a few days, carrying one small attaché case containing all her personal belongings, with a grey artificial astrakhan false hem sewn on to her childish reefer coat and wearing her first pair of adult stockings, Bluebell set off from Liverpool Central Station for Scotland. She left behind a family furore the like of which had not been seen since Mary had first taken Bluebell in fourteen years previously. Uncle George was furious, accusing Mary of allowing the girl to go to her 'destruction and dissolution'. George was fond of Bluebell and had always looked upon her as one of his own children. At that time, many people in the north of England thought touring parties were no better than travelling brothels. Mary did not let George know that she too had been anxious and had carefully checked on the Hot Jocks company, closely questioning Effie. But they were to be the last words George was to speak to Mary for a whole year, the longest and loneliest of Mary's life.

Just as the centre of a cyclone is its only calm spot, so was Bluebell, now tranquil and at peace with the world. During the train journey from Liverpool to Dunfermline, the forerunner of hundreds of other rail journeys she was to make, she knew for the first time where she was going.

There followed two of the happiest and most energetic years of Bluebell's early career. She was too young to have stage nerves, and everything was new to her. She had no idea how to apply make-up and simply picked up the art by watching the girls sitting next to her at the dressing room mirror.

She started in Dunfermline and was the baby of a show the dour Scottish audiences enjoyed. In one of her first letters home to Mary, she wrote, 'The other girls are much older than I am. Some of them are quite elderly – nineteen, twenty and one is even twenty-four!'

But they were pleasant girls. Bluebell was the only new girl in the company at that time and was rapidly absorbed into the show, one dance at a time, often learning one routine inside two days. Dance work was varied and energetic, involving highland flings, tap dances, kicking routines, in-line work and broken lines, acrobatic work and waltzes. The girls had to do a little of everything and were on and off the stage all the time, with a number of changes throughout the show.

Nothing could dampen Bluebell's ebullience and she could not have enough of this new life. Energetic as ever, she practised her ballet, barre work, acrobatic exercises and tap dancing at every opportunity; so much so, that on one occasion one of the 'aged' twenty-two-year-olds said, 'For Christ's sake, sit down! You make me tired just looking at you!'

The remark shocked Bluebell, with her Catholic upbringing, but later she became used to hearing such oaths. She liked and respected the other seven girls so much, she philosophically reckoned that even if they did break the third commandment, they all but kept the other nine intact.

Like the other girls, she earned two pounds a week and had to pay all her keep with it. Digs, where they ate all their meals, cost them about seventeen shillings each, and she sent a pound home to Mary each week. That left her three shillings for herself, and there were many necessities that swallowed that up. Early on she became the proud possessor of a black wooden make-up box with its own lock and key, an absolute prerequisite for all chorus girls and, bit by bit, she stocked it with all the greasepaint a dancer needed. Now and then she went to the hairdressers to have her hair trimmed in a straight bob – a hairstyle Mary had given her at the age of ten when she was no longer able to cope with the nightly curling up of her long hair. Little by little, Bluebell provided herself with the bits and pieces and general accoutrements a professional could not do without. The fortunate possessor of a good complexion, she never wore much make-up during the day and always abhorred the sight of a healthy complexion smothered by a lot of inexpertly slapped-on cosmetics in the daytime.

Every nine months, new sketches would be introduced into the Hot Jocks show – new dance routines and new acts – and then it would start all over again on the same circuit, which took in almost every part of Great Britain. Often there were two shows a day and matinees were always put on if it were a special day, such as a bank holiday, when there were likely to be more crowds. Occasionally, they played to empty houses, but such was Bluebell's constant exuberance at merely being on stage, that she 'gave' just the same to an empty house as to a full one. On the whole, it was a good venture for the people running this small, unpretentious show, and the company never worried about their salaries. In the small towns they visited, as well as in most of the big ones, it was the custom for each family to go out to the theatre at least once a week to see whatever was on, good or bad, just as in later decades the cinema became a weekly habit.

There was neither a chaperone nor a manageress for the girls, and the stage manager looked after them during the show. The rest of the time, the girls looked after themselves. That was why Effie had been so keen on Bluebell wearing adult clothes, for had there been any juveniles in the company the management would have had to engage a chaperone, which they could not easily afford and the girls did not particularly want. The only difference between a juvenile and a senior in those days was that a juvenile was a little girl in short socks and clothes or a uniform, and could be anything up to sixteen years old, while a senior wore adult clothes and could, perhaps, be only thirteen. Bluebell had no birth certificate to prove her age, and nobody asked for it; with her blue-eyed baby face, she could have passed for a juvenile had she needed to.

From Dunfermline they travelled throughout Scotland, to Dumfries, Edinburgh, Glasgow, Dundee and Aberdeen until, at the end of three months, Bluebell had seen more of Scotland than many a Scot! The Hot Jocks, many of them actually English, proved to be a great success with the Scottish.

It was during these initial three months that Bluebell had her first theatrical heartbreak, and the male leading dancer, George Clarkson, was the cause of it. During rehearsal one day, he gathered all the girls together to announce that he was planning a new sketch in three weeks' time, which would feature a new dance which had been sweeping the world like a prairie fire since its introduction in the USA the previous year – the Charleston. He intended to teach all of them this intricate and energetic dance and, at the end of the three weeks, he would choose the best one to perform the dance with him in the show.

Here was her big chance! Right from the moment she had first set foot on stage, she had envisaged becoming part of a star act – was it really to come so soon? With typical gusto, she threw herself into this new dance, practising hard during rehearsals, between numbers in the wings during the show each night, and even working through the steps in her mind as she lay in bed at night. She 'Charlestoned' until her knees looked like rubber and felt like plasticine, and the other girls teasingly assured her that she had long since outstripped them on the Charleston front. For three weeks, life became one long Charleston, but at the end of it, George Clarkson picked another girl called May.

Bluebell hid in her bedroom afterwards and cried bitterly. The episode left its mark on her and she could never forget the dance. Many years later, when the Charleston seemed as forgotten as the minuet, Bluebell resurrected it and brought it back into fashion with her Paris troupe in the late 1940s, and continued to include it in all her acts around the world thereafter.

After their tour of Scotland, the Hot Jocks company began their regular tour of England. They played Wigan, Wolverhampton, West Hartlepool, Manchester and then Liverpool's Rotunda Theatre (destroyed in the Blitz), where Mary and Bluebell had once gone to watch the stars whom they believed had to pay for the privilege of performing!

Having been away from home for more than three months, Bluebell wondered if she would notice any difference in West Derby. What would Aunt Mary think of her, with her smart bobbed hair and discreet daytime make-up?

As she got off the tram in the village, everything looked comfortingly the same. Idly, she noticed a big poster in Shillington's, the newsagents, stating WEST DERBY BEAUTY – SEE *DAILY MAIL*! and wondered how *The Daily Mail* had managed to discover anyone they could possibly depict as a beauty in West Derby!

Not only Mary, but Mrs Humphries and all the other neighbours around No.48 Deysbrook Lane welcomed her home. But when the others had put down the empty teacups and gone home, it was as if she had never been away. Mary's white head was bent over the fire as she boiled some eggs for tea.

'Have you seen Shillington's?' Bluebell asked. 'There's a big poster outside announcing a West Derby beauty. I wonder who it is.'

'It's you,' replied Mary, taking the saucepan off the fire.

'What do you mean it's me?'

'I sent your photograph into a national beauty contest the paper's holding. If you're in the paper today, it means you've won the local best, I suppose.'

'Why ever did you do that?'

'Why not? It's been accepted and printed now anyway. You can't do anything about it.'

Mary had not expected Bluebell back that day and it was sheer coincidence her picture should be in the paper the very day she arrived. She was not to know how many other times Mary had done the same sort of thing. Mary received ten and sixpence from the paper as a prize, but Bluebell did not reach the final of the contest. From then on, her friends in West Derby, particularly her best friend Dorothy Smith's elder brother Samuel, called her *Ten-and-six-penny face* and her stock reply was always, 'Well, that's more than you've ever got for your face!'

The girls in the troupe teased her too, but understanding what mothers are like, accepted that she had no part in it. During the same week, while Bluebell was at the theatre, Mary cut off half of the big hems she had previously put on Bluebell's skirts, because she decided she did not like her in such long, adult clothes. Bluebell cried bitterly, believing that the company would not have her back if she appeared in the cropped clothes. Mary was resisting her growing up all the way.

Mary nearly caused a commotion the day she came to the Rotunda Theatre to see, for the first time, Bluebell perform as a fully-fledged professional. Unblushingly she pointed directly at Bluebell on the stage and proclaimed from the auditorium in a loud, clear voice, 'There she is! That's my girl!!'

Somebody else in the front row was also watching Bluebell. When the company had been in Manchester the previous week, they had all noticed a tall, dark young man sitting in the same seat every night. They had thought it was for Bobby, one of the older girls. Most young men with a crush on a dancing girl usually lasted about a week and then were not seen any more after the show moved on to the next town. But on the first night at Liverpool, there he was again, in the front row and practically in the same seat. The next night he appeared again and to everyone's surprise, he sent a big bouquet of flowers to Bluebell – 'The Kid!'

Suddenly she matured in the other girls' eyes. To get a man to follow a show from one town to another was quite a thing, they assured her. Partly to show the others, she kept a supper date with him. After that, during the Liverpool run, they had supper together almost every night after the show. He was a shy young man, and on the last night he timidly intimated that he would like to continue seeing her the following week, when the show moved to New Brighton. But at fifteen, Bluebell decided she was too young to encourage him, or any man, and although she was pleased and proud at having her first 'date', there were no tears when she firmly finished the association.

This was the heyday of 'stage-door Johnnies'. Although this young man had not been one of them, there were plenty of them in every town. Usually, the girls joined in the spirit of flippant flirtation and looked upon the weekly date as a free supper ticket. Bluebell and the youngest girl in the troupe, Lily from Birkenhead, roomed together and shared everything from clothes to make-up. They even decided to share their stage-door Johnnies, but knowing the same young man would be taking out a girl from the following week's show, just as he was then dating her, killed any feelings of romance Bluebell might have felt for any of them.

So it did not take long for Bluebell to decide that stage-door Johnnies were a dead loss. It was like an eternal merry-go-round, with the boys knowing they would get a change of girl each week. Only in the big London shows, where touring was almost unheard of, and the girls were the spoilt darlings of the theatre, had some of them occasionally married a stage-door Johnny, some of whom had been peers of the realm. But that didn't happen to girls in little touring shows.

In any case, Bluebell was still far too much of a slap-on-the-back tomboy, and treated boys as if she were just another boy, a tried and proven method of discouraging any man. It had been the same ever since her friends at school had started to have boyfriends. When Bluebell had been about thirteen, a girl of the same age in Deysbrook Lane named Gladys had been regularly going out with a boy called Johnny. Johnny owned a bicycle, and Bluebell used to ask Gladys to ask Johnny to let her have a ride on it. He would answer, 'I'll give you a ride on my bike if Gladys will give me a kiss.'

Then Bluebell would implore Gladys to kiss him so she could have the ride. It never struck her to ask herself why he had never asked *her* to give him the kiss instead.

Bluebell could not understand why she always behaved in a tomboyish manner towards men. Being brought up by a single woman and going to a convent school had made her neither shy nor antagonistic towards men. It was just that they had never played a great part in her life, and she felt far more independent of them than most girls who normally learn to manipulate men before they can walk, when they first twist their own fathers round their little fingers. Perhaps this was where her education had been lacking.

Everywhere they went, the girls stayed in ordinary theatrical digs, where they called the landlady 'Ma', as they were all known, good and bad, in the profession. Sometimes they were delightful digs, where the 'Ma' was like a mother to them, in every respect, and the girls would gratefully take her a bunch of flowers, together with the rent, at the end of the week. But often the 'Ma' was an irritable and stingy woman whose only aim seemed to be to collect her money at the end of the week. Very seldom were there bathrooms in any of the digs. The girls' ablutions varied from a hip bath to a strip-wash in a pudding bowl, but usually consisted of a tin basin with a tin jug of cold water standing in it.

After a dusty day on the boards, the calls could be heard ringing downstairs, 'Ma, can I have some hot water?'

And, if the landlady felt in a generous mood, she'd call back, 'Not now, but in half an hour.'

Then they would get a kettle of water, which had been heated over the fire downstairs, but often it contained only a little drop one could hardly wipe over one's face. However, more often than not the reply would be, 'Hot water? No, we can't give you that. You've got water in your room,' and the girls would go disconsolately back to their tin jug of cold water.

People often used to say that it was outrageous that theatrical people on the Continent should have to work seven days a week. Yet in Britain, at this time, the Sabbath was usually the hardest day of the seven for members of touring shows. Then, they would have to be up early to pack their bags before making long, awkward journeys across the country on depleted Sunday train services, sometimes changing trains a number of times en route.

When they finally arrived at their next stop, their troubles would not be at an end, and often they would still be trailing suitcases through strange streets at eleven o'clock at night, trying to find digs.

Alfred Jackson's sixteen girls

THE JACKSON GIRLS

AFTER THE RUN AT THE Rotunda in Liverpool, Bluebell did not see her home again for over a year. Then she was given four weeks' Christmas leave, the last Christmas she was ever to have in her West Derby home. It was, as usual, unpaid leave and she had to find work during that time. A pantomime, *Sinbad the Sailor*, was about to play at the Rotunda Theatre. Bluebell was so anxious to get in to the show that she went along to the theatre the morning after arriving home in West Derby in the hope of being given an audition, although she knew rehearsals had already started.

The management took to her right away, for they were short of a girl, and rushed her on stage with all the other girls, who had been rehearsing already for a week. Rehearsals went on all day and while the other girls went out to lunch, Bluebell was told to stay on and practise the steps if she wanted to be in the show.

By the end of the day, she began to feel very cold, and then in turn hot and dizzy, and as they brought the rehearsal to a close, she dropped into the only dead faint she was ever to have in her early life. Aunt Mary's breakfasts had never been enough to sustain her until lunchtime, even when she had been a schoolgirl, and they certainly did not stand the test of a full day's rehearsal with no lunch. Had they known anything about her reputation for being tough, the rest of the company would have been even more worried than they were.

Mary herself was concerned when she reached home, but still woke her early next morning, cursorily asking, 'Do you think you're alright?' as she pushed her out to rehearsals again.

There was no doubt that Mary was the driving force behind much that Bluebell did in those days.

The following summer the show came through Liverpool again, where there was great excitement among some of the girls because the famous Alfred Jackson was auditioning there for his European touring dancing troupe. There was no need to tell any northerner about Alfred Jackson. He had been one of the original Lancashire Lads, a world-famous act consisting of the six children of one family named Jackson, who had come from Golborne, a small town between Wigan and Warrington. Their father had been choirmaster in the local church and had organised his children into a close harmony group and taught them clog dancing, among other skills. The Lads had perfected a very good musical comedy turn which they had regularly put on in village halls and out of doors on May Day festivals and Whit fairs.

By chance, when Alfred was only four years old, the manager of the Liverpool Empire Theatre missed a connection at Golborne railway station while on his way to Liverpool and wandered into the village hall to see the amateur show. His discovery of the Lancashire Lads led them first to fame in

Liverpool and then to London and eventually to every other province in the country. For twelve years they worked five performances a night without a break. They had gone on to conquer the Continent. They had sailed into Helsinki on the first icebreaker of the season, played in every country in Europe, met the Tsar of Russia and performed before numerous crowned heads of Europe.

They had finally split up in Budapest in 1907 when the eldest brother had married, and they all went their separate ways, to almost every corner of the globe. Their father, meanwhile, had started another Lancashire Lads group in England, one promising member being a boy called Charlie Chaplin...

After spending World War I in a German prison camp, Alfred had returned to Britain crippled with rheumatism, but had fought his way back to recovery, and with typical Lancashire cheek, had been the first enemy alien to perform in Berlin after the war. In 1922, he had started up his first girls' dancing troupe, 'The Eight Violets and One Rose', consisting of five English girls and three Germans. Few people had show business more deeply engrained in their soul than Alfred Jackson, but he also had a reputation for demanding absolute perfection in performance from anyone who worked for him.

His original small troupe had been a success at the Comic Opera in Berlin, but the Scala, Berlin, where he now had a six months' contract, was big enough for a much longer line. Jackson saw the possibilities of a magnificent line of highly-trained, disciplined British girls, and he was determined to get it. Right now, he was busy looking for girls from the north of England because he felt they had a greater capacity for hard work than those from other areas. The story was going around that he was auditioning hundreds in order to find just thirty girls.

Alfred Jackson's sixteen girls on the rooftop of the Scala in Berlin

Alfred Jackson's girls in Paris

Bluebell, however, had no desire to try for any other troupe. She was happy enough with the Hot Jocks, and by working with them she had developed as a dancer and was getting on well with everyone in the show. She was one of the favourites and was regularly in the front line on stage. To her, the Hot Jocks company was like a big family, the first she had ever lived with. It was Mary who finally badgered her into the audition with Alfred Jackson, and it was only for some peace at home that Bluebell went along to Daulby Hall in Liverpool, where the auditioning was taking place during rehearsals of the regular Alfred Jackson Girls.

Bluebell was instantly deterred by the atmosphere there. Here was a large, impersonal, echoing hall, with a piano playing very fast and somebody beating a tambourine. There were scores of girls, each with the same frizzy hairstyle and all working furiously and all doing different things at once, some performing fast kicking routines, others executing acrobatics, cartwheels, splits and rapid ballet turns. It was enough to make one's head spin. It seemed like a vast dance factory.

Mr Jackson and his plump-faced German wife, Elly, were there. Although nearing middle-age and already balding, Jackson still had the wiry grace of a dancer. Bluebell went backstage and changed into her practice things, a tight-bodiced, bloomer-skirted dress, white socks and dance shoes with ankle straps. She kicked for him, did the splits, a few ballet turns, some cartwheels and a little tap dancing.

It was the only audition Bluebell ever did in her life. Of all the Hot Jocks girls at this audition, she was the only one offered a coveted Jackson contract. And she turned it down, flat.

There was, of course, hell to pay when she returned home.

'The chance of your life, and you turn it down!' raged Mary. 'They'll never be after you again, mark you. And what excuse did you give?'

'I just said I was already under contract, which I am,' replied Bluebell. 'I can't let my own company down. Anyway, I didn't fancy it. It all looked too crowded and impersonal.'

'Well, I'm going up there tomorrow,' Mary announced, 'and I'm going to tell Mr Jackson we are very sorry about this but that they're to bear your name in mind. And if they need a girl, they're to let me know immediately, and then you can give a fortnight's notice to the Hot Jocks and go straight out to join them. You know very well your contract can be terminated with two weeks' notice.'

Arguing with Mary was like trying to slam a swing door.

'You know, Aunt Mary, you're always talking about missing me,' Bluebell said. 'But anybody would think you were trying to get rid of me, the way you want me to go abroad with this troupe. Why do you want me to go so far away? I can't understand it. Anybody'd think you'd be happier to have me at home!'

Little did Bluebell realise that even before she had come home on vacation, Mary had checked out the Jackson troupe. Another Liverpool girl, Lily Martin, whose mother was a friend of Mary's, was already a Jackson Girl and had been one of the 'Violets'. Lily had been taught to dance by a former Tiller girl, (John Tiller's 'Tiller Stars' danced at the Folies Bergère in the 1920s) and her widowed mother was a farmer.

All the time Bluebell had been away on tour with the Hot Jocks, Mary had kept in touch with Mrs Martin, and when Lily told her mother that Alfred Jackson was returning to

Liverpool to hold auditions, one of Lily's brothers had been sent post-haste from the farm to Deysbrook Lane to tell Mary. She had been overjoyed that Bluebell would be in Liverpool just at the right time.

'This could be your only chance of seeing places. And you could learn German too, think of it!' was one of Mary's arguments. 'You'll be grateful for this one day, I'm sure.'

What Mary learnt about the Jackson set-up the next day made her still keener for Bluebell to join them. The girls were paid two pounds a week, with all expenses found. If Bluebell went with them, she would only need to keep ten shillings for herself and washing and could send thirty shillings a week home to Mary. Mary's health had been gradually failing ever since catching Spanish influenza years before. Often, these days, she had to be sent home from the hospital where she still worked, and already they were suggesting that she should give up her job there.

It was with many feelings of relief that Bluebell rejoined the Hot Jocks after this brief but eventful interlude in Liverpool. Mary had one more attempt to persuade her to join the Jacksons, but Bluebell was adamant. This time, the Hot Jocks were going to Dublin, a city she had heard so much about, her birthplace, where she had twice lived, but which, of course, she could not remember. She loved the place. Mary's brother Peadar met her on the quay and, in true Irish fashion, insisted that she stay with him. She found him well established in a pleasant little villa of seven or eight rooms. He had married a dressmaker named Lily four years earlier, by whom he already had three sons: Peadar, Eamonn and Ferguson. Lily was an industrious woman and still took in dressmaking as well as efficiently looking after the large and growing family.

Jackson Girls, Berlin

Jackson Girls, 1931

Lodging with Peadar's family and becoming acquainted with this lively, white-haired man who had left his sisters due to her, made it an interesting week. The Irish in her responded to his volatility, and when he disapproved of her profession and would not allow any of his family to see the show, she did not mind.

Her Irish trip banished all thoughts of her recent Liverpool experiences out of her mind, and as they travelled straight from Ireland to their normal circuit in England, Bluebell settled down into the usual happy, restless routine to which she had become so accustomed, and very quickly began to forget about the Jackson audition.

It was not to be. Only three weeks after that contentious week in Liverpool, a telegram arrived from Aunt Mary:

GIVE NOTICE IMMEDIATELY. BERLIN OFFER.

This was followed rapidly by a letter from Mary ordering her to quit the Hot Jocks company immediately and accept this new Jackson offer. To prove it was all genuine, she enclosed their telegram, which read:

CAN PLACE BLUEBELL IMMEDIATELY. SEND HER TO SCALA BERLIN.

Troubled, Bluebell took Mary's telegram to the manager, Dave Westaway, and explained the situation.

'I think I shall have to leave,' she concluded.

'Do you think it's a matter of money?' he asked. 'We'll give you a ten-shilling rise if you think that will make any difference.'

'Knowing my aunt as I do, I don't think it'll make any difference. But I'll write and ask her.'

Mary's wired reply was prompt and imperative:

NO. MONEY NOT QUESTION.

There immediately followed a letter from Mary threatening to come and get her if she did not do as she was told.

It was with a heavy heart that she finally gave in her notice and packed her few possessions into the attaché case that had travelled so many miles with her around Britain, and with many tears, she left the company. She had grown very attached to them in the past two years.

Back in Liverpool, she found Mary had assumed the role of theatrical agent. She had handled all the correspondence with Alfred Jackson, who had written to explain where she could pick up the tickets for Bluebell's journey. She informed Bluebell that the Jacksons were changing three of the thirty girls currently appearing at the Scala, Berlin, which was a vast theatre on the lines of London's Coliseum or the Gaumont in Paris. In those days, girls under the age of sixteen could not work abroad without a licence. Fortunately, Bluebell was just over sixteen, which meant that she did not need a license to work abroad, and Mary had left the contract for her to sign.

Since she was not legally her parent or guardian, she had never had the authority to sign Bluebell's contracts, and as Bluebell had always appeared as a senior, it had not been necessary. But so determined was Mary to see her get this job, she had signed as her legal adoptive mother in applying for the passport, and obtained the countersignature of the priest at Saint Paul's Catholic Church in West Derby.

In addition, she had sent to Dublin for the birth certificate that none of them had ever seen, and without which a new passport could not be issued. She felt now, that in any case, Bluebell's future belonged to Bluebell and that there was no longer any danger of stirring up the archives in Dublin. Her fearful tenacity of Bluebell in Dublin sixteen years earlier, which had grown into a strong possessiveness throughout her childhood, was now subjugated by the ambition she felt for her – a selfless aspiration a genuine parent feels for a child when the ultimate sacrifice of parting is as nothing compared with the child's future success and happiness.

When it arrived, they poured curiously over the birth certificate, and Agnes made a special trip over from Tuebrook to see it too. It merely stated: *Margaret Kelly. Born of Margaret Kelly, née Margaret O'Brien. Father: James Kelly*. It did not give James' profession, neither did it give any further details about either parent.

Before Bluebell left, Mary handed her the document. Although she carried a British passport, it was her Irish birth certificate which was to help her through some of her most dangerous moments in years to come.

The average age of the Jackson Girls was very much lower than that of the Hot Jocks troupe or of almost any other troupe in Europe. One reason was that older girls could not have borne the tough life, the long tiring journeys in sleeper-less third-class railway compartments, the heavy chaperoning, and, above all, the strict discipline that was imposed on them.

The journey to Berlin was a hard one. The three of them destined for the Jackson line-up, two from Liverpool and one from Preston, left Liverpool station early one morning and arrived late at night in Berlin the following day. They travelled third class all the way, a great part of the journey on hard wooden seats on which they also spent the night. They had been forbidden to use the restaurant car by Mr Jackson, even if they could pay, on the grounds that strangers might speak to them. Living on sandwiches that very soon curled

Alfred Jackson's Girls

up at the edges and Thermos flasks of tea they had brought with them, they travelled by way of Harwich and the Hook of Holland.

As the struts of the hard wooden seats became increasingly more uncomfortable, Bluebell stared bleakly through the window at the flat countryside and read over and over again, to the rhythm of the wheels, *'Nicht Hinauslehnen – Ne Pas Se Pencher Au Dehors – E Pericoloso Sporgersi – Do Not Lean Out Of The Window.'*

With these phrases repeating themselves in her mind, she thought longingly of the known and seemingly secure life she had experienced with the Hot Jocks. *English wins in verbosity*, she reflected. It wins in other ways, too. *Why was she doing this?*

Alfred and Elly Jackson were at the station in Berlin to meet them and hustled them back to the *pension*[5] where the rest of the girls were staying, gave them a meal, and quickly packed them off to bed, in three separate rooms, each containing two double beds and three other girls, who were to show them the ropes. (Throughout all of the tours, the Jackson Girls slept four or even six in a room and two to each bed.)

The next morning, they were up early to rehearse in preparation to go on stage. Rehearsals were a daily occurrence for the entire troupe, and that night the new girls were to watch the show. It was a good thing that they had received an initiation into the troupe in that morning's rehearsal, for seeing the girls from the front that night was enough to have made them turn tail and run home, were it not for the fact that they were already under contract, already in Berlin and could not afford the fare back.

---

[5] French: boarding house

The work the Jackson Girls were doing was terrific. Even from the circle, they could see the perspiration rolling off them as they danced, with guardsmen-like precision, from one number to another for fifteen minutes on stage. They were not simply a fill-in number between acts, like so many chorus lines were; they were an act in themselves, and they completed four numbers in the quarter of an hour they were on stage.

When they finished, they ran off into the wings, and a screen came down to show a pre-recorded film depicting exactly what they were doing at that moment, changing into fresh costumes, which they completed in precisely one and a half minutes. The film and the girls synchronised, and as the screen slid up out of the way, the girls came on again to a storm of applause.

For yet another routine they went on dancing, at the same breakneck speed, and without a fault. They gave no sign of flagging, but gradually, towards the end of the act, their frizzy hair-dos began to wilt and drop out of curl. The three new girls sat in the circle agape; would they ever manage to do this work? Feeling shaky, they stumbled downstairs and went backstage. In the dressing room, the girls were all laid out on white sheets, panting, trying to get their breath back. Gradually, one by one, they sat up, went out onto the veranda for a breath of air, and drank from bottles of tonic water. Then they began to put their hair in curlers ready for their next appearance in the second show.

This horror at such incredibly hard work was a common sensation with new girls. One newcomer, Marie, was so terrified that she hid behind the piano and from there tried to make her escape, although later she became an excellent member of the troupe. Hard-working northern girls, no matter which well-known troupes they had danced with prior to their arrival, were always knocked flat by their first few weeks in the Jackson line.

To Bluebell, the thirty girls all working in line linked together by their arms, with their legs going so fast you could hardly see the shape of them, made her think of a huge factory – the same impression of them that she had formed in the Daulby Hall in Liverpool. The girls varied in height from 5ft 2 to 5ft 5½ inches, which made Bluebell one of the tallest. The line started with the shortest on the left and graduated upwards to the right, and she found herself the third from the right end.

As far as individual looks were concerned, they were not a glamorous troupe. Even in those days, Bluebell had high ideals of what she thought a dancing troupe should be like. These girls did not all have beautiful legs, and she thought it *a good thing that the speed of their work prevented the audience from noticing any individual limbs*. The music was fast and kicking – a rapid bang, bang, bang, bang, without cease. The rapidity of the work was the success of the troupe – their legs never stopped. The standard of precision of the line-dancing was as high as it has been before or since in any part of the world, and what the girls lacked in sophisticated glamour, they made up for with a youth and coltish lissomness which survived the rigours of any amount of hard work.

The difference between the work of the Jackson Girls and that of any other troupe lay not only in their speed and precision, but also in a curious little flick they gave to all the movements. They did not kick stiff-footedly, as so many lines did, making their legs look like poles; instead, each kick, no matter how fast, ended in a flick of the foot. When they kicked in a 'grand circle', for instance, every foot flicked as it began each upward ride; it gave an exciting crispness to each routine and helped the girls keep their rhythm.

Every morning at ten o'clock, Jackson took the girls to the theatre for rehearsal, no matter how energetic the show the night before. Generally, there was neither a piano nor an orchestra and Mr Jackson would hit out the rhythm on the tambourine hard and fast to give the girls their beat. If the girls were not working the way he thought that they should, he would fling the tambourine right into the middle of the line and start to walk out. But his exacting standards were respected and the girls would run after him, pleading, 'No, Mr Jackson, don't leave! We'll do it again!'

Bluebell had arrived in Berlin in September, when the city was cold and miserable. Life for them was very institutional, with the girls all living, sleeping and walking out together. They lived in a *pension* and had proper meals, but there were none of the usual advantages of living abroad, such as exploring the town and meeting the people. There had been far more freedom with the Hot Jocks.

However, the bathing arrangements were an improvement on the British circuits. There were no more tin jugs of cold water to wash in, although there was always a queue for the one bathroom. They had to be absolutely punctual for meals, with breakfast on the table by 9:30 am and would leave for the theatre half an hour later in a crocodile, two by two, for rehearsals or classes, returning in the same way for lunch.

It took Bluebell some time to get used to the idea of always walking in crocodile, like a crowd of schoolgirls, plump Mrs Jackson, with her plaited hair coiled round her ears and looking very German, walking in front and Mr Jackson bringing up the rear with Tessy, the German head girl, occasionally calling out, 'Keep your eyes front, don't look sideways!' whenever a man looked their way.

In the afternoon, if there were no further rehearsals or matinee performances, the girls were allowed to go out, but never alone, only in twos or threes, and it was strictly against the rules to speak to anyone unless they went into a shop to buy something. They would have to be back at the *pension* for high tea, before leaving in a crocodile once more for the theatre. After the show they were hurried straight home by eleven o'clock, and, before they went to bed, had to put their hair in tight curlers to give themselves the uniform appearance which was currently fashionable.

The show was vaudeville, consisting mainly of German acts, including a number of leading German stars. It was a great success. The girls were particularly inspired by the music to which they were dancing – provided by the band of the 'British King of Jazz', Jack Hylton[6]. The girls, however, stayed in a separate *pension* from the other members of the show and met none of them socially. Indeed, they were not allowed to speak to any other members of the company, even during the show.

Jackson's strict regime ensured that the youngest girls in his troupe were properly cared for, the youngest of whom were under sixteen. As mentioned, children of this age were allowed out of the UK only under special license and the girls were expected to report to the Bow Street Magistrates' Court before leaving England and again on their return. Jackson had to lay down a bond at Bow Street, for the considerable sum of £500 for each child under sixteen he took abroad. Furthermore, at every town on the Continent, he had to present them at the local police station before they could start work at the theatre.

---

[6] Hylton, known as the 'British King of Jazz', hailed from Lancashire, having been born plain Jack Hilton in 1892 near Bolton, the son of a cotton mill worker.

Jackson stood to forfeit his £500 bond if anything untoward happened to one of these youngest girls, and in order to ensure impeccable behaviour from these teenagers, he imposed the same stiff rules on all thirty girls. Being young enough, they more or less accepted it. However, many of them felt very restricted at never going anywhere or meeting anybody. Invitations streamed in, collectively and individually, to meet people, attend parties and so on, sometimes from quite eligible members of society, but Jackson would always say, 'You can just tear those up, we don't want anything of that sort.'

When anything went wrong during rehearsals, some of the older girls always chanted, 'It's the new girls doing it wrong again.'

Bluebell, being the tallest new girl and only third from the right end of the line, would invariably receive the ticking off. Eventually Bluebell remonstrated on behalf of the new girls, stepping out of line one day, rounding on the others and saying, 'Look here. Just how long do you have to be a new girl around here? I'm getting tired of it.'

But the new ones continued to take the blame until eventually still newer girls arrived. In fact, in every way Bluebell was getting tired of the whole situation. She decided she hated Berlin and being with this large crowd of girls. She would stay the six months and then go home. But after less than three months, she had grown to enjoy the life so much that she could not imagine doing anything else.

A testing time for Bluebell came after her first five months in Berlin, when the Scala contract ended. The troupe was to be split into two troupes. Fourteen girls were to be taken from the existing troupe and sent to dance at the Stadt Theatre in Vienna, where Jackson had a twelve-month contract. Mrs

Jackson would be in charge of them. The larger troupe would go on a tour of Europe with Jackson in charge.

It was instantly obvious to all the girls that the touring troupe would be the 'first team' and there was the inevitable last-minute competition for places with some girls trying to scintillate during the selection process.

Despite Jackson's fiery temperament, his rigid discipline and the constant hard work he imposed on those around him, the girls all fought to be in his troupe. Those who not only had performed the best and trained the hardest throughout the Berlin contract, but were also the most agreeable and the least trouble, were rewarded with places in the touring troupe.

Bluebell was one of the lucky sixteen. Right from the start, there seemed to be a rivalry between the two troupes and it was obvious that Alfred Jackson nearly always tried to keep the best girls for his own touring line.

At the end of her first nine months with the Jackson Girls, Bluebell spent her first leave in West Derby. But, as her stay unfolded, she realised with some dismay that she had grown away from the community of her upbringing. Liverpool seemed dirty and drab in comparison to the continental cities she had experienced, and the houses so small that she felt the walls were closing in on her when she was inside them. But more than that, she herself had changed, and, walking down the street in her continental clothes, she felt conspicuous. On her arrival, she had taken off her hat before reaching home, to avoid the stares of the people in her street. She felt the common sensation of children who enter a different environment from that of their parents. Her home was now on stage and her language that of the theatre which embraced the limits of her horizon and had become her whole life.

To West Derby, however, she was quite the celebrity. Bluebell was Aunt Mary's only topic of conversation throughout her absence. Despite her underlying feelings, Bluebell was glad to see old friends, the neighbours, the local tradesmen, the nuns at Freshfields sanatorium where she had first been encouraged to walk, and the priest at St Paul's who, far from disapproving of her career, now took a great interest in it. She had returned invested with the glamour of her European tour and had travelled more than any other youngster in the district.

As the local-girl-made-good, Bluebell suddenly found herself to be acceptable, even in the rather tight social circle of the more comfortable area of West Derby. Boys who had never spoken to her now sought her acquaintance and eligible young men invited her to dances at the exclusive tennis club. But Bluebell firmly rejected all advances and invitations. If in the past she had been considered to live on the wrong side of the tracks, then on the wrong side of the tracks she would remain. Mary despaired. Here was the first rung of the social ladder she had always hoped her girl would climb, and she was turning away from it! Mary decided that if Bluebell would not go out to meet society, society must come to meet Bluebell, and began to invite people to tea.

Mary had told the world and his wife that Bluebell could speak German, and it did not take long to find a German woman in the neighbourhood, whom she was able to invite to tea along with a number of guests whom she intended to be suitably impressed by Bluebell's linguistic abilities. There followed a miserable and embarrassing afternoon, during which Bluebell supplied monosyllabic 'Jas' and 'Neins' where she guessed fit during a peculiar and rather one-sided conversation in German. Doubtless the German lady guessed, but she did not give Bluebell away, and Bluebell decided then and there to learn German thoroughly when she returned to the Continent.

The brief three-weeks' leave was marked more momentously, however, by Bluebell's sudden engagement to Sam, the brother of her old friend Dorothy Smith – the young man who, as a boy, had called Bluebell 'Ten-and-six-penny face'. He had always looked upon Bluebell as a cute kid, but her sudden transformation into a well-travelled woman of the world bowled him over, and Bluebell also realised after all these years that it had really been for Sam that she had so often visited Dorothy in the past.

Sam was everything a teenage girl could wish for – tall with blue eyes and blonde curly hair, athletic and good at sports. He was twenty-one and a qualified engineer. At first, they went out together in a foursome with Dorothy and her boyfriend, but eventually Bluebell and Sam began to spend more alone together. Switching smartly from his former teasing elder brother role to that of attentive escort, Sam took her to the theatre and the cinema, never forgetting to present her with flowers or a box of chocolates, and would then take her out to supper. Strangely, despite her strong Catholic views, Mary did not disapprove of him, even though he was a Protestant, and when they asked her if they could become engaged, she was pleased, and even sang his praises to the rest of the family, though George did not approve of the match.

By the third week of the holiday, despite her engagement, Bluebell felt ready to get back to work. If it had not been for Sam, the vacation might have ended like a damp squib. Instead, she left as an engaged young woman, but without an engagement ring because Sam, who came from the same side of the tracks as herself, could not afford one. Once again, she was seen off at the station by Mary alone, as Sam was too shy to say goodbye to her in front of her aunt. But the night

Alfred Jackson's Girls

Jackson Girls

before, when they had parted, he had told her of his plan to emigrate to Australia, and she had agreed, in the flush of early romance, to join him there. As she set off once more on a third-class journey to Germany, she considered what a long trip to Australia would involve and how it might very well mean the end of her dancing career.

This time the journey to Berlin was more cheerful, made in summertime and with all the girls together. There was a light heartedness in the troupe because they knew that at the end of three months in Berlin, they would be returning to England for appearances in London. Berlin in mid-August had a happier aspect than the previous September when Bluebell had first gone, but after a week everything seemed very much the same. The same theatre, the same visits en masse to the zoo, the same remarks made by, it seemed, the same admirers, as the girls made the same crocodile march between the theatre and the same Pension Barbe. Herr and Frau Barbe still embarrassed the girls each day by going into the bathroom together, and the same girls giggled at that. However long they were to live on the mainland of Europe, continentals would seem strange to the prudish English girls whose mothers, it must be remembered, were of Victorian vintage, and this was a continental custom many English people found hard to accept.

If Berlin seemed the same, the girls returned with enhanced glamour and fame, and were quickly signed up for film work. Life became even more hectic when they were commissioned to dance in a movie called *The Three Kings*, starring Henry Edwards, going straight from the studios on to the theatre at night. The Jacksons never introduced the girls to any of the ordinary people of Berlin and some of the girls who were veterans of former British touring companies still hankered after the freedom of their old days.

In spite of increased work and rigid discipline, a few of the girls now learned to slip their shackles and the second run in Berlin gave some of the more persevering swains, who had tried to get to know the girls during their first run, a chance to meet them and even go steady with them. It was tricky, because Alfred Jackson, sometimes one of his brothers, and occasionally his father, always lived with them in the *pension*, and very little escaped their eagle eyes.

Occasionally, three or four of the girls would go out in the afternoon together, and while the others wondered around the shops, one of them would keep a coffee date with a young man she had met. Such meetings had to be very clandestine, for discovery alone with a man in a public place would have been enough to warrant the sack. The ideal arrangement was for two girls to go out together and separate to meet their dates, having planned a rendezvous afterwards, so that they could re-enter the *pension* together looking innocent. The fewer who were in on the secret meetings, the better, for not every girl in the Jackson troupe could be trusted to keep her word.

It might be wondered how the members of the troupe made the acquaintance of any member of the opposite sex in the first place, living as they were under such close guard. But occasionally, mysterious notes would be pushed under the dressing room door, addressed to individual girls from admirers who had managed to bribe the call boy or stage door keeper to deliver the *billets-doux*. Sometimes the boys would lie in wait for the crocodile to come along the street for the morning rehearsal, and then a note might be pushed surreptitiously into a girl's hand, at the risk of being noticed by Mr Jackson, who always walked at the back with the head girl, Tessy.

If he caught a man with a note, or 'molesting' his girls, as he put it, or even if a man merely followed the crocodile, it was not at all unusual for Jackson to become fighting mad. He never blamed the girls, for they were innocent little doves in his eyes. He had grown up a fighter. Child entertainers had been looked upon as sissy, and it had been the weekly ritual for him as a kid to have to correct this misapprehension by fighting the school bully during playtime each Monday morning at each new school he attended during his tours with the Lancashire Lads. So he had grown up not only a good dancer, but a nimble boxer. With the collective honour of sixteen young girls to defend, quite apart from the thought of the small fortune lodged at the Bow Street Magistrates' court back in London, it was small wonder Jackson was always on the alert.

In Hamburg during several late-night walks home from the theatre, the crocodile had been followed by a number of men. One evening, Jackson had only just managed to get the girls indoors with the door quickly closed upon them, before he had to turn around and square up to three or four ardent pursuers, and the girls had prepared for bed to the accompaniment of scuffling thumps in the porch.

After that, he marched the crocodile home through the back streets of Hamburg to avoid the 'molesters', until the police visited the hotel to enquire into suspicious reports that the Jackson Girls were walking through back streets by night and they wanted to know the reason why. A gang of men threatened to rough up Jackson after these episodes, but he always gave better than he got and never looked the worse for his experiences afterwards. The girls thought he actually enjoyed the occasional fight.

Any letters addressed to the girls were automatically opened by Jackson himself, and occasionally he would arrange a date for the senders – with himself. Such meetings always brought down the final curtain on any would-be romance.

One letter received in Berlin read: 'Four jolly English boys would like to meet four jolly English girls for dinner, drinks, et cetera, et cetera.'

It was undoubtedly the 'et cetera' that he didn't like, but when he met them, he kept his itching fists down and merely gave them the rough edge of his tongue to which they abjectly apologised. Perhaps they had heard of Jackson's fighting prowess…

So, it was with considerable daring that one of the girls called Elvie began regularly dating a handsome German named Kurt, a male ballet dancer from the Berlin State Opera Company. One day she came rushing into the bedroom she shared with Bluebell and two others, excitedly brandishing three tickets for the State Opera Ball and suggested that two of them should go with her. Her boyfriend had given them to her and had promised to bring along two other male members of the ballet company. They drew lots, and Bluebell was one of the lucky ticket winners.

For weeks, the beds and floor were covered with material for three dresses, all made in the same style because they had only one pattern. The style was typical of the 1920s: a tight sheath with masses of flounces round the hem. Bluebell's was in hideous wine-red crêpe, Gladys' in her favourite but appalling green, and Elvie's in the currently fashionable brown. The bedroom door was permanently locked in case anyone entered without warning, and the dresses were not improved by having to be hastily stowed away under the beds when anyone was admitted.

The whole thing nearly fell through just before the night of the ball. Alfred Jackson had been away in Vienna to check on his new troupe at the Stadt Theatre. While he was away, the girls heard he had received an invitation to the ball, too, and for a day or two they put the dresses away and could not even bear to look at them. It would be out of the question for them to go if it were even remotely possible that Jackson would be there.

However, he returned the day before the ball with his hand in a heavy plaster bandage. One of the Vienna troupe had been rehearsing badly and had responded in an unusually taciturn manner to Jackson's reprimands, with the result that he had lost his temper with her and, in his rage, had hit a door post with his fist and broken his wrist. This accident, though unfortunate for him, doubly compensated the girls. For once, he was not able to hammer his tambourine at morning rehearsals, and he declared he could not accept the invitation to the ball while his hand was swathed in bandages.

Hurriedly, they finished the dresses. A plan of action for 'Operation Ball' was prepared. They always worked seven nights a week, and on the night of the ball they would be on duty as usual, but when they arrived back at the *pension* at eleven o'clock at night, they would dress and escape. It meant climbing out of the second-storey window, crawling along the windowsill, and shinning down the drainpipe, sheath dresses and all, then walking to the ball, which was a good half hour's tramp away.

On the night, they went through the normal ritual. One by one they went into Mr Jackson's room to say goodnight, remark how well the show had gone, enquire as to how his hand was, and leave. Then they hurried into their bedroom and hastily dressed. There was a peremptory knock on the door. They froze.

Tessy's voice rang out: 'Girls, have you all washed your spats for the military number?'

'Yes.'

'Have you all washed your socks?'

'Yes.'

'Right. Goodnight, girls.'

… and she was gone. As they climbed out on to the window ledge, they heard Polly, the only girl in the room who hadn't a ticket for the ball, stalwartly chattering to herself covering their retreat. They had left their beds stuffed with pillows, knowing that after lights-out, Jackson invariably put his head round the door to make sure they were all in bed.

Their fears of discovery put an icy cold damper on their enjoyment of that evening. A polite, heel-clicking friend of Kurt, a ballet dancer named Karl, asked Bluebell to dance, while another, Otto, waltzed off with Gladys. Elvie and Kurt had already danced off into the thick of the maelstrom; but Bluebell was suddenly terrified of leaving the side of the room, and at the end of each dance skulked back to the shelter of the wall again. Now, at last, she was meeting a German at close quarters, and she did not know what to say. None of his charming hand-kissing, heel-clicking and pleasantries could put her at ease. Her fear of being caught made her tongue-tied, and her thoughts went around in tight, tense circles.

What if she were found out and sent home? It would be the end of her stage career. Mary would say George was right – Bluebell was going to her dissolution. No one could have enjoyed the ball less than she did, despite the fact that the ballroom was a-swim with famous film stars and film producers. It was only when she caught sight of the faces of the other two girls that she realised they too were suffering the same qualms. After a stressful hour and a half, they went home the same way they had come, on foot, leaving the handsome German escorts to enjoy the rest of the ball without them.

It was quite a climb to get up two floors by drainpipe, to the accompaniment of tearing noises as their badly-made, tightly fitting sheath dresses gave way at the seams. And when they finally clambered over the bedroom window ledge, Gladys' long rope of beads broke, and the rhythmic pinging as they fell on the hard linoleum floor was enough to rouse everyone in the house. Their nerves were all at breaking point, and Gladys began to cry. It was no good; crime did not pay.

The only blessing was that Jackson never found out. It was not difficult to guess what he might have done to those male ballet dancers if he had. Not long afterwards, he was involved in a fight with an over-eager American sailor who had sent the girls a letter to which Jackson had taken particular exception. Using his iron-hard plaster-bound fist, he had knocked him out cold and broken his jaw.

The Jackson Girls, like all prophets who make their names overseas, made a triumphant return from Berlin to the UK in November that year, for their appearance at the Coliseum in London, to the accompaniment of photographers' flashbulbs, reporters and flowers from known and unknown well-wishers when they arrived at Victoria station. As always, Jackson endeavoured to establish a professional rapport with the conductor at each theatre they played.

As anyone in show business knows, the musical director is one's key 'prop'. This time they had quite a distinguished conductor, but to their surprise, after the first few bars of one of the numbers during rehearsal, he rapped his stand and said, 'Alright, that's enough for me. I can see how the rest of it goes'.

And however much Jackson tried to persuade him to do otherwise, the conductor would do no more, leaving the rest of the rehearsal to Jackson and his tambourine.

Jackson had considerable misgivings about the performance that evening. Most of the work the girls did was complicated, with several changes of rhythm in the middle of the numbers. However, they got through the first routine in 6/8 time without incident. Then came one of their specialities. In the same fast 6/8 time they danced off, in line, and as each girl disappeared into the wings, she sprinted backstage across to the other side of the stage. So while the tail end of the line of girls was still dancing rapidly off one side, the other end of the line had already lined up at the other side and was dancing slowly on to the stage in 4/4 time. It always produced a roar of applause, especially on a wide and vast stage like the Coliseum, and also called for a quick change of pace on the part of the orchestra.

Which is exactly what did not happen! As they danced on again, with the last girls flying across from backstage and re-joining the end of the line which was still hidden in the wings, they went into the new routine with legs swinging slowly in half circles, but the orchestra had dried up. The conductor was frantically looking through his score, and the girls were still swinging their legs in half circles. Someone up in the gallery yelled out, 'What's wrong with the conductor?'

Eventually the orchestra leader came in with the opening bars of the slow number on his violin, and Tessy called out, 'Grand circle, girls!'

At once they went into the next step, swinging their legs in full circles, and, bit by bit, the orchestra joined the first violin, with the conductor lamentably following the players. But all sound was drowned out, now, by the audience who had burst into resounding applause at this show of discipline by the girls who had been, for a few moments, at least, bereft of their accompaniment.

Sophie Tucker was the star of the show, but the next morning it was the Jackson Girls who were given star ratings by the critics in nearly all the newspapers. That night, when they returned to the theatre, they were shocked, delighted and rather embarrassed to see their name now headed the billing outside the theatre in lights – above that of Sophie Tucker. Most of the stars, especially those from America, were considered quite sensitive about the order of billing, and the girls were worried about how Miss Tucker would take this change.

During the first routine that night they saw her standing in the wings watching them. She was due to follow them on to stage just before the intermission, and as she did so, she stopped them and, with a big smile, said, 'I think you kids are just wonderful!' in her warm throaty voice. It seemed this woman had a big and generous character to match her ample proportions.

Jackson was standing nearby in the wings, and for once could not complain at the breaking of his rule that no conversation take place between his girls and any other member of the company. They thanked her – such praise from the stars would stick in the youngsters' memories long after some of them had attained similar star status. For the rest of the run, Sophie Tucker stood in the wings to watch them every night.

In other ways, their rules were a little more relaxed. As they were on home soil, Jackson allowed them to visit their homes at weekends if they wished. Being in England meant one thing to Bluebell; seeing Sam again. During her month in London, they managed to meet every weekend. Sam came up to town on the first weekend and saw the show. The other weekends, Bluebell went straight to the station after the show on a Saturday night and caught the late train to Liverpool, arriving at five o'clock in the morning to be met by Sam.

It was an unusual treat not to have to work on Sundays, as they had on the Continent, but they were being worked so unusually hard the rest of the time, doing two shows a day and three on Saturdays, that Mr Jackson had installed a milk urn in the dressing room for them to help themselves from, in order to keep their strength up; yet they were still losing weight. But even after the three Saturdays shows, the overnight train ride to Liverpool was nothing to Bluebell if it meant seeing Sam.

In those days, it was unusual for a teenage girl to travel by herself through the night and when on one occasion Bluebell told Sam about a middle-aged man who had offered her his shoulder to sleep on in the train, Sam was silent. The following week he wrote to her saying he would meet her again at the usual time.

'And make sure,' he added, 'you don't sit by any man who offers his shoulder for you to sleep on!'

Sam was getting proprietorial. Good-natured as he was, it must have been hard for him to see his girl setting off on long European tours, however heavily chaperoned. When he saw Bluebell off after her last weekend in England, she was never to see him again. He left soon after for Australia, as he had always planned. And when, at the end of six months, he wrote asking her to join him, she knew her career had come to mean too much for her to be able to sacrifice it, even for Sam.

The subsequent year-long European tour which followed their run in London was much more extensive than the previous one, taking in Hamburg, Munich, Düsseldorf, Leipzig, Barcelona, Budapest, Copenhagen and many other European cities. But they always stayed in the same hotels and the second time in the same town brought the same pattern as before. The only major changes in the girls' lives were when they changed rooming partners, and even then, they had to ask permission first.

There was, however, constant change in their work. They altered the numbers and programmes every month and if they stayed in the same town longer than four weeks, they would still change their programme. With the continual stream of new routines to learn, there was every necessity for the daily rehearsals and it left them precious little time or energy for mischief, although they did what they could to make up for this.

Their whole life was an institutional one, revolving entirely around their work. Alfred Jackson did not praise them easily, and they worked like slaves just to please him and to hear him thank them. Older girls might not have bothered, but to these teenagers, he was a father figure.

When, after one particularly gruelling rehearsal following two all-night train journeys to Copenhagen, he showed his approval by saying, 'Alright, fellers…' – he always called them 'fellers' – 'Straight to the ice cream stand!' and proceeded to treat them all, they felt very happy. But if he were displeased with anyone, he would take her off the show for a night and put in a replacement, for now he took along a stand-in with the troupe. His temper was given full vent when a girl got her steps wrongly, and inevitably Tessy, the head girl, bore the brunt of it. She, in turn, would pass on the reprimand to the girl at fault. Jackson stood out in front of every single performance taking notes, and every slight imperfection was written down.

In the end, the girls themselves took a pride in the perfection of their work, and if one girl had so much as a thumb out of line, or let her head move, she knew she was not only in the doghouse with Jackson, but also with the rest of the troupe. Sometimes, Jackson would march up to the dressing room door to chastise a girl for a mistake on stage, only to hear, before he even knocked, the other girls rebuking her already. Jackson was like a stern father to them in many ways and would chastise his teenage charges like a parent. Invariably, they would cry and ask forgiveness.

Occasionally they appeared in a musical, instead of a revue, which provided a refreshing change. In November 1930, they took part in the first production of Stolz, Benatzky and Gilbert's operetta, *White Horse Inn*, in Berlin's vast, domed Großes Schauspielhaus. This light-hearted comic romance, later condemned by the Nazis, was a smash hit which went on to have long runs in London, Paris, Vienna, Munich and New York. To be in a show of this kind meant that Jackson had reached the top in Europe with his dancing troupe. Their regular numbers were cleverly worked into the show. They did the same line work, but adapted it to the songs of the show, songs which were to become as popular in the 1930s as those of *My Fair Lady* many years later.

One event marred that successful run. One of the girls, Ena Pavlova, who for months had been coughing incessantly, became seriously ill. The Jackson discipline was such that she took pride in not missing a performance, however ill she had felt, and she concealed the real state of health from everyone, including Jackson himself.

In the end, the girls had to hold her up on stage, and finally she collapsed during the run of the *White Horse Inn*. It was tuberculosis. They had to leave her behind in Germany, where she stayed in a sanatorium in the Black Forest for twelve months. Jackson paid for all her treatment, but it was too late and she died.

It is a well-known fact among stage folk that busmen's holidays are rife in their profession. If a performer has but one night off in a year, he or she is more than likely to spend it at a theatre seeing a rival perform. Bluebell chafed at not having the chance to see other troupes at work, though there was no other troupe in Europe at that time of the same calibre for precision work as the Alfred Jackson line-up. She had to content herself with a visit to a matinee performance by the State Opera Company, where for the first time she saw modern ballet. It was *The Green Table*, created by the young German choreographer Kurt Jooss in 1932. Set between both world wars, depicting the rise of the Nazi party, it comprised a series of tableaux depicting the futility of the human condition and the inevitability of conflict. The brusque, flat movements based on Greek dancing and classical ballet excited her. It was the forerunner of a method of dancing she was to use a great deal in the future herself.

After a month in Hamburg, the girls made an uncomfortable journey to Barcelona, as usual travelling third class, sleeping eight to a compartment – two on the racks, four on the seats, and two on the floor. There they performed at the Olympia Circus, encountering considerable difficulties. Planks of rough wood were laid down on the bare earthen arena for the girls to dance on. Jackson never let his girls perform in small theatres, but this venue was so big that the sound of the orchestra on the far side of the arena did not reach them for half a second, which made them look as though they were dancing out of step with the music. Jackson had to stand by the orchestra and conduct them from a distance while the girls tried to close their ears to the music.

But the girls got far more excitement out of another kind of arena altogether. Jackson formed them into their crocodile one day and marched them off to see a bull fight. Bluebell was prepared to dislike what she saw, but in the first few minutes she became a convert to the cult. Before the first bull was let into the ring, a man dressed in white appeared and stood on a small rostrum in the middle of the arena.

When the bull was released, he charged straight at the man only to stop dead against him, sniffing and snorting. The man didn't move. Eventually the bull ambled off, and after he had moved a few yards away, the man leapt off the rostrum and fled in the opposite direction, throwing himself over the fence just as the enraged bull reached him. Bluebell nearly fainted. Never had she seen such a curtain-raiser. But although she was to go to many bullfights again, she never saw the man in white again. Perhaps, she decided, he had tried it once too often.

From Barcelona, another gruelling two-day rail journey took them to Budapest. The train arrived just in time for them to drag themselves straight to the Magyar Theatre, where they were to perform, rehearse, unpack their costumes and get settled into the dressing rooms – which were appalling – and go to the hotel for a quick wash and brush up before rushing back to the theatre for the evening performance.

When they arrived at the theatre for rehearsal, hot and dusty from the train, they were surprised to find the orchestra already waiting for them. Jackson took out his tambourine to give the orchestra the beat and make sure they went fast enough.

The conductor was Alfred Marcus, a famous Hungarian musician who had spent twenty-eight years in the United States. He went through a few bars of the music with the orchestra for Jackson.

'No, no! Not fast enough!' Jackson shouted. 'Like this.'

He picked up his tambourine. 'Bang, bang, bang, bang, rat-tat-tat-tat, tat,' it went, like someone trying to break the world typewriting record.

'But that would be impossible,' said Marcus. 'I don't think the orchestra could do it. And if my orchestra can't do it, then I am sure' – he gestured towards the girls – 'I am sure these young ladies cannot do it.'

The girls, dead tired, were leaning on anything they could find on stage, while the conductor and Jackson argued.

One violinist glanced up and said to another in audible English, 'So these are the famous Jackson Girls, are they? So well-known for their discipline. Well, I'm disappointed. They don't look so disciplined to me!'

Jackson heard and turned to Marcus. 'Like to have a bet on that?'

And he turned to the stage. 'All right, girls, into line. The military number.'

They snapped into place and Alfred started to hit his tambourine at his usual pace. At the end of the routine, Marcus and the orchestra were gaping. Then the conductor's face spread into a huge grin.

'Very well. If the girls can do it, so can we!'

And so they did. That night the music that swept them on to stage and into their first number was the fastest they had ever danced to. The orchestra had outdone Jackson's tambourine at rehearsal, but now they were splitting themselves. Marcus whipped them into a mad frenzy and the line kicked faster and faster on the worst stage they had ever known. It had no spring and the girls could feel splinters penetrating their thin canvas shoes and stabbing their feet, and when they went crashing down into their abandoned Can-Can splits, each girl, in turn, winced as splinters tore into her thighs. But they went on dancing, their legs riddled with small wooden daggers, for the conductor had infected them with the same wild enthusiasm he had imparted to his orchestra, and it seemed that no matter how fast he conducted, the girls could match his speed.

It was a real test, and, as the routines went on, they could see Alfred Jackson's stunned face through a blur of smoke and noticed, with some satisfaction, that his arms hung limply by his side, his notebook and pencil forgotten. This was like no theatre they had ever known. It was almost a beer house. Instead of sitting in sedate rows of numbered seats, the audience sat at separate tables, drinking from enormous jugs of beer served by girls in embroidered blouses and full skirts.

As they danced off, the auditorium echoed with piercing whistles. Up until then, the girls had only known such a noise to indicate one thing – derision. It was too much. They had half-killed themselves to put over this performance tonight, rehearsing hard after a hellish journey, and then given their fastest-ever performance, surely a world record in precision dancing.

Some of the girls burst into tears and rushed to the dressing rooms. Even from there they could hear the whistles and by the time Jackson rushed in, a look of ecstasy on his face, the whistling outside was being well matched in the room by loud sobbing.

'Girls, they want you on again. Hurry!' he cried.

'What on earth do you mean?' lamented Tessy. 'Listen to them! They're whistling!'

'That's right – they love you! Now get on again, for heaven sake!'

When they returned to the stage, the audience was standing at their tables and still whistling, but as the line appeared, they burst into frantic applause and began to bang their beer mugs on the tables. It was a classic case of the audience contributing as much to the performance as the performers do themselves. Now it was not just the conductor, not just the orchestra, but the audience itself which fired the exhausted girls with their own wild delight, and the troupe went through the whole routine again at the same break-neck speed.

Afterwards, they took seven curtain calls. They soon learnt that this was not simply opening night enthusiasm. Nightly, for the entire three months they were there, the Hungarian orchestra whipped itself into the same frenzy, as audience after audience stood and cheered. The girls loved it.

Bluebell loved Hungary and set to work learning Hungarian. In Budapest, the note-passing from amorous young men became an active sport, and frequently she would be walking in the crocodile and suddenly find a note had been pressed into her hand asking for a date. They were always in English, or an attempt at English, and occasionally she went for a coffee with the sender. These young Hungarians were charming, but emotionally they simmered and steamed like their own hot thermal baths, where Alfred Jackson disappeared each day for several hours, leaving the girls with somewhat more freedom than usual.

Most of the girls, however, made for the baths too, out of sheer necessity, for they were bitten to pieces by bugs. All the rooms in their nineteenth-century hotel were padded in heavy plush velvet, and fleas abounded. They would go to bed dead tired, only to wake in the middle of the night scratching madly. As they were also spending their days in Budapest making a film called *Eton Stockings*, which involved rising at 6 am, they got little sleep.

By the time they left Budapest, they had changed hotel three times to escape the bugs, but the pests seemed to love the girls as much as the audiences did. 'Buggypest', they decided, was a more appropriate name for Hungary's capital city.

As the tour went on, some of the girls made more and more daring sorties. On the Côte d'Azur, at Juan Les Pins, the girls broke out in a rash of disobedience, keeping dates with men in the audience who sent their messages tucked into bouquets of flowers, which Jackson invariably tried to intercept, going out for drives with the men of the orchestra, and generally tempting providence too far. It was innocent enough, as the girls generally kept the dates in groups.

Certainly, Jackson would have been very suspicious had he seen the head waiter climbing up the fire escape to the girls' bedroom at night, but it was always for the most innocuous of reasons – to bring up a tray of cream cakes and éclairs, which they all adored. The girls always cultivated the head waiter, for he was often a useful collaborator. Once, they even made an early morning swimming date in the Mediterranean with him, but Jackson found out, not only about that, but about the drives with the musicians and the coffee dates with gentlemen admirers and threatened some of the culprits with instant deportation.

But he didn't carry out his threat, for it would have spoiled the line-up on stage. He threatened to deport them again at Danzig when he discovered a newspaper picture of his girls sunbathing at a Danzig swimming pool. The troupe was so famous now that it was impossible to avoid publicity altogether.

It was only when they reached Belgium that things came to a head and a number of girls were finally sent home after they had been found on their way to a midnight rendezvous with some British engineers who were staying in Brussels at the time.

The girls were encouraged to associate with very few people during their tours, and these were usually limited to professional dancers who could help them with their work. Jackson's own brothers and fellow Lancashire Lads of former days sometimes turned up and gave the girls some coaching in tap dancing or acrobatic work, and Jackson's father, whom the girls adored, sometimes joined them. During a tour of Italy, one of the girls bought a mandolin and drove everyone mad trying to learn to play it. In retaliation, the girls armed themselves with their own homemade instruments, and, by the time they had reached Northern Europe, they had formed a band.

When Jackson Senior discovered this, he was delighted and, to the girls' dismay, decided to train them properly. Before long he had a number of them playing the banjo and, using a tuning fork to conduct, rehearsed them on long train journeys until they had become a passable group. They felt that with a little more encouragement, perhaps he might have formed a troupe of Lancashire Lasses.

They met all the former Lancashire Lads at one time or another, including Charlie Chaplin, who came to the theatre specifically to watch them. Before he left, he turned and pointed at a girl who was clowning around for the others on stage and asked, 'Who is she?'

'That's Bluebell.' Jackson answered. 'An Irish girl.'

'No need to tell me that!' Chaplin replied.

The only outsider whom Jackson introduced to the girls had been the sad case of a Danish boxer, a man of enormous proportions, a former heavyweight boxer of international repute. Alfred, who was an old friend, was distressed to find him in a mental hospital when they reached Copenhagen. Like many stage people, Jackson liked sportsmen, regarding them as fellow members of the entertainment business, and decided he must get his friend out. He took the girls along with him and gained admittance for himself to the cell where his friend was confined, although he was warned by the warder that the man was dangerous.

After only a few minutes' conversation with the old fighter, Jackson was convinced he was only punch drunk and secured his release. That night the boxer was the troupe's guest of honour in the hotel, and although he did a few crazy things, such as helping himself to the entire cauliflower from the waiter's vegetable tray, the girls did not giggle, nor did they think he was anything but harmless. In fact, he was a great deal more harmless than many of the young men they had encountered who had their wits about them.

It was very tempting, travelling around foreign countries, to see beautiful clothes in shop windows, sometimes priced quite moderately. Bluebell's own purchases did not go much further than a few small pieces of embroidery in the street markets of Budapest and if she saw anything very attractive in a shop window, she knew she could not have it. Some of the girls, who had been with the troupe longer, possessed some very smart outfits but Bluebell never seemed to have any money to spare after sending home thirty shillings of her weekly wage of £2.

Laundry, stockings, handkerchiefs and other small necessities took all of her ten shillings pocket money. It was lucky the frizzy hairdos she had to wear damaged the hair and kept it short, obviating the necessity of too many visits to the hairdresser.

When she went home on leave, she never had any money saved. If she had not sent home the thirty shillings regularly, she knew Mary would have written to the management, and she would have been in trouble. Sometimes she wished very much that she could keep the money for a couple of weeks, to buy what she needed, and occasionally she asked Jackson if she could, but the reply was always, 'No, not this week. Wait a few weeks and I'll try to arrange it.'

But the permission never came.

By now Mary had given up her job at the hospital and, when Bluebell next visited home, she was surprised to find a little blonde, blue-eyed toddler in the house. Mary had taken the child in temporarily. On subsequent vacations, Bluebell was to see a succession of little girls whom Mary took in for a while, all with blue eyes and blonde hair, just like her. In every case, Mary changed the child's name, and always added her favourite name, Sylvia, to the new one. She kept them each for a year or eighteen months, until the Catholic church, from whom she had received them, found families to adopt them.

Eventually Mary took in a baby, christened her Wendy Sylvia, and tried to keep her. She grew into another blonde, blue-eyed child, and Mary, enrolling the child in dancing lessons, hoped to achieve the same results with Wendy as she had done with Bluebell. But it was not to be; Mary was not strong enough now to look after a child, and the authorities finally removed Wendy and had her adopted by a married couple in Tuebrook.

Mary had never regained her strength after having had Spanish influenza following the war and she was now quite frequently ill. Having become so attached to Wendy, Mary frequently went in search of her after she had been adopted, standing pathetically outside the front gate of her new house in the hope of glimpsing the child through a window, until eventually the adoptive parents had to call in the police. There was no doubt she would never cease to miss Bluebell, and sometimes, in a fit of depression, she would say, 'If I'd known you were never coming back, I would never have let you go on the stage.'

But Bluebell knew Mary did not mean this. Had it not been for Mary's drive, Bluebell might very well have stayed at home. She shuddered to think what she might have become.

THE FOLIES BERGÈRE

BLUEBELL'S VACATION GAVE her a breathing space and an opportunity to assess her position. She was no longer engaged, and therefore free in every sense to concentrate on her work, but she was no longer sure whether she was truly happy with the troupe. This was rather a shattering realisation, for the troupe was her home, her family and her whole life. But there was a Bluebell whom West Derby knew, and had known well since her babyhood, and there was a second Bluebell, whom she had created – the sophisticated, independent, well-travelled and ambitious young woman.

It was wonderful to be away from home, to be independent of the environment of penury that had been her habitat during her upbringing. She was now acutely aware of the absence of material things at home.

Her early life had made her build up a protective wall around herself. While she got on well with the girls and enjoyed the camaraderie of the troupe, the privations of her childhood in West Derby prevented her from relaxing with them and,

The facade of the Folies Bergère

The front cover of a programme

emotionally, she kept her distance. The girls often referred to her as 'The Duchess', because of her reserve and dignified bearing.

One occurrence that amplified Bluebell's sensitivity about her background came at the end of that vacation, when Mr and Mrs Jackson made an unexpected call at Deysbrook Lane to inform her that the troupe was leaving on an earlier date than scheduled. They had never visited her home before and she was out when they called.

When she returned and heard about it, she burst into tears. For people of that standing in her profession to see her home and experience the background from which she had come was enough to shatter her eggshell pride. It was tough, she decided, for a young girl in her teens, who had no father and no proper family. While she did not feel unequal to the people she worked with, she did not feel she could ask them into her home. She felt very strongly that if ever she were to have children, they would have a place they could bring friends home to.

Throughout the following tour, she went on pondering where she was heading with her career. Would she continue, indefinitely, touring the music halls of Europe, always walking in a crocodile, never speaking even to the show people she worked with? Did she always intend to rough it on tour, for theirs was a gypsy life compared with that of the girls who stayed put in one city, year in year out.

On tour the girls were their own wardrobe mistresses, for they never had any dressers. They were supplied with plain white canvas shoes with bar straps, onto which they had to apply gold or silver paint, which would make the shoes dry up and shrink, so that the girls had to dance whilst enduring considerable pain from pinching, iron-hard shoes. They would become increasingly difficult even to put on, the paint would crack and more paint had to be applied to conceal the cracks. Any mending and running repairs to costumes, the girls had to do themselves. Breaks between numbers were often filled with frantic sewing sessions. Any marabou and fur trimmings that had grown tatty had to be replaced, socks and gloves which returned with holes from the laundry – one could never be sure of the laundering from country to country – had to be darned. After a year of two shows a night and extensive touring involving constant packing and unpacking, the costumes became very worn.

Their next tour took them all over Europe again, working in elegant theatres, vast arenas and circuses, both indoors and out. In one town, they performed out of doors with the audience sitting in a natural auditorium flanked by palm trees. When it suddenly rained, there was a concerted dash for a closed theatre adjacent to it, the girls making for the stage, while the audience raced inside and fought their way into seats. Sometimes it was so hot the perspiration trickled down their legs, leaving long, streaky, white marks in their leg make-up. Performances were stepped up to five shows a day during one part of the tour, and they all noticeably lost weight. The tour became a blur of railway stations, hotels, band calls, opening nights and applause.

Yet each venue remained in their memory for a variety of different reasons. Bologna was memorable in that the entire audience consisted of men, while in Milan, the stage of the Odeon theatre was so highly sprung that it came up to hit them at the beginning of the first kicking routine and broke up the line. As the slightest mistake by one girl could trip up the whole line, the stage beneath them reacting like a bucking horse had catastrophic results.

It was also in Milan that there was a near riot, when the Jackson Girls' vigorous and repeated arm movements in one of their routines was mistaken for a fascist salute, causing sections of the audience to stand and cheer, while others tried to fight them. In Brussels, the King of Belgium came to see them. In Berlin, they were given free supplies of stockings for an advertisement and in Leipzig, each girl was lent a brand-new car, straight from the factory, complete with chauffeur, for the duration of their stay.

The troupe made a triumphant entry into their next port of call, Chemnitz, eighty-five miles away, in sixteen identical open tourers, each containing a chauffeur and a girl. By this time, press photographers could not leave them alone and increasingly bizarre photo opportunities were concocted by promoters wherever they went. In Stockholm, for instance, the girls had to run a handicap race against some of Sweden's leading athletes round the hallowed 1912 Olympic track, to the accompaniment of clicking shutters.

Christmases were spent either working or at Mrs Jackson's family home in Frankfurt am Main, and it was only at such times that Bluebell had a chance to stop and think again. Although she never let it show in her dancing, she was beginning to feel the effects of over two years' continuous touring. In effect, she was growing up and becoming too old for the stringent regulations imposed on the troupe.

It is possible that Alfred Jackson did not notice that some of the girls were getting beyond the schoolgirl age and were consequently becoming less amenable to discipline.

One of his most essential props was a small silken Union Jack on a miniature mast, which was placed on the group's dining table in any hotel where they stayed, no matter what country they were in.

If, according to Mr Jackson, the girls had not danced well, the flag would be lowered to half-mast. If bad news came from England, or indeed anywhere in Europe, such as when Ena Pavlova died, down the flag went again. In fact, the flag came down with such monotonous regularity that the other guests in the hotels must have thought them a pretty poor troupe. There were times when the girls felt the flag a rather childish idea, as all too often, its position on the mast merely reflected Jackson's mood of the day. Yet the flag must have had a good psychological effect on them, for they always aimed at having it at full mast.

After two years, still aged only nineteen, Bluebell was appointed deputy head girl to Tessy and was invested with additional responsibilities. In her new position, she now had to set an example to the other girls which meant exercising more discipline, both on and off the stage. Just as she had been the demonstration pupil at the Vine Street Dancing School in Liverpool, now she was regularly called out by Jackson to demonstrate steps to the rest of the troupe.

The promotion temporarily alleviated her feelings of restlessness, but it could not lessen the fatigue of constant travel. She began to dream of putting together an act of her own, but without money, such an ambition was completely unrealistic.

In the end, it was her continued indigence which caused a major change in her life. How strange it is, Bluebell reflected in later years, that such crucial corners in life are turned, not through one's own will but by sheer chance.

Once more, the Jackson Girls were due to have a much-needed month's break and, as usual, it was to be unpaid leave. The Jacksons, now aware of her home circumstances, realised that Bluebell could not afford to take it. As it happened, one of the girls in the other troupe in Paris had become unwell, so the Jacksons asked Bluebell whether she would like to take her place during her month's leave, instead of returning to Liverpool.

Mrs Jackson's troupe, although still considered to be the Jacksons' 'second team', had nevertheless struck gold. During the Jackson Girls' first tour of the Continent, they had been visited at Hamburg's Hansa Theatre by a tall, dark and influential impresario. Bluebell remembered that morning's rehearsal very well, for it was more like an audition, and the girls had to wear their stage costumes instead of practice dresses. Instead of rehearsing, they had gone straight through all their routines for the distinguished looking visitor. His name was Paul Derval, managing director of the Folies Bergère[7] in Paris, considered to be the leading cabaret music hall in the world.

One or two of the girls knew of it but, having been brought up in Liverpool, they had not heard much about such places. Besides, northern France had never been on their touring itinerary. Bluebell had not even heard of the Folies Bergère. Indeed, Derval was the first Frenchman she had ever seen, and she was still young enough to be disappointed that he was not a short man with a Van Dyke beard.

---

[7] The Folies Bergère was the first music hall to be opened in Paris. Designed by Plumeret, it was a direct imitation of the Alhambra Theatre in London's Leicester Square, a music hall which became the model of all Parisian music halls. It opened in Paris on 2nd May 1869 as the Folies Trévise, offering light entertainment, including operettas, popular songs and gymnastics. 'Folies' was simply another word for 'theatre' and 'Trévise' was the name of the street into which the stage door opened. However, the Duc de Trévise objected to his name being used for a place of entertainment, so in September 1872, it was renamed 'Bergère' after the nearby Rue Bergère.

Many artists and writers were drawn to the Folies Bergère, and Édouard Manet's famous painting *Un bar aux Folies Bergère*, depicting a barmaid at the theatre, was exhibited at the Paris Salon in 1882.

Paul Derval, director of the Folies Bergére, 5th November 1932

Derval had brought much success to Paris' première nightspot since his joining after the Great War. A superstitious man, he insisted that the title of every revue or show consisted of thirteen letters (the same as the Folies Bergère). Under his direction, the place had become famous for spectacular costumes and fabulous sets, and he presented to Parisian audiences the greatest names in show business. Former Lancashire Lad Charlie Chaplin, Maurice Chevalier, the legendary actress and singer Mistinguett (at one time the highest-paid female entertainer in the world) and the 'Black Venus' Josephine Baker, the loose-limbed dancer and singer (who caused a sensation when she appeared scantily clad in a short skirt made of artificial bananas, bracelets and a beaded necklace), all graced the stage.

Derval had been pleased with what he had seen of the Jackson Girls that morning at the Hansa Theatre, and signed a contract there and then with Jackson. He was known to be very selective with dancing troupes and, having heard of the great successes the Jackson Girls were having all over Europe, had travelled especially to Hamburg to see them, as he was looking for a new troupe for the Folies. Jackson told Derval that he could not give him this touring troupe, but he could offer him a troupe of the same quality, which, in fact, he did.

Jackson selected the best of Mrs Jackson's Vienna troupe – who were finishing their contract at the Stadt Theatre – added a few more whom he auditioned in England, left his touring girls for a month to rehearse them in Paris, and moulded them into a troupe as well trained as his other girls. The troupe performed in the Folies Bergère under the name 'The Sixteen Helen Jackson Girls'.

The touring troupe often heard what a wonderful life the Helen Jacksons led in Paris. Instead of living in a hotel, the Parisian team occupied a private apartment, and had only one show a day. The costumes at the Folies Bergère were fabulous, and there were wardrobe mistresses and dressers to look after them. The girls never wore anything from an old show so each new show meant fresh and elaborate costumes. Even shoes were thrown out and replaced with new ones, and bathing suits were made-to-measure each girl.

Now Bluebell had a chance to taste this kind of life for a month. She travelled from Germany to France alone, feeling unusually excited about her holiday work. She had no difficulty slipping into the routines, for they were nearly the same as the ones she had been doing all along. Bluebell was accustomed to performing in large theatres, so the Folies Bergère did not overawe her during rehearsals. But it was only when they fitted her with her costumes that she realised the difference between the Folies Bergère and almost any other theatre in the world. There was possibly only one other organisation that draped, and sometimes undraped, the girls in such magnificence, and that was the other Folies, still being presented by the Broadway impresario Florenz Ziegfeld Jr. on the other side of the Atlantic, in New York.

The Folies Bergère audience appeared more illustrious than any other Bluebell had seen. Nearly everyone appeared in evening dress. Here, the daring styles which originated in and become synonymous with the 1920s were sported by audiences *par excellence*: red lipstick, *garçonne* bobbed hair[8], costume jewellery, sling-back shoes and coloured nail polish, not to mention the aroma of Chanel No.5. Dotted amid the audience, there was always a sprinkling of stars of stage or screen, who sunned themselves in the stares of adulation turned on them by the rest of the audience during the intermissions. Indeed, if American screen icons came to Paris,

---

[8] French: page-boy haircut

their attendance at the Folies was more or less expected. It was not unusual to see Gloria Swanson, the silent screen's most successful and highest paid star, who earned $20,000 a week in the mid-1920s, or Clara Bow, the original 'It girl', in the audience. Each night brought new excitement to Bluebell, as she identified famous faces beyond the footlights.

There were three dancing troupes at the Folies, representing three different nationalities, and all doing different kinds of work. Between them they covered practically every kind of dance. The Jackson Girls were famed for their trademark line precision work, which included kicking, tap dancing and acrobatic dancing. And there was a Russian ballet company, Le Ballet Stella, consisting of a dozen male and female dancers, who kept mostly to classical ballet work, wore tutus and wigs, and whom Bluebell often watched, spellbound. She still considered ballet the supreme form of dancing.

The third troupe, the Spark Ballet, consisted of nudes. They were all German girls, tall and attractive, but they did not actually perform ballet as their name suggested, limiting their movements to musical comedy work instead. Even in those days, the Folies Bergère presented more nudity than any other theatre, and, being in Paris, the wholeheartedness with which it was presented was not only permissible, but expected. With all his peacock feathers, Ziegfeld, on the other side of the ocean, was never quite so daring, and that is perhaps where the Folies scored every time over the Folies.

Life seemed so much easier to Bluebell here than with the touring troupe. There was usually only one show a day, with two matinees a week and, with Mrs Jackson in charge, the discipline was not so severe. Mrs Jackson had taken and furnished a flat in the Rue de Paradis, an eight-minute walk from the theatre, and all sixteen Jackson Girls, together with Mrs Jackson, two maids and a dog, lived there. They still

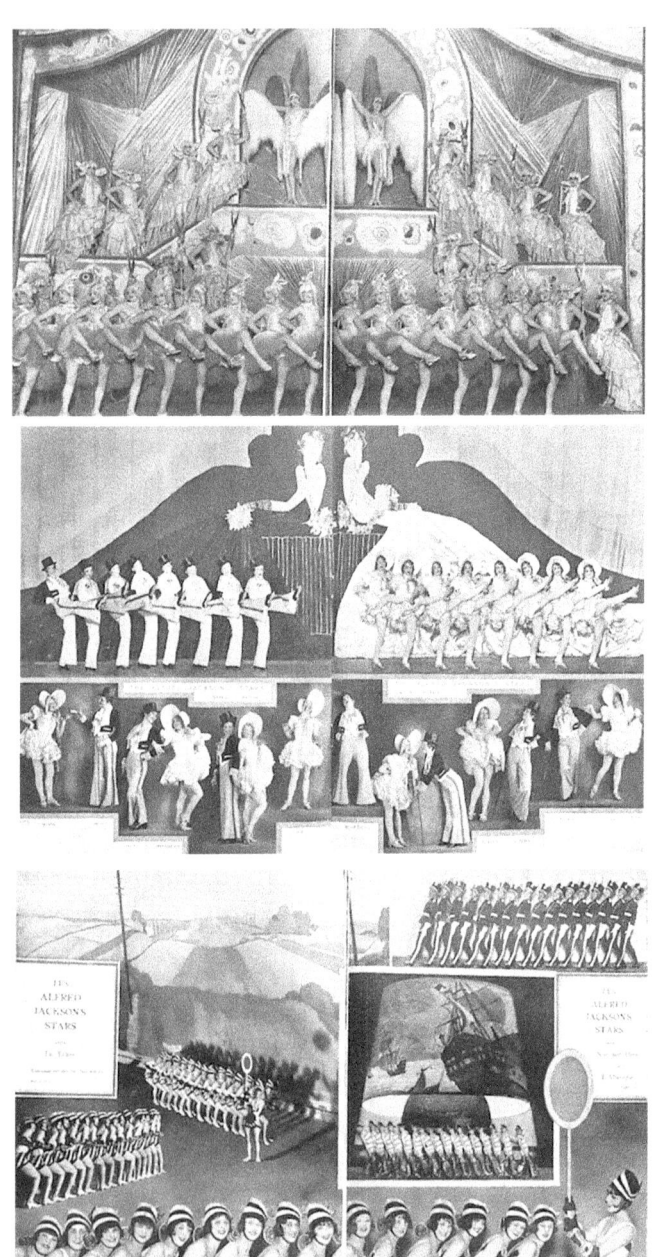

Theatre programmes from the Folies Bergère

rehearsed every morning, and still walked in crocodile to the theatre, which must have amused the sophisticated Parisians but, unlike her husband, Mrs Jackson did not come to the theatre every night.

Paris seemed to Bluebell more spectacular and exciting than any other city she had known. Already she spoke fluent German; now she avidly set to work to learn French in the short time she had. After two weeks she had fallen in love with Paris. She went to see Mrs Jackson and asked her if she thought her husband would allow her to stay with this troupe.

'Yes, why not?' was her easy-going reply, but the request brought a long-distance telephone call from Alfred.

'What do you want to stay there for?' his voice crackled over the line. 'Don't you like being with me?'

'Yes, I do,' Bluebell reassured him hurriedly, and then proceeded to come out with a number of flimsy excuses as to why she wanted to stay in Paris.

She did not tell him the real reason – how wretchedly tired she was of touring, how she knew that the next tour would be almost a duplicate of the last one, and of the one before. Alfred was in Liverpool auditioning at the time, so it would not be hard for him to find someone to take her place in the touring troupe. Reluctantly, he agreed.

Bluebell settled down and unpacked her suitcase properly for the first time in five years. It was remarkable how well the girls in the Paris troupe got on with each other, considering they were all living on top of one another. Their flat consisted of a main room, which served as a living and dining room, Mrs Jackson's bedroom, and three other bedrooms, into which the sixteen girls were crammed, mostly six to a room. There was only one bathroom, but the scramble for it every

Bluebell (foreground) with her girls backstage at the Folies Bergère

morning was a good natured one. Mrs Jackson was far less of a disciplinarian than her husband, a thoroughly domesticated *Hausfrau*[9]. She had never been in show business herself and was far happier helping the German maids with the cooking, and supervising the preparation of the girls' meals, than watching out for faults in the dancing line.

---

[9] German: housewife

Performances at the Folies Bergère

MARCEL

DAILY REHEARSALS WERE conducted by the head girl and it was her responsibility to enforce Alfred Jackson's non-fraternising rule as far as the rest of the Folies Bergère company was concerned. The girls chafed against this, but they could see that in many ways it saved them a great deal of heartache and trouble. The other two Folies troupes mixed freely with the rest of the company and suffered from the resulting emotional upsets at the hands of fickle beaux, to which off-stage dramas the Jackson Girls became interested observers.

Bluebell noticed, for instance, that the pianist in the Folies orchestra was one of the most assiduous Don Juans in Paris. Indeed, no man could have had more opportunity to follow such a pursuit than at the Folies Bergère. He was an intelligent man, and although he was by no means good-looking, many women found him attractive.

Margot, a beautiful German girl in the Spark Ballet, was very much in love with him, and sometimes he took her out; but sometimes, also, he took out other girls, with the result that Margot spent half her time in tears. Bluebell decided she did not like him. Such a fellow, she said to her head girl one day, would cause ructions within any company, first going out with one girl and then with another. Such was the stuff dressing room hostilities were made of.

Bluebell had received a number of notes from different men in the orchestra asking for dates but, still fearing that to step out of line might mean the sack, she always threw them away. It had been different on tour. She knew she would be moving on at the end of the week or the month, and the occasional date could not lead to a more permanent involvement. Anyway, since Sam, she had not met anyone who moved her sufficiently to care.

One night she was dancing on stage and glanced down into the orchestra pit. There was 'Don Juan' himself, gazing up at her from his piano. One of the violinists also noticed him looking at her.

'You looking at Bluebell?'

'Yes.'

'Well, don't bother. You won't get anywhere with her. We've all sent her notes. There is nothing doing.'

The pianist went on playing. He looked up again at the stage.

'Hmm,' was his non-committal reply.

If there was one thing that attracted the attention of Marcel Leibovici, the Romanian pianist of the Folies Bergère, it was the challenge of an uninterested girl.

One of the other acts was using the stage the following morning, so the Jackson Girls rehearsed backstage. The orchestra was there, and the conductor was discussing the music with one of the singers.

It was the usual chaotic rehearsal scene, except that Bluebell noticed the pianist using these odd moments to play, seemingly, to himself, snatches of brilliantly executed works by Ravel and Debussy. She had never heard him play this kind of music before. It sounded heady and exhilarating. She did not realise that here was a time-old habit of the cock showing off his feathers, and that she was the one meant to be impressed.

'Bluebell, would you get the tambourine, please?'

It was the head girl, putting some of the girls through their country number, 'Way Down Home'. Bluebell slipped out and down into the passageway that led under the stage. It was a well-frequented route used by the artists on their way to the stage.

In her short cotton practice dress, she hurried along in her usual absent-minded way, but suddenly was brought to a halt by a form which seemed to fill the whole passage.

'Bonjour, Bluebell,' a voice said softly.

It was the pianist. She looked round furtively. If anyone caught her speaking to a man, there would be trouble.

'Bonjour.'

'Comment allez-vous?[10]' he asked.

She was trapped.

'Très bien, merci.[11]'

---

[10] French: How do you do?
[11] French: Very well, thank you.

She knew how to say that, but that was about all.

'Vous ne parlez pas Français?[12]'

'No, do you speak English?'

'No.'

'Sprechen Sie Deutsch?[13]' she suggested, whilst rebuking herself inwardly for this concession – now she would never get away.

His face lit up and the conversation continued in German. He told her he had been watching her dance with admiration, his usual opening gambit, but Bluebell could only think of hurrying back to the rehearsal. It was the first time any member of the company had talked to her. Although she found him quite charming when he spoke and his manners were impeccable, she soon forgot all about it.

Two or three days later, he did exactly the same thing again. When she left the stage, he must have darted out from the orchestra pit to waylay her. She was determined not to become involved with him, but he was persistent and, after six months of assiduous persuasion, she agreed to their first rendezvous outside the theatre. They met discreetly in front of the Église Saint-Laurent near the Gare de L'Est. Bluebell had to take one of the girls into her confidence – Phyllis Norman – a good friend who agreed to go out with Bluebell that afternoon, leave her near the church, and meet her at two minutes to five outside their apartment in Rue de Paradis. They had to be back for tea punctually at five o'clock.

That first date consisted of coffee in a small café where they could be reasonably certain that they would not encounter

---
[12] French: Do you not speak French?
[13] German: Do you speak German?

anyone from the company. There followed one of the most interesting afternoons Bluebell had ever experienced. Marcel talked freely of his life, a life that in many ways matched hers in hardship. In addition, he was a true Continental, had stood on his own two feet for many years now, and was, in every sense, a man of the world, whereas she had travelled Europe only in the protective cocoon that Jackson had spun round all of them. Born in December 1904, he was six years older than Bluebell and was the son of Jacques Leibovici – an outstanding violinist – who had given up a promising career for the love of a woman whilst still at the Conservatory of Music and Drama in Bucharest. Jacques had become an insurance salesman, a husband, and, in the fullness of time, the father of four children, the youngest of whom was Marcel, named after the French novelist Marcel Prévost, famed for his writings about feminine issues and whose books Marcel's mother had been reading during her pregnancy.

The family had lived in the university town of Iași in Moldavia, one of the leading centres of cultural, academic and artistic life in Romania. It was about thirty miles from the Russian border, although this varied according to the latest political agreement, so Marcel grew up speaking Russian alongside his native tongue, as well as the French and German he learned at school. To Bluebell, he seemed extremely erudite, for he had read widely in several languages, including works she had never heard of, by such writers as Dostoevsky.

Marcel had taken after his father in musical ability and, at the age of eighteen, went to Vienna to further his musical studies. In September 1923, he arrived in Paris with just 800 francs in his pocket. After renting a room and a piano in the Latin Quarter, he had run out of money within a month, and survived only through the occasional paid engagement he managed to find.

He had hoped to attend the Conservatoire of Music, but his chief ambition, to be taught personally by Gabriel Fauré, director of the Conservatoire, was dashed by the composer's death in November 1924. The Conservatoire offered him a place on condition he received coaching in harmony in advance. These lessons, scheduled for six o'clock in the morning, necessitated his leaving his room in the Latin Quarter before light every morning to walk across the sleeping city as he could not afford public transport.

One day his teacher asked him to describe the symbol in musical notation for a double sharp (*double-dièse* in French). Marcel could not immediately remember the word 'croix' and while he hesitated, his teacher snapped, 'Is it your religion which prevents your saying it?'

Marcel walked out.

Until then, he had not pondered the fact that his father was a Jew. He himself had no religious beliefs, but now his pride kept him from his great ambition to study at the Paris Conservatoire. Instead he enrolled at the rival Schola Cantorum de Paris, one of the biggest music schools in the world, founded in 1894 by Charles Bordes, Alexandre Guilmant and Vincent d'Indy. Here the emphasis was on the study of late Baroque and early Classical works, Gregorian chant and Renaissance polyphony. With large class sizes of between sixty and seventy, including many mature students, it provided a thorough training in harmony and counterpoint for the young Marcel.

Then, like so many musicians with the best of classical training behind them, he had turned to the world of 'Le Jazz' to obtain a livelihood.

'Not that I dislike jazz! In fact, it is not at all against my nature to play jazz or swing,' he added. 'I have always adored it. You know, Ravel does too. Whenever Jack Hylton comes here, I do my best to get to hear his band perform.'

Hylton had forged a strong connection with France through his tours, which culminated in a presentation at the Paris Opéra in 1931 of his jazz arrangement of Stravinsky's one-act comic opera *Mavra*. His love of France showed in his choice of repertoire and collaborations; he recorded with Maurice Chevalier amongst others.

In fact, Marcel could not have chosen a better period or place to witness jazz at its most exciting in Paris. The Quintette de Hot Club de France was formed in 1934, a few years after his first date with Bluebell, and Stéphane Grappelli and the virtuosic jazz guitar player Django Reinhardt, who was the same age as Bluebell, were already making their marks in the clubs of Paris and welcoming into their circle visiting American jazz musicians, such as Duke Ellington.

Marcel insisted that the most wonderful music in Paris was to be heard at the Folies Bergère. Life at the Folies, he told Bluebell, was truly exciting, something that he was sure that she, too, would discover. Swiftly changing the subject, he added, 'I have wanted to get to know you since you arrived. You know what they call you in the orchestra?'

She shook her head.

'*Blue-belle-jambes*[14]'. He flashed a wicked smile. 'And some of them call you *Blue-belles-cuisses*[15]. And if you don't know what I'm talking about – look it up!'

That night she glanced down from the stage into the orchestra pit. Marcel was looking up at her, still smiling.

---

[14] French: Blue beautiful legs. This is a play on the word bell/belle – belle means lovely in French
[15] French: Blue beautiful thighs – another play on words

Marcel enjoying his task of auditioning for Bluebell Girls

After that, life became hectic and exciting. Marcel was the most persistent wooer she had ever known. No wonder he had caused havoc among the girls in the other troupes. Bluebell was frankly scared of becoming too involved and thought it might be a good idea to ration the dates. They were dangerous, if only from the point of view of the Jackson rules. Once more she sheltered behind the barrier she had built for herself so long ago, the barrier of politeness, which had shielded her from even her closest friends in the Jackson troupes. She became a typical *prude anglaise*[16]. But this seemed to intrigue Marcel all the more.

The head girl was rather like a gendarme[17] and was always there when the girls least expected it and always watching. Getting a message to Bluebell required ingenuity on Marcel's part. The stage door of the Folies Bergère was 150 yards from the end of the road that it was situated in and the Rue de Paradis, where the girls lived, was just a few minutes' walk away. After the show or rehearsal, the girls would go out through the stage door in two-by-two crocodile formation and turn right at the end of the street. The head girl walked outside the crocodile, sometimes on the curb, and sometimes at the back, to make sure nothing happened during the few minutes they were exposed to the wide, open world. Marcel had to estimate how far along the line Bluebell would be walking.

As they left by the stage door, he would rush to the front of the theatre, down the other side of the block, along the parallel street to the one they were walking in, and come back to try to intercept her the moment she turned the corner before the head girl did. If he succeeded, he would slip a note into Bluebell's hand. Usually she walked beside

---

[16] French: English prude
[17] French: a constable

Phyllis Norman, who would not talk of it to anyone. But if he missed her, Marcel had to dash to his car, drive around another block and wait for the crocodile in the entrance of a café just around the next corner. Always, their meetings were outside the Église Saint-Laurent. Then if they had been caught together, it would look like a happy coincidence that they both attended the same place of worship.

Eventually, Marcel's car following the crocodile became quite obvious, for he frequently missed her on the first corner, and everyone knew that he was following for Bluebell. Ultimately, they realised that the head girl must also have had her suspicions, and Bluebell reluctantly suggested to Marcel that perhaps they ought to stop seeing each other.

'Nonsense!' he exclaimed. 'What is it they say in your country? If you cannot beat the opposition, join it! Only in this case, we'll make the head girl join us. I know she has a secret boyfriend too. We can make up a foursome and, once in the conspiracy, she won't dare to talk.'

Bluebell was surprised at the readiness with which the head girl agreed. She had known all along about Bluebell's secret relationship but had been unable to pin them down. Or perhaps she had not wanted to. Bluebell got on very well with her and also knew that she was a favourite with the Jacksons.

After that, there were many happy outings, sometimes in still larger groups. Bluebell had at first been so wrapped up in her new-found romance, that she had not noticed that many of the other Jackson Girls had regular dates. With no matinee and their afternoons free almost every day, there was plenty of time to fraternise.

Mrs Jackson was only too glad when the girls volunteered to take her dog for a walk although, all too often, the poor thing ended up tied to a café table leg while the girls did their courting. Bluebell often wondered what would have happened if only that dog could have talked!

These blissful days came to a sudden end little more than a year after Bluebell's arrival in Paris. Alfred Jackson brought his touring troupe to the Olympia in the Boulevard des Capucines in Paris, and then decided to stop touring. He would retain only one troupe at the end of the four-month run at the Olympia, and that would be at the Folies Bergère. Moreover, that troupe was not necessarily going to be the one already there. He quickly found out about many of the girls' romances, went up in a sheet of flame, and began a round of sackings. He replaced most of them with his touring troupe.

Bluebell, miraculously, was kept on. Her relationship with Marcel must have reached the Jackson' ears, but the older couple remained very fond of her, as she was of them.

The touring troupe thought the easy daily schedule at the Folies Bergère sheer bliss after the rigours of the tours, and the old camaraderie, together with the easier life, engendered a very happy atmosphere, both at the theatre and at home in the flat. Now Bluebell was back with old friends again, including Marie. The Rue de Paradis apartment echoed with Lancashire accents. Life was very sweet.

As the previous show at the Folies had come to an end, some of the Jackson Girls left of their own accord. One or two of them married their boyfriends, including the head girl, whose beau was no less than the Greffier du Tribunal de Commerce de la Seine, an impressive title meaning that he was worth about five million francs a year, even then. The girls called him 'Bags', short for 'money bags', and the head girl left the troupe with all their unnecessary good wishes.

Tessy once more took over as head girl and was as grateful as the rest to settle down in one place at last. Some of the other girls joined different acts, and one even joined an adagio act, performing acrobatic stationary balances. Others became showgirls. Most of them wanted to stay on in Paris to be near their boyfriends.

Bluebell had forgotten about the practical jokers among the touring troupe. Usually the girls kept these among themselves, but from time to time one of the girls could not resist a practical joke on stage of the expense of the stars of the show. The French screen actor André Randall sang in the style made world famous by Al Johnson. For his final appearance in the second half, he would kneel down to sing 'Sonny Boy,' with the girls grouped around him, harmonising. He never appeared without a wig or a hat covering his totally bald head. 'Sonny Boy' was his final number and when he finished, there would be a blackout on stage, followed by applause. Then the lights would go up again, and there would be a final blackout.

One night during the first blackout, one of the girls quickly brushed his wig off his head, and when the lights went up again, he was seen kneeling there, but with a spotlight gleaming on his large, shiny bald pate. There was a gasp from the audience, then a raw of laughter and applause. But this did not mollify the star. Almost dancing with rage, he tore off stage as soon as the curtain fell, grabbed the stage manager and buttonholed Jackson, lividly declaring, 'I was brutally assaulted on the stage! Brutally assaulted!'

Marcel loved such episodes, and, to Bluebell's chagrin, tried out some of his own. By now the Jackson Girls had become a speciality in the show, taking part in other acts and helping with conjurers' tricks. In one act, when some of them sang 'Swanny,' Bluebell had a bar's solo, of which she was inordinately proud, entailing singing, a capella, just four notes to the words, 'oh me, oh my!' This little cadenza was her high moment in the show, but on one occasion, as she sang her four precious notes, she was horrified to hear Marcel helpfully picking out the notes on the piano, as if she could not pitch them correctly on her own. *All right*, she thought, *if you want to give me notes during the performance, I won't take notes from you after the show.* And although Marcel was waiting around the corner for her with a little note apologising, she swept past in the crocodile without taking it.

The next day, Marcel tried something else. It was a matinee on a fine afternoon and the house was far from full. Bluebell was doing another little solo piece. In a country scene, she had to sit on the edge of the stage with a fishing rod, and it was Marcel's job to put a gleaming fish on the end of her line for her to land. On this day, she hauled up her catch – and landed an old boot instead! Marcel had obtained his chief's permission to do it, and there was nothing Bluebell could do except fume.

Sometimes worse things happened by sheer accident. One of Jackson's latest gimmicks was for the girls to have 'jinks' on their shoes. These were small iron discs, like those of a tambourine, built into their heels.

So proud of the perfection of the troupe's precision work, he wanted the audience to hear as well as see the synchronisation. If a girl made one false move out of step with the line, it could be heard as well as seen. Every movement had to be in perfect rhythm and unison. To impress the audience still further, this particular number was the fastest, most complicated they had ever attempted.

It was a gala night, and the audience was packed with big names, impressive titles, white ties and tails. All sixteen girls were kicking away fast and hard when they heard Georgie yelp. At the same time, her right shoe, still jingling, sailed high over the audience and hit a man, apparently, slap in the face!

Poor Georgie continued to dance until the end of the number wearing only one shoe, but afterwards was too scared to go to the dressing room. She waited in the wings to hear the worst, while the stage manager went out front to investigate. It was a long time before he returned, beaming behind an enormous bouquet of flowers, which he presented with a flourish to an astonished Georgie. Tucked among the flowers was a little note that read: *Well aimed! I would be honoured if you would meet me for dinner after the show.* Then it gave her victim's name and address.

'*Quelle chance!*[18]' exclaimed the stage manager. 'He was holding up his opera glasses at the time and all you managed to do was to smash those. *Vraiment*[19], he is born under a lucky star!'

And as the opera glasses belonged to the theatre, no damage was done to the patron. But he did not get his date – Jackson saw to that. The episode reminded the girls of a similar incident in the early days at the Scala in Berlin, when the troupe had been doing a high kicking routine during which somebody's shoe had flown up into the rafters and never come down. The audience had spent the rest of the performance waiting for a shoe to fall on their heads.

When Bluebell returned home to Liverpool for a holiday, it was her first for two and a half years. Throughout that time she had worked without a break, except for a week after her shoulder had been dislocated by another girl catching her arm awkwardly during a number. Even then Bluebell had fought against the anaesthetic in the hospital afterwards,

---

[18] French: What luck!
[19] French: Truly

telling the doctor through the gas mask that she had to be on stage again that evening. But when she came to, her shoulder was in plaster and she chafed for a week until she could get back to work.

On her return to Liverpool, she found Mary had moved house, to another small house in Mercer Place, around the corner from her old home. Her new home was imaginatively sandwiched between the Threlfall's Derby Arms and a coal depot, but Mary was delighted with it because it had two tiny bedrooms upstairs, instead of the solitary one she had in her former home, and also running water. As ever, Mary had a little orphan living with her, but now, instead of sleeping downstairs on the sofa or with a neighbour, Bluebell was able to sleep in one of the bedrooms.

Mary had not changed at all but she insisted that Bluebell had. Bluebell, now twenty, had, like many girls, been transformed by her time in Paris and Mary recognised the extra chic her adoptive daughter displayed. Bluebell had continued to send Mary nearly all her money, but by dint of careful saving, she had managed to buy herself some Parisian clothes. They were by no means *haute couture*, merely clothes from the '150' shops, where one could buy dresses, coats and suits, in fact any kind of clothes, for exactly 150 francs (the equivalent of £1 in 1930) and no more.

Although Mary was the same, everything seemed very different. Dorothy Smith, her former fiancé's sister, had married and left the district and both her parents had died, so there was no one to tell Bluebell how Sam was getting on in Australia. Indeed, throughout the years to follow, she was always puzzled that she never heard from him again.

The break in routine made her feel restless again and once more, she wondered where all this would end. Subconsciously, she was slightly envious of the former Jackson Girls, who had been sacked from the Folies the year before and who had joined other acts.

But when she returned to Paris, events began to turn in her favour. Tessy had returned to Germany to see her mother, who was gravely ill, and would not be returning in the foreseeable future. As deputy head girl, Bluebell now became head girl, with all its attendant responsibilities. It also brought her in another ten shillings a week, which seemed like untold wealth to her then. A new girl was brought out from England to make up the line and she had to be rehearsed. As head girl, Bluebell had plenty of work to do to fill her mind, and her restlessness was assuaged a little. Only now and then did she stop and wonder where all this would lead, or whether she was simply heading down a cul-de-sac, as did so many dancing girls, with nothing but early retirement at the end.

Her own problems, such as they were, were subjugated by those of others. As head girl, she was included in many of the business conferences held by the Jacksons, and she knew that financial trouble was brewing. Alfred Jackson had income tax problems. The French government had slapped on a 'foreigners' tax', in addition to those he was already paying. They also claimed foreigners' tax for the sixteen girls he had out in Paris previously – those who had formally performed at the Folies. On top of this, they gave him half a dozen titles, such as *maitre de ballet, proprietor de dance, troupe directeur*[20], and so on, and were taxing him on each count. His accountant told him he might have to work for twenty years to pay all these taxes, and the British Embassy recommended he consult its own lawyer. A recent devaluation did not help matters and was the main cause of this heavy taxation.

---

[20] French: ballet master, dance master, troupe director

Events suddenly came to a head when rumblings were heard that the Folies Bergère itself was in tighter financial straits than usual. It seemed unbelievable; it was still the leading music hall in Europe. True, the shows were lavish and expensive, and no cost was spared to present the biggest spectacle on the continent, but surely over the year the returns more than made up for that?

One day, the director, Paul Derval, asked the whole company to assemble on stage after the matinee performance. A large, untidy and perturbed crowd congregated, including the musicians. Bluebell could see Marcel with a non-committal expression on his face. It was he who had first intimated to her that there was something wrong. As he had risen through the ranks, he was recognised in the management. He was also a close friend of Maurice Hermite, the *chef-d'orchestre*[21], and George Triel, the general manager.

Derval walked on stage. In a few crisp sentences, he explained that business was bad. He was asking everyone to accept a ten percent reduction in their wages. Either that, or the theatre would have to close.

Everybody agreed to the cut, on a temporary basis, except Jackson, who could see that, in any case, he was nearing the end of the road. His income tax troubles certainly would not permit him to take a reduction at this time, and if Derval did not agree to continue at the former rate, it was a get out for Jackson. Derval released him from his contract.

The following day, after morning rehearsal, the girls were gathered together in their apartment and told that the troupe would be disbanded and their contracts terminated in a month's time. Jackson was leaving for Germany with his wife

---

[21] French: Conductor

immediately after the show that night. It seemed as though he could not shake the dust of France off his heels fast enough.

His announcement was greeted with a stunned silence. Then he added, 'As you will be remaining here for a few more weeks without either Mrs Jackson or myself, Bluebell will be in charge of you. I'm leaving her to wind up any final details that may crop up, and if you need any help, ask her.'

Now it was Bluebell's turn to be stunned. She was to be left in charge of the whole troupe! Not only that, she was to preside over its demise, performing the last rites as the troupe disintegrated. What should have been a challengingly enjoyable experience was overshadowed by the end of the Jacksons as a troupe. Would there ever be its like again? And what about the girls? Did this mean returning to England and going back to the old round of touring? Would she ever be able to face that after Paris? Suddenly, she went cold at the thought of it. *She would be out of a job. She must work. Aunt Mary… and how could she leave Marcel?*

'Bluebell!'

It was Alfred.

'Come with me.'

He also beckoned Elvie. She and Bluebell were the only orphans in the troupe.

'I know it's a bit more difficult for you two than the others,' Jackson said. 'Although I know my brother might take on most of the girls in his show in London, I think you two have deserved a free holiday. What do you say to coming to stay with us in Frankfurt?'

Elvie was elated. It solved two problems for her at once as she was quietly in love with a German whose home was near

Frankfurt. It was arranged that she and Bluebell would join the Jacksons in Germany at the end of the month, when the troupe disbanded.

That night the troupe danced as they had never danced before. Although in many ways Jackson had verged, at times, on being a tyrant in their opinion, the girls thought a great deal of him, and some almost idolised him. He stood at the back, blinking hard, as they finished to the usual storm of applause. He knew that it was the last time he would ever see a troupe of his in action.

He and his wife left that night, after the girls had returned to the apartment. Bluebell went with Lily, who had been one of his original 'Violets', to see them off at the station.

Before he boarded the train, Jackson said, 'You've both been very good girls. I hope things will go smoothly, Bluebell.'

He patted Lily on the shoulder. 'If all the girls were like this one, you wouldn't have any trouble.'

The train left the station, and with it, the end of a chapter.

Alfred Jackson Girls, Bluebell centre top

THE BLUEBELL GIRLS

AS THEY WALKED TO THE theatre the following morning – they could not get out of the crocodile habit – Bluebell wondered how the girls would take to her as temporary leader. She did not want the standard of their dancing to decline during the few weeks she was in charge. A dancing troupe is rather like an orchestra. They can learn their numbers and perform quite a few pieces without a conductor. But in the long run, they have to resort to one.

Once changed, they all lined up on stage. Bluebell faced them. As she looked along the line, she knew she need not worry. Yesterday she was one of the girls; today they were accepting her leadership without question. They were the finest troupe in Europe, like a stud of highly trained thoroughbreds. It seemed a tragedy that within a few short weeks, not only would the troupe be scattered, but the friendships and camaraderie that existed between them would come to an end. Without Bluebell needing to bang a tambourine, the girls rehearsed for her as hard as they had ever done for Jackson. She knew their finish would be climactic.

But as their performance built up to a crescendo right up to the last night, so in reverse ratio did their formerly comfortable life taper off in their apartment. Alfred Jackson had taken nothing with him in the way of furniture, but before he left, he had promised various items to different people he knew in Paris, including the concierge.

While the girls were still living there, the beneficiaries arrived to take their pieces away. By the end of the month, they had no knives and forks, all the fuel had gone, and even the lights were turned off! There was enough food to eat, but they ate it somewhat romantically, with their fingers by the light of candles stuck in bottles. However, Jackson had done the right thing by the girls. Whatever his tax troubles, he had paid them in advance for the remaining month of their work, and all their fares home were covered.

There were quite a few tears when they all finally split up. Bluebell and Elvie saw everyone off. Many did not know what they were going to do. On the whole, this hard-working bunch was like Bluebell in that they could not afford to stay out of work for long. But in her case, she could not even afford to stay in London looking for jobs, as many of them planned to do.

The holiday in Frankfurt with Alfred and his wife was restful and at first Bluebell welcomed the change. They were all anxious to hear how the other girls were getting on, and were delighted when Alfred's brother, 'J.W.' Jackson, and Lily Martin telephoned from London one evening. J.W. told Alfred he was opening up at the Leicester Square Theatre in London and that he had been able to take in a number of the Jackson Girls. Would Alfred give his permission for them to dance some of his old numbers, which had been such a success on the Continent?

Alfred not only agreed, but offered to send his brother all the costumes, too. Lily was to be the head girl of the J.W. Girls in London. She had seen eight troupes go through Alfred's hands, and she knew all the work.

By this time, Bluebell and Elvie had been in Frankfurt five weeks, two of which had been spent on holiday with the Jacksons in Bavaria. Now that Alfred was giving his brother carte blanche with his routines and even handing over his costumes, Bluebell realised that she had missed an opportunity.

For a twenty-year-old, the weeks of inactivity dragged by. She could not expect Alfred to send money home to Mary indefinitely. Her aunt was her responsibility. While she had thought herself in clover, being looked after during those weeks, the other girls had found themselves jobs. The troupes would all be complete by now, while her career had been marking time.

Subconsciously, she knew that one reason why she had agreed to join the Jacksons in Frankfurt, was her innate fear that once she returned to England, she might never see Paris – and Marcel – again. The step across the Channel was, for her, a big one. But now she could no longer hesitate. Elvie had expressed no opinion. She had said nothing of her own private life recently. Once Bluebell had made her decision to return home, Elvie agreed, resignedly. Never talkative about her life, Elvie had suffered a heartbreak during the past few weeks and never mentioned one word about it. It was all over between her and Kurt and she was ready to go home.

The Jacksons were sorry to see them go. With no children of their own, they enjoyed having young people about. Soon after they left, they invited Tessy from Berlin, who had now lost her mother, to live with them. It was the last Bluebell saw of Alfred Jackson. He never returned to show business, although he had many offers. He had certainly packed more into the first half of his life than most do in a full lifespan, and intended to enjoy his retirement.

At the end of the decade he was, for the second time in his life, caught in Germany when war broke out, but this time he managed to get out into Switzerland, where he was able to follow his favourite pursuits – fishing and skiing. Later, Mrs Jackson, a diabetic, died, making a last request that Alfred and Tessy marry. This they did, and the two eventually retired to a peaceful life in Devon.

It was a dull, dismal day as Bluebell got off the train at Victoria station. London was giving her a wet welcomes. Liverpool, she knew, would, no doubt, be even wetter, and she was due to board a train home within a few hours. The weather certainly suited her mood, for she felt incredibly depressed.

Elvie, also unhappy, had gone on home to the south of England, and Bluebell was now alone with her dejection. After leaving her one case in the left luggage office at Euston station, the London mainline terminus which served Liverpool, she went into a Lyons' Corner House for some egg and chips.

What was she to do now? Were all these years of dancing to be wasted? Bitterly, she thought how money always counted when you wanted anything badly, even a job. She still wanted more than ever to have an act of her own, but that would take money, and as usual she had none. She still sent most of her earnings to Mary, and now she had no earnings, and no savings. Alfred Jackson's kindness in giving her a free holiday had resulted in her missing the boat the other girls had caught with his brother J.W. at the Leicester Square Theatre.

The closure in Paris of such a wonderful troupe had been tragic. There were other troupes in Britain, of course, which might be her only hope but she doubted she would be satisfied with a slower tempo after the speed precision work that had been the hallmark of Alfred Jackson's teams. With a few hours before her train left for Liverpool, she decided to make her way to Leicester Square. She would just have time to look in on the J.W. Girls at the theatre as they were getting ready for their evening performance.

It was strange to go to a theatre where the stage door keeper did not know her. Standing on the pavement, she felt like an outsider as he grudgingly telephoned up to the dressing room to enquire if Lily, Bluebell's old friend, was there. Cagily, he told her he 'wasn't sure' if she would be.

'Well, well, if it isn't Bluebell! What are you doing here?'

She turned, and there was J.W Jackson smiling down at her. The stage door manager glanced across at her with rather more friendly interest.

'I'm in London for a few hours before leaving for Liverpool,' Bluebell explained. 'I've only just arrived from Germany today.'

'Have you got a job?' he asked. Like all the Jacksons, his remarks and questions were forthright and direct.

'No, I haven't. But I'll find one as soon as I get home, I expect,' she said, rather too brightly.

'Would you like to work for me? You can start right away!'

It took her breath away; but now she recalled the many times J.W. had called in to see his brother at the Paris apartment in Rue de Paradis and how frequently he had asked her, 'Well, Bluebell, when are you going to leave my brother and work for me?'

It had been a standard joke between them and Bluebell had always laughed it off with, 'I don't know… When Mr Jackson chucks me out, I guess.'

She almost laughed now, with relief. Immediately and delightedly, she agreed. But more was to come.

'Well, where would you like to work, then? Paris or London?'

She had forgotten he still had a troupe at the Casino in Paris. This was more than she ever expected. Paris was more her home now than any other place. And Marcel was there, too. Again, there was no hesitation.

'Paris, please!' she answered, and felt like whooping.

'Alright, you can leave in the morning. I'll fix you up to stay somewhere in London tonight. Come along with me now and I'll get you your train ticket.'

'You've gone over to the opposition?' Marcel asked, when she returned to Paris the next day.

'Oh, not really,' Bluebell answered. 'Most of the others have gone over to J.W. in London.'

'I only hope you will be happy,' he remarked.

As she turned in early to be fresh for a hard morning rehearsal, Bluebell wondered what Marcel meant. She need not have bothered for, instead of rehearsing as the Alfred Jackson Girls had done, at concert pitch, she found the J.W. Girls merely 'marking'. This meant that they did the steps and went through the motions of the routines, as dancers do when they are only reminding themselves of a number, but they did not extend themselves. Milly, the head girl, showed Bluebell the routines and helped her with her steps, and within three days she was ready to go on.

With all her experience as an Alfred Jackson girl behind her, it did not occur to her to watch the show from the front before taking the stage with the J.W. Girls. This was a terrible mistake. As she went on stage for the first time with the troupe, she threw herself into her newly-learned routine with the same gusto that she had always applied to her dancing; but after only a few bars, she realised that she must look mad to the audience, for the rest of the line was still 'marking', as they had done in rehearsals.

To Bluebell, they were not dancing at all. She tried to subdue her dancing and restrict her movements to the level of the others, which is the first requisite of a precision dancer but, as the routine wore on, she felt increasingly frustrated.

At the end of the performance, she went back to the dressing room in silence, verging on tears. Her balloon of happiness had been pricked and much of her joy in being back in Paris evaporated. If she had not been the lone Alfred Jackson girl among all these others, it might not have been so bad – something could be done about it. But these girls just would not dance – not in the way she recognised it – and she was in a minority of one. She knew she could never be happy or even comfortable dancing like this, and she would always stand out like a sore thumb in the troupe.

After two days, she went to Milly and told her she would have to give in her notice. Within forty-eight hours, J.W. himself was on the phone from London. He wanted to know why she wished to leave. Bluntly, she told him.

A few days later he wrote to her, suggesting that if she would stay on after the two months at the Casino, he would either put her in a new troupe, or send out a fresh troupe to join her. Bluebell knew that by making this offer he was doing her an honour that perhaps no other dancer had ever received

Preparing for performances. Leader Magazine, 1949

from him. For him to offer to build a troupe around her was certainly more than she had asked for. There was no doubt that the old rivalry between himself and his brother had been aroused.

For the first time, Bluebell fully understood why the Alfred Jackson Girls had been the best in Europe; the secret was plain, undiluted, hard work. There was no short cut to success and these girls at the Casino would never earn the same reputation as the old troupe. It was not their fault; it was simply that they did not have a dynamic, driving, bullying personality like Alfred Jackson to intimidate and browbeat them until they were fired up and tempered to perfection. Having tasted that perfection, surely no girl could stand for second best.

Though she was all too aware that her decision would mean leaving Paris, she replied with the assurance that her mind was made up and that she would leave at the end of her contract. J.W. then came over to Paris and they talked about it at length, but it was all to no avail. Bluebell knew she would never be happy without an extremely hard-working troupe to dance with. In the old days, the Alfred Jackson restrictions were supportable because they knew that, as a troupe, they had something to be proud of. Now she still had to endure many of the restrictions of communal living, but to what purpose – for marking on stage?

One afternoon J.W.'s son Bill, noticing that Bluebell was depressed, invited her out for a coffee. Seeing that she needed cheering up, he bought her a Pernod instead. It was the first alcoholic drink she had ever had, though it tasted innocently enough of the aniseed balls she used to suck as a child in Liverpool. When she arrived home the other girls had to hide her. It was not unknown in Jackson troupes for the management to smell a girl's breath when she returned from an afternoon's outing. This would not have been necessary that day – Bluebell was staggering. She was not sorry; it dulled her senses for a few hours and took the edge off the misery she was experiencing at the thought of leaving Paris and Marcel.

Now she knew what Marcel had meant when he had hoped she would be happy. He did not seem surprised when she told him how miserable she was; it was good to be able to talk to someone who was in the profession and understood. Both Marcel and Bluebell knew this would probably mean they would have to part again. Maybe eventually she would forget him, and Paris, and the sort of dancing to which she had become accustomed.

As the weeks went by, she prepared herself once more for the break knowing that this time she would certainly be returning to Liverpool. She began to look at Paris as one does a loved person whose days, one knows, are numbered. It was a balmy and warm July, and Paris looked very beautiful. When one door closes, another opens. That had happened before when J.W. had offered her this job at the Casino just when she thought she would never see Paris again. But this time, it had been she who had slammed the door shut. Providence might not treat her so leniently again.

But a door did open, the most important one of her life. One day, only a day before J.W. was due in Paris to see her, Marcel came around to her digs. Bluebell was feeling depressed at the imminent parting and was slightly hurt when she saw Marcel turn up with his face wreathed in smiles.

'Today,' he said gaily, 'I am only a messenger boy. I cannot give you any explanation, but Paul Derval has sent me to ask you to come to see him right away.'

That was all Marcel would say. With only an hour and a half before her next performance at the Casino, Marcel drove her straight over to the Folies Bergère. Feeling like the prodigal son, Bluebell went through the familiar stage door and climbed the stairs to Derval's office. With its dark wood, leather chairs and hard settees, it looked more like an Edwardian lawyer's office than that of the management offices of the most spectacular music hall in Europe. Solid and methodical, Derval looked more like an industrial magnate than an impresario, although he had been a comedian in Vaudeville before becoming director of the Folies Bergère. It was his boast that he could remember the name of every girl who had ever danced there. But why did he want to see her? She glanced questioningly at Marcel as he manoeuvred Bluebell into the director's office as he explained that he would need to come in with her in order to translate into German anything she did not understand in French.

Derval rose from behind his king-sized desk and shook her hand. Indicating two chairs, they all sat down.

'How lovely to see you again, Bluebell,' he began. 'I heard you were back in Paris. How are you getting on at the Casino?'

He tossed her the question as though he knew the answer and did not need a reply. Bluebell explained that she was leaving at the end of the run. His beetling eyebrows went up, and his eyes and mouth down in that well-known Gallic facial 'thumbs down'. Suddenly, his expression relaxed, and looked straight at her.

'We're putting on a new show in October. Would you like to have a troupe of your own here?'

Bluebell could only look at him in astonished silence.

'I have always thought you had a great deal of authority with the girls,' he went on. 'I am sure you could gather together a good troupe and produce the quality and standard we need here. The girls would be under individual contract to us, of course, so you need not worry about that. You would have a separate contract with us as troupe leader, head girl, choreographer and dancer as well.'

This, at the age of twenty-one, was something she had never envisaged. She was still thinking of her own personal career, and how she could get into an act or form one of her own. It was a providential offer which would not only be a wonderful opportunity for her, but would gather together again all those girls flung apart by Alfred Jackson's retirement.

She listened, stunned, as Marcel translated the details of the contract she would sign and those of the contracts the girls would have into German (for they still only conversed in that language together). Perhaps Derval was a little surprised that a twenty-one-year-old should haggle over wages, but before she even wrote to any of her former dancing colleagues, she wanted to be able to offer them a more substantial wage than they had before. This was necessary because she insisted that they should be allowed to live more freely than they had done as Jackson Girls. Most of them were now over twenty-one and quite capable of looking after themselves. She was not to receive payment for presenting the troupe, as Jackson had done, and all she would receive would be an extra 10 francs a day, to cover her expenses. Even if she had wanted to, she could not have afforded to run a large apartment like the one they had all occupied in Rue de Paradis. It was decided that the girls would receive 2,100 francs a month and would therefore be among the highest paid dancing girls in Europe.

As she left the office with Marcel, they met the Folies Bergère producer, Maurice Hermite, in the outer office.

'So, we are going to have you back, yes?' he said, beaming.

It seemed that everyone already knew about it. Marcel was looking pleased; he and Maurice were old friends and Marcel assisted Maurice with the musical arrangements for each new show. The management at the Folies was rather like a large family and now Bluebell, a former Jackson Girl who had previously never been allowed to speak to another member of the company, was to join this prestigious family.

Later, she asked Marcel whose idea it had been in the first place to invite her to form a troupe. He simply smiled enigmatically, and she knew that it was more than likely he planted the seeds of the idea, probably in the mind of Maurice in the first instance, possibly directly negotiating with Paul Derval himself. Perhaps it was this thought, more than any other at this time, which made her truly happy, since nothing could be more indicative that Marcel wanted her to remain in Paris.

From then on, life became a hectic turmoil of letter-writing between shows at the Casino. Bluebell had two months left there, which meant that the moment that show ended, she would have to go straight into rehearsals for the new Folies Bergère show. This would also give the other girls time to hand in their notices, if they were working. Fortunately, they had all exchanged addresses before the final split of the Jackson troupe.

Bluebell knew that those girls who had gone to the Leicester Square Theatre with J.W. Jackson had long contracts which they could not break. But two of the former Jackson Girls were already back in Paris. Bessie, who had always been one of the sweetest and most sympathetic girls in the Jackson troupe, was still dating Pierre Samin, a flute player at the Folies, and could not get back to Paris quickly enough. She had managed to have an audition in London for a troupe, which was appearing at the Olympia in Paris, and she had talked Georgie into joining her. But just as Bluebell had felt dissatisfied at the Casino, so they too were getting restless at the Olympia. They, too, hankered after the exacting standards of precision work. These girls were doing five shows a day, because the Olympia was now a cinema, and at that time it was quite normal for films to be interspersed with live shows. Cinema audiences, not yet fully weaned from stage shows, were being given both on the same plate.

Anxiously, she waited to hear from the other Jackson Girls to whom she had written. One by one, the letters came in, all expressing delight at the chance of getting together again in Paris. Bluebell had managed to secure no fewer than six former Jackson Girls and with Bessie and Georgie, that made eight. She needed four more. Georgie partly solved this problem by persuading three of her former colleagues at the Olympia, who had been thinking of leaving, to join her instead. They were still one girl short, but Bluebell was confident enough to set off to see Derval to assure him that she could supply a troupe.

She walked down the road towards the Metro that day feeling very satisfied with the quick response the old Jackson Girls had shown. As she walked, she saw a beautiful blonde swinging along the pavement towards her and wondered whether she, too, was a dancer. She certainly looked as if she could be. Only then did she realise she knew her. It was Elvie, but what a different Elvie! The last time Bluebell had seen her was that miserable, wet day when, equally dejected, they had parted at Victoria station in London, having returned from their holiday in Germany with Mr and Mrs Jackson.

It seemed that having lost her job and her German boyfriend, she had transformed herself in every respect: her mouse brown hair was now a startling ash blonde; her face and even her personality had subtly changed. She had become a girl who turned every head in the Champs Élysées. It was obvious that, from now on, she was going to enjoy every minute of her life, a dangerous thing to do, perhaps, but not so dangerous, she had decided, as to give her whole heart to one man.

It was seeing Elvie's transformation that first opened Bluebell's eyes to the beauty potential of every woman who subsequently passed through her hands in the years to follow. Elvie, having returned to Paris, was working in a small show, but she immediately agreed to join Bluebell at the Folies Bergère. Bluebell now had her twelfth girl, found at the eleventh hour.

That day, Paul Derval gave her the contract and the rail tickets for those who were travelling out from England. When they arrived, the girls could hardly get over their new freedom: no more crocodiles, no more living on top of one another in one apartment. They agreed to split into pairs and lived in small hotels – Bluebell sharing digs with Georgie. The girls had Bluebell's promise that once the show was underway, they would dispense with daily rehearsals.

They started rehearsals the day after the girls arrived from England.

As Bluebell went on stage that morning and saw all of them lined up for the first time, she thought how lucky she was to have these former colleagues for her first troupe. For a start, they were all friends. Some were older than Bluebell. There were the Jackson Girls: the tall, dark Denison twins from Bradford; blonde Elvie with her new look; golden-haired Bessie Bird from Newcastle; Olga from Manchester; Phyllis, a Liverpool brunette; blonde, svelte Georgie from London; and the three girls from the Olympia – Valerie, Joanne and

Elaine, all remarkably glamorous blondes with a lot of hard work in front of them to bring them up to the standard of the former Jacksons.

When her contract at the Casino ended, Bluebell suddenly found herself having to stretch a rehearsal pay to cover rent and meals. She lived in a tiny, cupboard-like room in a small hotel, and tried to do without food as much as possible. She was fortunate that her appetite and diet had never amounted to much. Her hotel was in a little street in front of Square Montholon near the Rue Lafayette. The room contained a bed, a table and a stool.

The other girls occasionally came to her for loans, which she tried to give whenever possible. The entire responsibility of the troupe had devolved on to her, and now she appreciated how free of these cares she had been as a Jackson Girl. She had to find the girls' accommodation, meet them when they arrived, organise financial arrangements for those who wanted to transfer some of their money to banks in England, see to working permits in France, approve costumes, work on choreography, supervise rehearsals, and consult with Maurice and Marcel over music. The business of running a troupe, which later became so routine, seemed frantic and new. There was also the small matter of her own dancing to keep up.

Marcel called on her one day and looked about him at her diminutive headquarters. Then he looked at her and invited her out for a meal. He was amused when she hesitated to accept. It was typical of Bluebell that she should refuse to accept charity, even from Marcel. Ruthlessly independent, she knew that having started on something as she had done with this troupe, she wanted to show her ability to carry on with the job all the way. It was her eggshell pride, again, coming between her and a square meal.

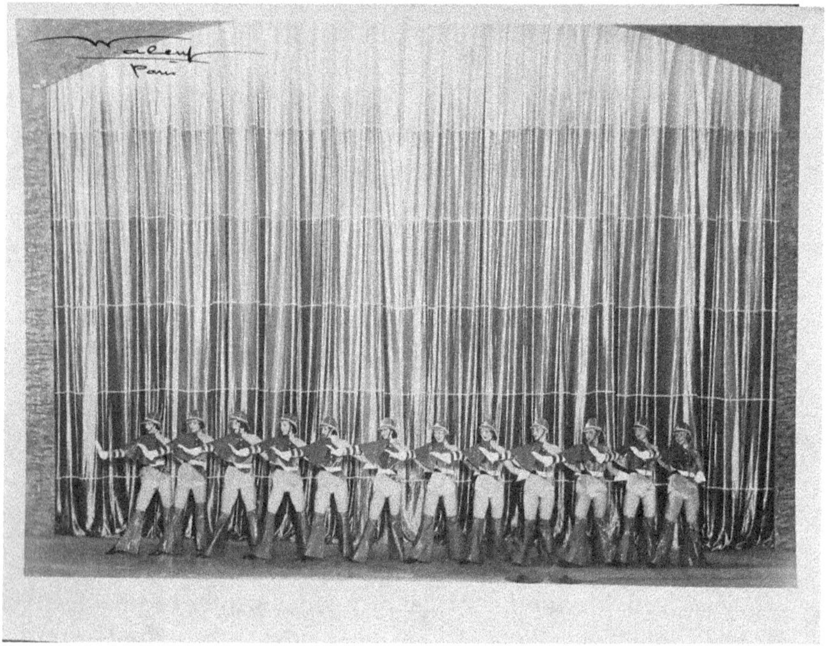

*Bluebell Girls at the Folies Bergère in their 'Policemen' routine –
part of 'La Revue d'Amour' produced by Paul Derval in November 1932*

Rehearsals went on all day and every day, lasting altogether for about three months. Bluebell was engrossed in perfecting the five numbers, each involving plenty of choreography and different from anything they had done before as Jackson Girls. She still kept to precision work as she was not yet experienced enough to attempt any other kind of dance work. In fact, Bluebell's choreography was never adventurous. One former head girl, Eleanor Dare, in later years described it as 'old hat'.

So absorbed was she in the rehearsals that it never occurred to her what the troupe was to be called. Maurice Hermite, the producer, together with his assistant Pierre Larrieu and Marcel, not to mention Paul Derval, had not thought of it either, until they were faced with presenting their new programme. 'The Folies Bergère Beauties' or 'Les Folies Bergère Belles' were suggested but it was Marcel who suggested the name by which they and subsequent troupes were to become so famous.

'Why not call them the Bluebell Girls? It's a pretty name, especially to Continental ears. Belle means beautiful. It's a name no one has heard before. And Bluebell is, after all, the troupe leader.'

Derval agreed to the suggestion, and so, without Bluebell being aware of it at the time, the Bluebell Girls came into being.

For days before the opening, Bluebell began to feel extremely nervous, a new sensation for her. She could not sleep at nights and her appetite disappeared. She knew that once the show started, she would feel better. She would also have her own dancing to think about, which would help to allay her nerves. She was aware that she would not notice any mistakes if she was in the dancing line, and wished she could stand at the back, like Alfred Jackson, and watch, so that at least she could know the worst.

It was a policy that no one at the Folies Bergère had their name up in lights outside the theatre. Instead, when they closed the grill outside, they hung large portraits of the stars of the show on it, and Bluebell was among them. She was thrilled and took to walking up and down the Rue Richter to see if people were looking at it. It was unbelievable to see her picture with its prim caption 'Miss Bluebell', alongside those of André Randall, the leading lady and other principals.

At last, the opening night came. The costumes were marvellous, better than they had ever been. It was obvious that if the Folies Bergère had been going through a bad time financially only a few months earlier, it was on top again now. Thanks to nearly three months of rehearsals, the Bluebell Girls were perfect. The first number was received with tumultuous applause and the intermission was spent in the dressing room, with other members of the company constantly putting their heads around the door to congratulate them, including members of the Ballet Stella and the Spark Ballet, who were still with the company. The numbers in the second half were more elaborate and spectacular than those of the first and were even better received. By the time they reached the complicated grand finale, they were almost dazed by the heady stimulant of applause.

After the show, Bluebell was invited to join Paul, Maurice and the rest of the management at the opening night Champagne supper at the Bagatelle Club next door to the Casino de Paris in the Rue du Clichy. As Bluebell stepped out of the chauffeur-driven car, she glanced up at the casino where only three months earlier she had been merely one of the dancers. After so many weeks of difficulties, scratch meals, complicated business problems, doubts and worries –

a period akin to purgatory – she could hardly believe that this was her, Bluebell Kelly, not only dining in one of the most elegant restaurants in Paris and drinking Champagne which she had never tasted before, but enjoying the company of the management of Europe's most famous music hall. It was like a wonderful dream, and she began to think what Mary would have thought, if only she could see her now.

'To the future of the Bluebell Girls!'

Bluebell was jolted out of her reverie. Maurice was raising his glass to her.

'To the world's youngest troupe leader,' smiled Paul Derval.

MISTINGUETT

IT WAS, OF COURSE, ALL too good to last. Month after month went by and the name of the Bluebell Girls became well known throughout Paris. But one day, about six months after the opening, Paul Derval sent for Bluebell and told her proudly that they had signed up Mistinguett for the next show, opening the following autumn.

'She's coming in to see the show tonight, so I thought I'd warn you,' he said. 'You see, I want to keep you on for the next show, and if she likes you tonight, you're in it. But as she is going to be the star, it all depends on her.'

Bluebell knew all about the famous and almost legendary 'Mist'. She was born plain Jeanne-Marie Bourgeois, and had danced in Paris at the turn of the century, and was the spirit of comedy who also played in straight dramatic roles.

She had made both songs and dances world-famous by the way she had put them across, from the dance 'La Valse Chalouopée' at the Moulin Rouge, of which she was part-proprietor, to the song 'Mon Homme' twelve years earlier

Bluebell girls and boys in 'Le Bois de Boulogne' wearing orange and grey outfits. Eleanor Landreau, sister of author Sylvia, top left.

Bluebell Girls starting the infamous 'Danse de Grenouilles'.

at the Folies Bergère. She was a veteran of the vast Folies Bergère stage.

When Bluebell arrived in Paris, the city was still reverberating from the news that Mistinguett's sketch entitled 'Le Salon de Madame du Barry', in which she had portrayed the mistress of Louis XV avoiding the guillotine by suggestively raising her skirt to reveal the famous legs, had been banned by the police commissioner after royalists had vehemently protested. This was remarkable considering some of the shows that passed in Paris! Mistinguett, popularly known as 'La Miss' or 'Mist', was now at the height of her fame. So great in the profession was she that no management could engage another act for a show in which she was starring without her permission.

Bluebell hurriedly assembled the girls and told them that afternoon. They had to be good that night as all their jobs depended on it. Of all the numbers, the *pièce de résistance* was a strenuous routine they performed dressed as frogs. It was not a glamorous number, but quite spectacular. The decor portrayed stagnant swamps, full of 'crocodiles' and other water life. Realistic tropical trees and fronds made of rubber hung down; backstage, there was an elastic curtain depicting a lake, which had holes in it that the audience could not see. At the end of the number, the girls turned their backs on the audience and jumped through the green fronds, through the holes into the 'water'. The dancing consisted of the most energetic leaps and intricate movements, and the troupe was proud of the fact that they almost outdid real frogs. They squeezed into their tight-fitting frog costumes early that evening and went through the number over and over again in the dressing room.

Eventually, Bluebell went to the door to see what stage the show had reached. To her horror, she found that the number following the frog number was already on. They had missed their cue! Just for once, the call boy had forgotten to call them down, and on this one occasion they had been too busy to notice. As the show was so fast-moving, they had gone straight on with the next act, and no one out front had noticed, including Mistinguett. The girls had missed their big chance to show her what they could do.

Derval sent for Bluebell two days later. He looked positively unhappy as she went into the office.

'I'm sorry, but Mist is going to bring over a new troupe from England,' he said. 'So I'm afraid I shall not be able to renew your contract.'

Mist, apparently, wanted a completely different type of troupe, something new. The troupe she engaged were trained by Buddy Bradley, the first African-American dancer to choreograph an all-white show in London, to which he had moved in 1933 after failing to find acceptance in the United States. His troupe consisted of tall English girls and his trailblazing choreography involved new, snaky movements and tap-dancing, all very modern and very different from the precision work for which Bluebell's troupe was known. The Bluebell Girls were, in effect, finished. They had another six months of the contract to go.

Bluebell told the girls right away. To be rejected like this in the first show could be regarded as a failure, yet they knew they had been a success; everyone who had been to the Folies Bergère had greeted them with acclaim, except Mistinguett. The most Bluebell could do was to promise her girls that she would do all she could to get a contract for the troupe somewhere else.

The door always seemed to be closing on her and she was not sure whether another would open in time for her to get her foot in before having to disband the troupe. She had a team of fine, good-looking dancers. They had already made a name for themselves in Paris, and she did not think they would be a hard sell.

A door did open. With the growth of the film trade in Paris at this time, there was also a great deal of movement within the theatrical world. Bluebell heard, through the show business grapevine, that Jacques Charles, one of France's most famous producers, long-associated with the Casino de Paris and Moulin Rouge, was to become the producer at the Paramount Theatre in the Grand Boulevard.

Charles had produced all of Mistinguett's appearances at the Casino and had travelled throughout the world producing shows. News reached Bluebell that Charles was looking for a troupe of girls, and immediately she went to the Paramount to see him. As at several other large theatres in Paris and, of course, the Leicester Square Theatre in London, they were planning to run films and live shows alternately throughout the day, with the chorus line putting on pre-concert shows designed to reflect the theme of the movie. Other cinemas of the time, such as the Alhambra and the Gaumont-Palace, employed vocalists of the 'chanson réaliste' school, such as Damia who was renowned for her songs and tragic roles, and the cabaret singer Lys Gauty, for the same purpose, their songs of despair standing in dramatic contrast to the dancing of a chorus line.

Bluebell did not have to tell Jacques Charles much about the troupe, for he had seen them several times. She explained that they were finishing at the Folies Bergère, and at first, she was afraid that Charles might think the management no longer wanted them and therefore decide they would not be good enough for the Paramount either. But Charles knew Derval well, and he had heard all about the circumstances of the Bluebell Girls' present position at the Folies Bergère.

To Bluebell, it seemed too good to be true when, without hesitation, he agreed to engage them. But there were catches: Bluebell would have to engage a further twelve girls to fill the huge stage of the Paramount; more seriously, the contract was for only two weeks. She had to gamble on making a hit right away, and hope a further contract would be offered, otherwise she would be involved in a big loss which did not bear thinking about, since she would be bringing out twelve girls from England at her own expense for only two weeks.

Needless to say, she hadn't the money to pay for all this; her extra 10 francs a day for being troupe leader at the Folies Bergère had been more than swallowed up in additional expenses, and a significant proportion of her salary was still being sent home to Mary. She would have to borrow funds for this project and work like a fanatic to make sure she made a success of it.

Hurriedly, she placed an advertisement in *The Stage*, Britain's theatrical journal, and called an audition. It was the first advertisement she had ever put in this paper, and there were to be many more in the years to come. She took a couple of days off, put her deputy in charge of the troupe, arranged for the reserve girl to fill the gap, and went over to England.

Bluebell always tried to keep to the principle of never engaging a girl without seeing her first, and also, if possible, the girl's parents. As she walked into the Max Rehearsal Rooms in Soho's Great Windmill Street for the first time, she could not, by any stretch of the imagination, have envisaged that several decades on, she would still be auditioning in the same rooms.

She had no agent, and as she sat down behind a table in the large bare room which had been allotted to her, a caretaker came up and asked if she were Miss Bluebell's secretary. At twenty-two, she did not look much like a troupe leader. For years to come, parents accompanying their daughters to auditions would ask, 'Aren't you a little young to be in such a responsible position?' Yet she found they never seemed apprehensive about putting their daughters in her care after they had talked to her for a while.

From time to time, at the Folies Bergère, the secretary would ring up to the dressing rooms and tell her there was a newspaperman there to speak to her, and when she came down to see him, the reporter would say, 'No, he would like to speak to Miss Bluebell,' and nothing would persuade him that Bluebell was not merely the head girl sent down to get rid of him.

As she sat there waiting to conduct the auditions on that very first occasion, she smiled to herself and could hardly believe that it was only eight years ago that she had first toured with the Hot Jocks company and boys had called out after her in the street, 'Does your mother know you're out?'

Eight packed years.

She found, however, that she was not nervous as she took her first audition; she knew what she wanted and was determined to find girls of 5'7' or over if possible. If Mistinguett wanted a troupe of tall girls, then so did Bluebell, a precept she kept to ever afterwards. Many times in the years to come, it was to break her heart to see a very pretty girl who was a beautiful dancer but was two inches too short, so could not join Bluebell's troupe. Once, a girl of eighteen, who had gone right through the Sadler's Wells Ballet School, came to be auditioned. She had grown too tall to get into the Sadler's Wells Ballet Company, and yet she was too short for Bluebell. Bluebell's main stumbling block in auditions was nearly always height. Consequently, for every girl she engaged, she had to audition about twenty.

Young women from every kind of troupe and every part of the country came to that first audition, enabling Bluebell to engage most of her twelve additional girls for the Paramount. The remaining gaps were filled by other former Jackson Girls who were drifting back to Paris after many varied and mostly unsatisfactory experiences in other troupes. Two of the girls had nearly starved to death in London; another had been robbed in Monte Carlo. It was a sorry tale, but now Marie and the two Olgas were both back, and the team, now designated 'Les Bluebell Paramount Girls', seemed almost complete again.

Bluebell found herself embroiled in a turmoil of rehearsals; once more, she was caught up in the world of obtaining work permits and booking hotels, but this time, the girls would be contracted to her. For the first time, she felt she was truly, in every respect, their troupe leader.

As soon as the run at the Folies finished that October, the girls went straight into the show at the Paramount. At the end of the two weeks, the Paramount managers sent for Bluebell. It was Bluebell's crucial moment, but she need not have worried; they were delighted with what they had seen, and signed up the troupe for the whole season, six months, until the following May.

It was a hectic job: if the film was a big one, it went on for a fortnight or, at the most, three weeks. If it was not so big, it might last only a week and a whole new show would have to be choreographed and rehearsed for the next film. Jacques Charles would come to her the day before they started a new show with, 'Next week we are going to have a film with a Spanish flavour,' and the theme of their new show would have to mirror that of the new film. So for instance, Bluebell choreographed an elaborate Oriental show to go with the film version of *The Mikado*, with all the girls draped in Japanese kimonos. The following week saw the girls dressed as aviators and dancing before a backdrop depicting a huge aeroplane for a famous John Ford movie of 1932, *Air Mail*.

On the morning of a new show, the girls would have to be at the theatre at six o'clock, often yawning and with their eyes practically stuck together with sleep. They would rehearse with a piano in a practice room under the stage until nine-thirty, when the first programme started, and then be back to change for the new show soon after midday.

There were to be four shows a day, with five on Saturdays and Sundays, and the girls would have little respite, because the first would start at one-thirty in the afternoon and the last at ten-thirty at night. It was a good thing that most of them had the rigorous stamina and training of being Jackson Girls in the past, for their current schedule was enough to break the average dancer.

Occasionally, girls overslept. Once, when Bluebell was dancing at the Paramount in her own troupe, she had gone to bed, exhausted, at midnight and, with her last thoughts, reminded herself that she had to be up at six o'clock for a change of programme rehearsal the next morning. She had woken up with a start to find her clock said a quarter past seven. Leaping out of her bed, she had flung on some clothes and torn through the streets to the Paramount. It was only when she reached the building in the early morning winter darkness that she realised why it was all bolted and locked, and the streets empty; somewhere, a clock struck three; when she had squinted at her clock from her bed, it had actually said twenty-five minutes to three, not quarter past seven!

Now, for the first time, Bluebell's name was up in lights. In hundreds of electric light bulbs, 'Les Bluebell Girls' shone and could be seen at a great distance. As at the Folies Bergère, when her picture was first mounted outside the theatre, she walked up and down outside, looking at it, and if one bulb was off, she would report it to the management. It was exhilarating being only twenty-two and having one's name in lights already, and it was certainly the Paramount that helped her to become well-known across France. Other people in show business who worked at nights had the opportunity to come along and see their show in the afternoons, and in this way, the reputation of the Bluebell Girls spread where it would be most effective – among people in her own profession.

One afternoon, Mistinguett herself came to see a film and stayed to watch the live show. Wherever Mist went, she was treated like royalty, so her visit to the Paramount was accompanied by the usual reception of obsequious managers, producers and hangers-on. After the girls had done their numbers, she turned to the management and said, 'Well, I did a silly thing there. These girls are the ones I threw out at the Folies, and they're much better than the ones I put in their place!'

Other people, apart from Mistinguett, were also beginning to notice the Bluebell Girls, and gradually they began to be invited to perform one-off engagements elsewhere. Bluebell was delighted when the Committee for Social Work and Charity for Aviation held their 'Gala des Ailes' in March 1934, at the Theatre des Champs Élysées, and requested her troupe to dance, alongside stars of the Paris stage and circus and well-known classical musicians. They were performing for Albert Lebrun, President of France from 1932–40, General Victor Denain, the Minister for Air, and a number of the most famous aviators in France, as well as other leading members of French society.

It was all very well having one's name up in lights, receiving praise from the great Mistinguett, and appearing in charity galas, but spring was coming and the Paramount would soon be dropping its live show for the summer, having already signed the girls up for the following winter season. But the tide of recognition was turning, and within days of Bluebell's signing with the Paramount for the following winter, Paul Derval sent for Bluebell again. He asked her to return to the Folies Bergère and supply no fewer than two troupes for their new show the following autumn.

This time, the Bluebell Girls at the Folies would be her own troupe, under contract to her alone and she would receive top billing as 'Miss Bluebell, Maitress de Ballet'. Mistinguett's earlier insistence that Les Bluebells leave the Folies Bergère had, in effect, given Bluebell her greatest career boost to date.

Now offers for summer shows began to pour in for the Bluebell Girls from far-distant places: Italy, Ostend, Geneva, Nice, Le Touquet, Rouen, Bordeaux, Baden-Baden and Le Tréport in Normandy, known as the most British sea resort in France, where, the girls reckoned, 'all the retired majors used to fly across the Channel in chartered planes' for wicked weekends. It was amazing how widely their fame had spread.

From looking for work, Bluebell suddenly found herself looking for girls, more girls and still more girls. She went to England and back to the Max Rehearsal Rooms many times, travelling backwards and forwards by boat across the Channel throughout the whole of that summer.

This time, she was determined more than ever to find tall girls. They looked better on stage. She found that tall statuesque English girls were tremendously popular on the Continent. Whereas in England, men seemed to get a complex about girls taller than themselves, Continental men loved women they could look up to in every sense of the word. They liked English girls with their fair, peachy complexions, long clean limbs and fair hair. They also seemed to like their naivety and even their prudishness.

Already Bluebell was losing girls through marriage, although usually she tried to persuade them to stay on afterwards. Married girls, she found, were often more settled and therefore able to concentrate more on their work than some single girls. But in those days, husbands did not expect their wives to continue a dancing career after marriage and some, frankly, did not like to be reminded that their wives had ever been dancers, even though, had they had never appeared on stage, they might never have met in the first place. Dancing at that time was often thought a suspect career, even though most chorus girls had less energy left over for mischief than many office girls.

The management of the Casino de Concours in Bordeaux, a beautiful open-air theatre, wanted the Paramount girls for the summer show, but as they were already booked for other places, Bluebell promised another troupe of the same calibre. Sixteen tall new girls, destined ultimately for the Folies Bergère, were brought over to Paris, and she selected the stalwart and indefatigable Big Olga from Manchester to be their head girl. They rehearsed the girls hard in Paris and they left with Olga, who gave her word to Bluebell that by the opening night she would have them licked into shape. Bluebell was to travel down to Bordeaux two days before the opening, with costumes and music.

By this time, Marcel and Bluebell were working as a team on new productions, for which Marcel arranged and composed the music. Generally, when Bluebell started on the choreography of a new show, Marcel would begin by playing a few melodies with varying rhythms, and then they would hope that inspiration would come to her. They worked painstakingly on the Bordeaux show, during the afternoons before Marcel had to be at the Folies for the evening performances.

Finally, Bluebell left Paris at nine o'clock in the evening, two days before the Bordeaux opening, armed with costumes and music. It was only after the train had pulled out that she realised that she had left the music in the taxi! Frantically, she leaned out of the train at the next stop, thrust some money in to a porter's hand with a scribbled message to telephone Marcel at the Folies Bergère in Paris to tell him what had happened. Fortunately, Marcel received the message at the theatre.

After the show that night, he gathered together the orchestra leader, the two musical arrangers of the Folies, and all the musicians who were able and willing to sit up all night, to make copies of the orchestral parts at his apartment. Sitting with the manuscript spread out on tables, coffee tables, on the bed and even the floor, they worked, living on black coffee, throughout the whole night and the following day, and Marcel put the completed new score on the nine o'clock train the following evening.

It was a very battered-looking crowd of musicians who reported for duty in the orchestra pit of the Folies Bergère that night, but Bluebell was able to take the score and orchestral parts off the train at Bordeaux at dawn the following day and present it to the conductor of the Casino orchestra for rehearsal at nine o'clock that morning. The director of the Casino never knew about the near mishap, and the original copies of the music were never recovered. Bluebell had a tough twenty-four hours keeping the whole episode to herself with her fingers firmly crossed in the hope that Marcel could work the miracle that he did. All the same, the reproachful look he gave her a few days later when she returned to Paris was enough to make her a hundred times more careful in the future. She was learning the hard way that troupe-leading entailed more than simply looking after the girls.

Little did she realise that she was soon to lose the services of such a valuable trouper as Big Olga. In the two weeks in Bordeaux, Olga had indeed licked the girls into shape and throughout the run it was proposed, or rather hoped, that these new girls would have assimilated all thirty numbers of the Bluebell repertoire. Such a task would normally take a year, but Olga could be relied upon to train the girls well. She had a tough time, though. One girl could not do the splits; another had to be vaccinated. All these problems are the small headaches usually met by troupe leaders. One girl absconded during the first week after sampling the bitter taste of hard work in rehearsals, and Olga literally had to chase down the railway line after her. The girl got away, though, and another had to be found quickly to replace her. But on opening night, Bluebell was amazed to see these new girls give a performance equal to any of her old time-tried troupe.

Once again, the Bluebells topped the show, although, with the exception of Olga, they were all fresh out from England. The only disturbing thing was, in fact, Olga. Throughout the show, she could be heard coughing, even during a solo song by the leading lady who turned and glared at her on stage. Olga was one of the most robust girls Bluebell had known, so she assumed she could not possibly have caught a cold in sunny Bordeaux, and that she must surely have just a frog in her throat. If you looked at the troupe, Olga, with her athletic build, dark glossy hair, china blue eyes and pink cheeks, always looked the strongest and most healthy. Indeed, a few days after Bluebell had returned to Paris, she had a cheerful letter from Olga telling her of the girls' continued success and informing her that she had won a long-distance race in a local swimming gala. There was no end to the energy the girl had.

Within two weeks, however, Bluebell was urgently recalled to Bordeaux. Olga had collapsed. She was suffering from double pneumonia and rheumatism and the doctor had prescribed a medicine which contained a certain percentage of arsenic. One of the other girls had been charged with the job of administering the medicine to Olga, but, in her usual independent way, Olga had helped herself and was unconscious. She was still insensible when Bluebell arrived. She waited by her bedside until Olga came to. Twenty-four hours later, when, looking near to death, she opened her eyes, looked at Bluebell, and said, 'God, Bluebell, you must have thought I'd tried to do myself in!'

Before Bluebell returned to Paris, the doctor promised her that lung X-rays would be taken, and the director assured her that he would not let Olga return to the troupe. However, Olga was not to be cast aside quite so easily. After the X-rays had been taken and sent away to be analysed, Olga got up as if nothing had happened and went to the theatre. Before the director could stop her, she had gone through the whole show and collapsed again. After she had somehow changed, the director grabbed her by the arm and marched her out to the ornate wrought iron gates of the Casino.

Clearly distressed, he said, 'If you were my daughter, I would forbid you ever to go on the stage again. You're a very sick woman. I'm not telling you what your trouble is, but my wife died recently from what I think is wrong with you. Now, you're going out through those gates and you must never come back through them again.'

And with that, he walked her through the gates and put her in a taxi.

Within no time at all, Bluebell received the reports of the X-rays: Olga had tuberculosis. She was very ill by this time and had to return straight home to Manchester. She was put on the train at Bordeaux and Bluebell met her in Paris. At every juncture of the journey, her way was smoothed for her by friends, many of them Bluebell Girls. Those who had been her former colleagues remembered how, as a Jackson Girl, Olga had always shared a room with Ena Pavlova and had been there when Ena finally collapsed before being taken to the sanatorium in the Black Forest, where she had eventually died.

Olga, herself, was to spend five years in a sanatorium before she recovered and the wish of the director of the Casino in Bordeaux was granted in that she never did dance again. Throughout the whole of her illness, until 1939, when she was finally discharged from the sanatorium, subsequent Bluebell troupes, whether they had known her or not, clubbed together and sent Olga her wages; having been taken ill abroad, she received neither sickness benefit nor insurance. It helped her to buy the extra food she needed and to continue to pay her parents the £1 a week that she had always sent home during the years she had danced.

RED STARS, BEAUTIFUL LADIES AND PARAMOUNT GIRLS

FROM THE BEGINNING OF the next season, when Bluebell opened with troupes almost simultaneously at the Folies Bergère and at the Paramount, her own regular active dancing career was virtually at an end. With three large troupes dancing at the same time, she no longer had time to dance herself but established herself as a 'swing' girl for both the Folies and the Paramount, which meant that when any girl was off, either through sickness or vacation, Bluebell would take her place.

There were twenty-eight Bluebell Girls at the Folies now, sixteen in one troupe and twelve in the other. Bluebell recalled the Jackson days when he made all the blondes in the troupe curl their hair up tight to look fluffy while all the brunettes had to wear their hair sleek and straight.

Now she decided on a much more daring idea. Her troupe of sixteen would all be redheads and named 'Les Bluebell's Red Stars' and the remaining twelve would be platinum blondes to be billed as 'Les Bluebell's Beautiful Ladies'. Those girls

with mouse-coloured or fair hair dyed their hair blonde and the brunettes went red.

It was a sensation, as it was believed to be the first time this idea had been tried out in Paris or, come to that, anywhere else. Their first appearance in the show was always startling. The curtains swung back slowly upon a dark and apparently empty stage, with the orchestra playing softly. Then, out of the darkness, at the back of the stage, the line of twenty-eight blondes and redheads slowly advanced from the darkness and, as they moved forward, so the light became brighter and the music louder. This simple method of presenting the girls at the beginning of the show to the accompaniment of a crescendo of light and sound, combined with the startling colouring of the girls' hair and their magnificent height and stature, never failed to get applause, even before they started dancing.

Of course, there were accidents. As even Paris hairdressers were not what they are now, many of the girls preferred to peroxide their hair themselves. One girl, thinking her hair would become really ash blonde if she left the peroxide on all night, wrapped her head in a towel and went to bed like that. Well, her hair was ash blonde in the morning, but… it was still lying on the pillow when she got up! The poor girl had to wear a wig until her hair grew again, and even then, the first quarter inch grew out ash blonde as the peroxide had penetrated into the roots. Fortunately, she had a northern sense of humour and used to have fun going into the hairdressers to ask for a shampoo and set before whipping off her wig and saying, 'Here you are. I'll be back for it later!'

Another girl left the peroxide on a little too long and miserably watched her hair go down the drain as she washed it through afterwards in the sink. She, too, had a wig, but she was more sensitive about it than the first girl, which was

Miss Bluebell in 1936 with the girls lucky enough to appear in The Great Ziegfeld

not helped when it fell off on stage during a number. Her wig fell down over her eyes once during a precision number and the audience had rocked with laughter. After these two mishaps, Bluebell could see herself presenting the first all-bald dancing troupe in the world and issued instructions on 'How to Peroxide Your Own Hair'!

The presentation at the Folies Bergère was as fabulous as ever and the costumes were breathtaking. In the red, white and blue finale, there were sixty people all moving about on stage at the same time. The Bluebell Girls were all dressed in blue Viennese gowns, smothered with blue sequins, and the dress rehearsal was, as usual, a frantic mess, with people yelling directions in all languages and each girl desperately trying to follow her own colour. But after the opening night, the critics announced that the Folies had excelled itself, especially with its water scenes, for which a real swimming pool had been built into the stage.

It was exciting to run a troupe in Paris in those days. All over the city, there were *panneaux de publicité* [22], portraiture heads taken by Colette Harcourt, the famous Parisian photographer, and full-length pictures six yards by four yards in size. There were five or six of these outside the Opera House at one time, in the Étoile and along the Champs Élysées, and they had to be replaced every three or four days because people kept stealing them. Throughout a season, thirty to forty thousand had to be printed. Bluebell troupes were in demand and now Bluebell had her first post office savings book. It was hard to believe all this was happening to her.

Her Paramount girls were by no means overshadowed by their blonde and red-haired colleagues at the Folies Bergère. At this time, some magnificent films were being released, one

---

[22] French: billboards

of the most spectacular being *The Great Ziegfeld* (1936), the film story of the life of the great Florenz Ziegfeld, who had died only four years earlier. To accompany the film, which was to run at the Paramount for three weeks, Bluebell had to create a 'Ziegfeld Folies' in Paris. For this she was given thirty-two more girls, to add to her sixteen, who came from dancing classes and other troupes.

The forty-eight girls were all on stage standing in groups talking together when Bluebell arrived for rehearsal and was introduced to them. Some were Russian, some were French, some English. Bluebell listened to the music, then called out, 'Now, would you all mind forming up into a line please?'

But they could not get into a line, even on that huge stage, and although they all crammed together, with their shoulders hunched, it was still impossible.

'Well, please go into a semi-circle then,' she suggested.

A huge semi-circle of forty-eight girls formed itself slowly on stage and Bluebell stared at them. Looking around the stage, she thought, *I'll never be able to do anything with this!* and she could feel herself beginning to cry. Then she pulled herself together and kept telling herself, *It's your job, so you've got to do it. You can't walk out now!*

It was the first time that she had dealt with such a large number. So immersed was she in her Jackson Girl background, she did not at first realise the simple solution which, just at the moment when she thought she was defeated, presented itself. It occurred to her that she had at her disposal a big tessellated staircase, so she broke the formidable semi-circle into grouped formations, positioning half of the girls on the staircase and half of them on the great stage. Even then, she needed all forty-eight girls, exotically dressed and waving enormous Ziegfeld-like ostrich fans, to fill the enormous space. Bluebell had discovered 'broken line dancing'. Old Ziegfeld himself might have been pleased with the result. Young Bluebell had taken another step forward in her career.

Bluebell's tight daily schedule of shuttling backwards and forwards between the Folies Bergère and the Paramount did not allow for political problems; but at about that time, one of the most influential men in French politics was Alexandre Stavisky, a financier who, from being a penniless Russian refugee, had become a multi-millionaire in only four years. His wife, Arlette, formerly a Chanel model, was one of France's most beautiful women. He was a banker, owned a number of businesses, was the proprietor of the Empire Theatre in Paris, and enjoyed the patronage of some of France's most eminent politicians of the day.

However, Stavisky was also the most spectacular swindler of the inter-war years, his wealth having grown from the issue of fraudulent bonds based on the surety of what he claimed to be the emeralds of the late Empress of Germany – which were subsequently found to be made of glass. In the early days of 1934, his exposure imminent and embroiled in public scandal, he disappeared. *L'affaire Stavisky* produced large-scale rioting all over Paris and to a mob attack on the Parliament buildings. By 6th February, people were describing it as a civil war, 'France's Second Revolution'. That night, Marcel and Bluebell made sure that they saw every one of their Folies Bergère girls home and then hurried across to the Paramount, where the girls would already be finished.

They found the boulevard a mass of swarming rioters. Cars were being overturned and newspaper kiosks thrown to the ground. Knowing that the girls would be trapped in the theatre, they had to get to them somehow. Finally, they abandoned the car several blocks away and made their way via back streets to the stage door of the Paramount. They found all the girls there, terrified. By now, the way that they had come into the theatre was blocked by rioters, so they were trapped too. There was nothing for it but to stick it out in the theatre. Most of them slept on the dressing room floors that night and expected to be able to go home the next day; in the end, they were trapped inside for two days.

Fortunately, there was a restaurant adjacent to the theatre and they managed to slip in there for their meals. The girls were becoming more than a little fed up with the sight of their dressing rooms when the whole disturbance suddenly ended with the discovery on 8th February that Stavisky had died of gunshot wounds to the head, in a chalet in Chamonix. Officially he had committed suicide, but it was widely speculated that he had been murdered.

By now, Bluebell Girls at the Folies Bergère and the Paramount were doing some film work by day and after-midnight cabaret work, as well as their regular work. They were in demand everywhere and even danced by moonlight at a pigeon-shooting party in the beautiful public park, Bois de Boulogne. After-midnight work was usually limited to a ninety-minute cabaret somewhere, although one agent once tried to twist a contract so that the girls would have to do a five-hour cabaret after midnight, wear costumes that would give them the appearance of being completely nude, and mix with the clients as well. It was the first time Marcel ever threatened violence, and the contract was torn up.

Though Bluebell never countenanced her dancers mixing with clients, she did put pressure on some of them to become nudes: her girls were either dancers or nudes (who did a limited amount of dancing). If she noticed a girl had a good figure, Bluebell would tell her she wanted her to be a nude; if the girl did not agree, Bluebell would say, 'I'm sorry, I haven't got room for you and you'll have to go,' and the girl would have to fall in with the plan. However, Bluebell would not have sacked her if she stood their ground; but the threat was there, and the girls believed that she would have done it.

Never did Bluebell allow her girls to mix with clients in the theatre or nightclub where they worked. This was a hard and fast rule that Bluebell always enforced and only if a girl had special friends or relatives who had come over from her homeland, did she let a girl sit with them after the show.

Various managements attempted to break this rule and persuade the girls to go out front and mix with the clients, but they never succeeded. Granted, it was accepted in some places of entertainment, but for Bluebell's girls, work began and ended on stage, and managements usually agreed, in general, that, if anything, a troupe of beautiful girls with the elusive quality of unattainability drew more clients than one to whom familiarity may have brought contempt. A prudish English idea, perhaps, but it worked. Many a young English blood returned to 'Blighty' after a trip to Paris and boasted how he sent a message backstage and invited the best-looking young woman to join him at his table. But you can bet your bottom dollar that she didn't accept; for if a Bluebell Girl were to be seen out front with a customer, she could expect only one thing – the sack.

By 1934, and at the age of just twenty-four, Bluebell was the foremost troupe leader in France, with troupes in three Paris theatres: the Folies Bergère, the Théâtre des Variétés and, for a while also, at the Circle Medrano. Bluebell Girls also danced at the Bal des Petits Lits Blancs that year, and for every year until the start of the war. Staged at the Opera, the largest theatre in Paris, the Bal des Petis Lits Blancs was the biggest charity show of the year in France and similar to the 'April in Paris' Ball at the Waldorf Astoria in New York, the Royal Command Variety Show at the Palladium in London or 'La Nuit D'Août' at Monte Carlo. The sixty-four girls danced on a narrow silver bridge (the Pont d'Argent) over a sea of 8,000 upturned faces!

That year, Bluebells were dancing even in Buenos Aires, and an invitation came for another troupe to dance at Radio City, New York, but two weeks before the girls were due to leave, the United States refused work permits. This was a pity, because it meant that, due to the war, it was to be another twenty years before Bluebells would dance for the first time in the USA, although at the time, the Buenos Aires success more than made up for the New York disappointment.

'The Continental', which the French star Jean Sablon sang with the Bluebell Girls at the Folies Bergère, was the hit song of the season in France, and it seemed to reflect the carefree mood of Europe, which was riding a happy wave-crest. Nobody seemed aware of the Teutonic rumblings in their midst, or, if they were, they did not want to hear them. Life in Paris was one of bright lights, sunny parks, romance and swimming pools. Bluebell Girls, who were all so much in demand and now the highest paid dancing girls in Europe, travelled everywhere by taxis, rather than the Metro.

The Paris of the 1930s could easily go to one's head, especially with Champagne a shilling a glass. English girl dancers working a seven-day week on the Paris stage probably drank far less than the average office girl in England of the time. In fact, many of them did not drink regularly at all, generally waiting until a special occasion, when some of them were known to dive in head first and come up soaked. Most of them developed no more than a craving for good strong tea, and many were the times that small hotels and dressing rooms were nearly burnt down due to a hidden paraffin stove bursting into flames or electric kettles fusing and whole buildings plunged into darkness when the girls attempted to satisfy the English desire for tea made the English way. Many was the mother who was begged to bring over some tea on her next visit, and Bluebell was no different having hers, a special mixture, sent out from Liverpool.

Some girls could take alcohol, others couldn't. One night, when the girls went on at the Folies for their first number, Bluebell could see that Evelyn, a beautiful blonde, was definitely out of control. Her make-up was smeared, her headdress was on back to front, and she gave the impression that she had fumbled so with her dressing that, at any moment, she might become as undressed as the official nudes. The other girls were desperately trying to cover up for her by steering her through the routine.

Bluebell was furious. As soon as Evelyn staggered towards the wings, still guided by the other girls, at the end of what seemed to Bluebell an interminable number, Bluebell caught her and guided her off – right out of the theatre – and gave her the sack. At the end of the week, though, she 'did an Alfred Jackson' and took her back. But the shock cured Evelyn!

Another girl, Ida, at the Paramount, knew her limit and was conscious of her weakness. Invariably, if she were invited to a party by a man, she would decline the invitation unless she could find a friend from the troupe to accompany her. This was because the poor girl needed only a couple of drinks, before the evening would disappear into oblivion.

Sometimes, a young woman's off-stage activities led to trouble in the theatre. Josephine Baker, one of the most pleasant and popular people in show business, was already a big star in Paris. When she returned to visit America in 1936, her boyfriend remained in Paris.

For a *divertissement*, he fell in love with Mabel, one of the Bluebells at the Folies. Josephine's boyfriend installed

1934

The 16 famous Bluebell Girls.
Marie Waugh (third from left), Bessie Bird (fifth from left)
(both dancers from Newcastle) at The Paramount Cinema, Paris.

Mabel in Josephine's beautiful apartment and even gave her Josephine's clothes, jewels and furs!

It was a cold, early winter when Josephine returned from America to start her run at the new show at the Folies, only to find she had neither an apartment to go to, nor warm clothes to wear. She had to sleep in her dressing room until accommodation could be found because, when he heard Josephine was on her way back, her boyfriend had moved Mabel out and disposed of the apartment.

Almost with poetic justice, the man became ill and it was then that Mabel went to Bluebell and Marcel to ask what she should do. They told her that whatever she had left of Miss Baker's property, she should give back. Until then, they had known nothing of the whole sorry story. When Josephine found that Mabel was a member of one of the Bluebell troupes at the Folies, she told Derval she would refuse to sign her contract unless the girl went and he asked Bluebell to remove Mabel. Normally, Bluebell would have defended any girl in one of her troupes, but, on this occasion, she willingly transferred her.

A more light-hearted version of the same story was to take place a year later. Mistinguett was still the brightest attraction in Paris. She was such a great star that producers had to allow a four-minute hiatus in the normal schedule of a show to allow for the applause when she first appeared on stage. She could do anything – dancing, singing, comedy, sketches – and in 1938, the theatrical grapevine buzzed with the news that Mist was signing for a new revue at the Théâtre Mogador. This time, Mistinguett requested that the management ask for a Bluebell troupe to appear in her show.

Mist must have been about sixty by then, but she looked much younger and, even at that age, her legs were fabulous.

She was 5 foot 4½ inches with fair but not particularly blonde hair and protruding teeth. Nobody would have called her beautiful and her voice could only be described as *canaille*[23]. It had a strangely acid quality, perhaps considered vulgar, and it was probably a good thing that microphones came into use more towards the end of her long and meteoric career, for they would certainly have sharpened this fault.

Yet when Bluebell met Mistinguett on stage at the first rehearsal, she realised why she was so great. She looked like a star and dressed like one too. Her vivid and radiant personality must have come from an inexhaustible supply of *joie de vivre*, which had survived a lifetime of struggle and more than a few heartbreaks. Bluebell admired her more and more as she saw her perform each night, putting across that presence – star quality – the ability not only to shine when she felt like it, but also to put it across night after night, whatever happened.

Something did happen, though, which nearly stopped the show as far as Mistinguett was concerned – and a Bluebell Girl was the cause of it. Mist's current escort was a young man named Carlos. He was a very tall, good-looking Brazilian dancer and her partner in the show. Unfortunately for Mist, Carlos had a wandering eye, and it very soon alighted upon a pretty red-headed Bluebell called Irene.

Before long, Carlos and Irene were meeting clandestinely and at first neither Mist nor Bluebell knew anything about it. Mistinguett was the first to find out and it soon became obvious that she was performing under a great emotional strain and some of the company knew why. Already, she had several showdowns with Carlos about 'this Bluebell Girl'.

---

[23] French: harsh and common

One night, at the end of the finale, Mistinguett fainted dead away on stage just as the final curtain came down. When she came around, she was violently sick.

Then she stood up, shot a flaming look at the redhead, and in front of the entire company said, 'I feel like killing that girl there.'

The next morning, Bluebell was sent for by the management. Mistinguett was there in the office. Bluebell was told by the producer that Irene would have to go.

Bluebell felt the request was unreasonable. If it had not been one of the Bluebell Girls, it might have been any other girl in Paris that Carlos would have chosen to flirt with.

'I'm sorry,' Bluebell said, 'but this girl is under contract to me, not to the management. There are another four months of her contract to go. I've no reason to dismiss her, although I shall discipline her for what's happened. If you insist on her dismissal, however, I must ask you to pay her off for the rest of her contract, which is until the end of the show.'

'How much would that be?' Mist asked.

The Bluebell Girls were well paid. When it was worked out, Mistinguett sat down resignedly.

'Alright, let her stay on,' she said bitterly. Then, her eyes flashing, she said, 'But she must not look at Carlos again, or I will kill her.'

Suddenly Mist began to cry and fumbled in her handbag. Instead of taking out her handkerchief, she produced her diary.

'I don't see why he should cost me still more money,' she wept, feverishly turning the pages. 'Look, I gave him 30,000 francs six months ago, and here – recently, another 50,000, nearly 80,000 in all. This boy has already cost me so much, I don't want to lose him now.'

Everyone felt embarrassed. Here was the old sad story of a wealthy but ageing woman finding her man only capable of cupboard love, for the sake of personal gain. Yet, at the same time, it was a relief. For, it seemed, Mistinguett was weighing up her loss, not so much in heartbreak, but in francs. Of course, the story had the usual sequel. Irene did not keep her word and went on trying to see Carlos, but she went the same way as most, and Carlos' eye went on wandering. Not long after that episode, Carlos, looking for a change of scenery, began a torrid affair with a pretty Parisienne and Irene caught them together in her apartment.

In the years that followed, Bluebell almost forgot about this Brazilian dancer and the havoc he had wrought. Not until eighteen years later did she hear of him again, when he wrote to her from Brazil asking for a Bluebell troupe to dance in a big cabaret he was running there. But he didn't get one, not because Bluebell thought he might still cause trouble, but because, in his contract, he insisted on the girls going out front and sitting with the customers. Wherever Bluebell saw this insidious clause in a contract, all chances of doing business with her were killed.

The demand for Bluebells mushroomed fast towards the end of the 1930s and business boomed with such a great rush that at times Bluebell had difficulty remembering how many troupes she had. Europe was flourishing and America had forgotten her depression.

In the programme at the Folies there were advertisements enticing wealthy patrons to sail to California for a holiday for $477 or to travel by coach to North Africa for 1,700 francs; another advert proclaimed that the Bluebell Girls '*ont été transportés de Londres à Paris par les avions British Airways Limited,*' *(aller et retour)*[24] for 490 francs. Men looking like Rudolph Valentino, with their black, greased hair and centre partings, and women with pencilled, thin eyebrows, wearing their hair like smooth silk skullcaps, featured on the adverts.

To dine in an elegant Paris restaurant with an orchestra cost only 14 francs, '*boisson comprise*'[25]. Folies Bergère patrons were urged to move on after the show to applaud the celebrated can-can at the cabaret Bal Tabarin in Rue Victor-Massé. If they looked closely enough, they would have noticed that the same Bluebell Girls were doing the can-can as those they had watched an hour earlier at the Folies.

In the meantime, down in Monte Carlo, a troupe of Bluebell Girls were roused from their sleep, at three o'clock in the morning, to put on a special performance for King Gustav of Sweden, who later returned the favour to the same troupe when they performed in Stockholm; he sent a squad of his army officers to squire the girls around the city and show them his summer residence, Drottningholm Palace.

Over the years, Marcel had become indispensable to Bluebell, not only in her work, but also to her life. Bluebell wanted to marry, but not to settle down; her childhood and youth had done for that. Security is what she continued to aim for in life, long after she had achieved it. At that time, Marcel could not offer much financial security if she were to give up her career, although that was something she could not imagine doing. But he was an excellent business manager, and together they made a good team. Moreover, Bluebell was sometimes troubled with the thought that they had come from different religious backgrounds. Even though Marcel

---

[24] French: have been flown to Paris and back by British Airways Limited.
[25] French: including one drink

had never actually practised his, Bluebell did and, at the time, believed very fervently in her Catholic faith.

There were many obstacles between their romance and marriage. Nevertheless, Marcel gave more and more of his spare time to managing Bluebell's business and when he took his first holiday in nine years from the Folies Bergère, he used it to travel to Naples by car to look after a Bluebell troupe there!

Always an incredibly fast driver, he tried to do the journey in one day and ended up crashing his car later that night. Fortunately, he was not hurt, but it was a fine way for a worn-out musician to begin his first vacation in nine years.

THE THREAT OF WAR

THE MUNICH CRISIS OF September 1938 erupted during Marcel's working holiday in Italy; things were beginning to look very black politically. Earlier that year, Bluebell had been in Baden-Baden for a one-night gig with her girls and had received a month's pay for one night's work. However, the sight of swastikas scrawled on the wall at the back of the theatre, in telephone booths and in lavatories made her realise that this was something more than a political philosophy; it was a national disease. While they were there, the girls had referred to Hitler as 'His Gilpotts', so that the Germans would not know who they were talking about.

While Marcel was looking after Bluebell's troupe in Italy, she knew he would seek advice from the British Consul there if an emergency arose, but after his return to Paris and, as crisis followed crisis, she worried about them. So she sent a wire to the head girl, Pris Blythe, suggesting she should consult the British Consul. Back came a letter from Pris telling Bluebell that all was calm on the Italian front and that the British Consul was 'no effing good'. Pris added that the

1938 at the Folies Bergère, just as the threat of war was beginning

girls in Venice were having a marvellous time, out riding every day with the Italian cavalrymen stationed in Veneto. Having received only a waffling and hedging reply from the British Consul, she had put the vote to the girls, and they had elected to stay and fulfil the contract. But Pris felt she should, nevertheless, put another call out to the British authorities to check on the situation.

Replying to Bluebell, she wrote:

'As soon as I received your telegram in Venice, I picked up the phone in my hotel room and asked the switchboard to get me the British Consul. I reckon she must have been putting calls through to different consuls all day and by this time was getting rather muddled and put my call through on somebody else's line. As soon as I heard it was the Consul speaking, I blurted out "There are eight of us British girls here. What do you advise? Do you think it will come to a war and what should we do?" Well, do you know, Bluebell, there was a deadly hush. Then a rather cold voice answered, "This is the German Consul speaking!"'

In spite of the Munich Agreement and the promise of 'peace in our time', there was an increasing realisation that the new Folies Bergère show they were currently rehearsing would mark the end of an era in the history of many theatres, the end of many careers, of freedom and travel, of life as only Paris knew it and for many, perhaps, life itself. Almost as though the management instinctively knew that this would be the last year before many years of economy and rationing, 'Madame La Folie', the 1938-9 presentation at the Folies Bergère, was the most extravagant of all the pre-war shows.

Its 'One Thousand and One Nights' scene was the most fabulous so far and the shimmering sequinned costumes that the Bluebells wore for the 'Manon's Revenge' scene, comprising enormous headdresses and four-foot ostrich feather fans, were the most glamorous they had ever worn.

The nudes were never more seductively attired than in an Arab number called 'Syrie' and the story of Lady Hamilton's romance with Lord Nelson was lavishly portrayed, with the stage a-swim with satin crinolines and foot-high wigs. The Folies Bergère was to ride high into the dark years ahead.

Many have lamented that the Bluebell troupes never performed in London but, in fact, they did. That autumn, Jacques Charles asked Bluebell if she could muster one hundred Bluebells to perform at the Earl's Court Exhibition Centre in London that December. It was a mighty challenge, for she would have to do this without calling on the services of any of her troupes, all of which were working a seven-day week in Paris.

Fortunately, some of her dancing troupes were becoming free and a number of former Bluebells, who had only recently retired to marry, could be persuaded to stage a comeback for a short contract in London. Choreographing and rehearsing them made her previous work at the Paramount in 1936 with forty-eight girls in *The Great Ziegfeld*, which had at the time nearly reduced her to tears, seem like child's play. The one hundred girls were split into two vast troupes: one a ballet troupe, the other a kicking line. The head girl of the ballet troupe was Pris Blythe, who had by now returned to England for good. The kicking line was headed up by Dodo Felton, her former Buenos Aires head girl, as both were seasoned troupers. Pris' troupe worked the first half of the show and Dodo's the second.

It was a truly testing time for Bluebell and both she and Marcel travelled to England for the opening. Her girls had always appeared in foreign lands with success, but so often prophets develop clay feet when they return home. However, she need not have worried, for Londoners loved them. For Bluebell, the resounding triumph in London meant more to her than any other success. It was the memory of this particular show which kept her going throughout the year that was to follow, and she kept the poster showing her one hundred girls at Earl's Court in her office at home thereafter. It was like a grand finale of the careers of all the pre-war Bluebells. Afterwards, they were to be scattered far and wide, some back to France and to French husbands, others to the United States and American husbands, but most back to their hometowns and the boy next door in England.

After the final performance, Marcel and Bluebell made their way across London to Euston Station to make her first visit to Liverpool in six years – and Marcel's first visit ever. As they walked on to the Liverpool-bound platform, Bluebell recalled the last time she had been there – the cold and miserably wet day she had left her one small suitcase in the left luggage office after the collapse of the Jackson troupe six years earlier; how she had gone to a Lyons' Corner House for a plate of egg and chips and how, by sheer good fortune, she had decided to call in at the Leicester Square Theatre to see her friends who had been lucky enough to get jobs right away with Alfred Jackson's brother.

On such a slender thread of chance had hung the fate of her whole career. Had she not called in to see them, she might never have bumped into J.W. Jackson at the stage door, and he would not have sent her back to Paris – and Marcel. She would not have been there for Derval to offer her the task of starting a troupe at the Folies Bergère. And the great Mistinguett who had – quite inadvertently – dealt the next ace in her favour and caused her to form the first troupe under contract to herself at the Paramount, would never have featured so crucially in her life; one that had now become a rushing torrent of success, excitedly surging on and on.

With a constant deluge of work, this was the kind of life that Bluebell, with her northern upbringing, loved and welcomed, the kind of life she could not do without. Gone, years ago, were her own personal stage ambitions. The woman-in-the-wings role was a greater part than that she could ever have achieved on stage.

While she sat on the train as it travelled northwards to Liverpool, her thoughts were projected forward to Aunt Mary. There was a woman in the wings, if ever there was one. Bluebell smiled as she thought of the times when, as a child, she had organised her own little charity concerts with the other little girls who were her pupils. Some of these concerts had taken place at the Alder Hey Hospital, where Aunt Mary had worked, and all the children had received presents afterwards from the patients. She recalled how, during one Christmas concert at the hospital, she had gone on stage to do her speciality number, a balloon dance, and after only a few bars her balloon had floated near the Christmas tree and burst on a candle. Bluebell had nearly dissolved into tears, but Aunt Mary had been standing in the wings ready for such emergencies and had thrown on another balloon before Bluebell could even lose her step.

Yes, all through her career, Mary had been her woman in the wings, but she had repaid her aunt in full. She still sent money home to her and from time to time Mary would ask for an additional lump sum. Once, when she had urgently asked for £25, Bluebell had sent it immediately, thinking it was for an emergency. When she had asked her afterwards what she had needed it for, Mary wrote back saying: '*For a piano. I'm going to learn to play.*' Bluebell had heard from the rest of the family that this was so that she could accompany one of the little waifs she had taken in for a while, whom she was teaching to dance. Mary was finally doing things she could not have contemplated previously; indeed, every three to four months, true to her eccentric self, she startled the family by sending a card from some fashionable holiday resort.

Mary was just as Irish as ever. How Bluebell had laughed when she had sent her a photograph of Marcel; the picture was a full-faced one, quite a good one, except that nothing could conceal the fact that his hair was receding. Mary had written back with, '*Why does he cut the front of his hair so high?*' Now she was going to see for herself. It was only right that she should meet the man Bluebell was by now engaged to marry.

It was a memorable visit, this last one to Liverpool before the war. There were so many old friends to see and to whom she wanted to introduce Marcel. Bluebell wanted as many people as possible to share her happiness. More than anyone, she knew that Big Olga, still recovering from tuberculosis, would like to be at their wedding in Paris and they made a special trip to the sanatorium near Manchester to invite her. Though she only had a few more months before her discharge, she was unfortunately not yet well enough to make the journey to Paris.

There is rather a mystery as to when Bluebell and Marcel were married. In France, there is a separation between the church and the state, so a couple first have to be married at the town hall in Paris. It seems they had their town hall wedding at the beginning of March 1939 and began married life in a *pension* in Rue Blanche in the Montmartre district. It was a noisy road on a busy intersection in the heart of cabaret land, right opposite the Moulin Rouge and only minutes away from the Folies Bergère itself.

Bluebell still kept in touch with old Bluebell Girls, although, as usual, she had her hands full looking after her current girls at the Folies and elsewhere. A neighbour in the Montmartre district was Bessie Bird, now Madame Pierre Samin, and they saw each other every day. It was a warm, sunny morning when Bluebell took a large bunch of flowers to the clinic in Avenue Juno to visit her the day her son, Michel André, was born.

'Not so long for you now, either,' Bessie had said, smiling, looking at Bluebell.

In fact, Bluebell had less than a day to go before her own son was born. Terrified of going into the clinic too early and having to wait unnecessarily in a tense, clinical and antiseptic atmosphere, she called an afternoon rehearsal and spent the entire evening performance climbing up and down the spiral staircase that led between the dressing rooms and the stage of the Folies Bergère. From there she went on to a late-night movie starring Ginger Rogers and Fred Astaire and stopped for tea in a bistro in Place des Ternes – anything to delay going to the clinic. Finally, Marcel had to carry a prostrate and protesting Bluebell into the Bologne clinic, where Patrick was born on 13th July 1939.

Marcel and Bluebell continued to speak German together until 2nd September 1939 but after war was declared on the 3rd, they decided that from then on, they would speak only French together. Their son should be brought up to speak French and English, for they had no particular wish now for him to grow up speaking German.

At this time, Bluebell already had a war casualty staying with her. Babs Fox, a pretty blonde and former Folies girl, whose husband Lambert, like Bessie Samin's, had been mobilised and sent away, had come to stay. Eventually, both Babs and Bessie were to learn that their husbands had become prisoners of war. Bluebell and Babs were together the day war was declared in France and the first air raid warning sounded almost immediately. The two girls tore into a shelter followed by an excited Frenchman who dashed in behind them shouting about a gas attack. Everyone was panicked into putting on their gas masks, but, after a few minutes, Babs noticed that all eyes were turned on Bluebell and then saw the reason why: Bluebell's mask had no filter, just a large hole, and if she was still alive, there was clearly no gas attack. Sheepishly, they all took theirs off. Bluebell hadn't even noticed her mask was incomplete!

By this time, there were no domestic servants to be had and Bluebell had only Paulette, her nanny, to help with Patrick. Babs helped with the cooking and shopping until December, when she was due to leave with Bluebell's troupe bound for San Remo and Rome. Italy was still neutral and Babs and the rest of the girls had no qualms about their trip. Bluebell knew that should anything happen, they could return straight home to England by boat.

The Folies Bergère, like all other theatres in Paris, closed down the day war was declared and the Bluebell Girls in Paris had nothing to do. Two months earlier, in July, Bluebell had a troupe of twelve girls in Zürich, but because of the crisis they had been sent home to England after fulfilling only one month of their three-month contract. Now, during those first few peaceful weeks in Paris, which should have been recognised as the calm before the storm, Bluebell heard from the director of the Zürich cabaret asking if she were willing to send some girls back there to complete the contract. Switzerland was not likely to be embroiled in the hostilities, he explained, and it seemed a safe enough place to send a troupe. Marcel wired back to Zürich:

ALL OUR TROUPES FREE – READY TO JOIN YOU. SEND MORE DETAILS.

Half an hour after Marcel had sent the wire, two gendarmes called and asked him to accompany them to the police station. There he underwent a severe inquisition. *Was he a military leader? A secret agent? A spy? Then what was his business? His profession, then? All right then, why did he have a foreign accent?* Bewildered, Marcel answered all their questions, but the police were not satisfied. Finally, the police chief took out Marcel's telegram and laid it before him.

'Then what does this mean, please? "All our troupes free – ready to join you. Send more details,"' he snarled. 'If you are Romanian, then to whom are you offering troupes and why does your message go to a neutral country like Switzerland? I presume because it is en route for Germany?'

Marcel laughed with relief and after he had explained the play of words to the gendarmes they, too, saw the funny side. In French, the word 'troupe' is spelt the same, whether it applies to military personnel or dancing ones. As it was, Bluebell never did send that troupe to Zürich. She decided that although Switzerland would doubtless remain neutral throughout the war, it would be a far more difficult country from which to get back home to England when the girls' contracts ended than it would be for the troupe in Italy, who would have an escape route via the sea.

Bluebell wanted to return to England, just as everyone in foreign parts at that time wanted to return to their homeland. She was registered with the British Embassy in Paris and expected them to contact her or advise her to go home when or if the situation worsened. These were the blissful months of the Phoney War. For nearly a year, nothing seemed to occur, and then it all happened far too quickly.

Bessie, with her husband now mobilised, decided for her infant son's sake to return home to Newcastle and spend the duration of the war with her parents. Bluebell asked her to look after the Folies Bergère girls who were going home to England on the last train out from Paris. Bluebell, however, still had the contract to fulfil in Italy, beginning in December and, as long as any of her girls were on the continent, she felt it her duty to remain there also until the end of their contracts, so that she could arrange their safe passages to England.

Despite the politically tense atmosphere, the girls in San Remo were a great success, and the regular bulletins she received from Babs left her in no doubt of their continued success with the Italians. But early in the New Year, she received a begging letter from Babs explaining that her husband, Lambert, was due home in Paris for ten days' final leave. It was their last opportunity to meet before he left for the front line, and, by implication, possibly the last time they would ever see each other. Bluebell knew she would never cease to blame herself for not doing everything in her power to arrange for them to spend Lambert's leave together. But now she had no other girls to call on. There were, in fact, no Bluebell Girls in Paris for the first time in seven years.

There was only one thing to do:

OK, she wired back. RETURN IMMEDIATELY. WILL TAKE YOUR PLACE.

Although she had not danced for six years, she saw no reason why she should not still be able to dance in one of her own troupes. She knew all the routines, because she had choreographed them herself, and during rehearsals was always demonstrating and joining in, and she was still naturally supple.

After her séjour in San Remo, when she returned to Paris, Marcel received his first order to enlist as a foreigner in the army and he went to the Rue Saint-Dominique, where foreigners were being enrolled for the services. After queueing for four whole days, he signed on; now there was yet another reason for them to stay on in France. As it was, Marcel's call-up was delayed until March, then April, then May, until it was too late.

Bluebell had always been unhappy that they had not been married in church. Because of their mixed religions they had a civil marriage, but now she persuaded Marcel, in case anything should happen to him, to have another marriage in a Catholic church, to which he equally agreed. She petitioned the Archbishop of Paris, who referred the case to the Vatican. Marcel had an interview with the Archbishop, during which he promised that the children of the union would be brought up in the Catholic faith. Thus, at the end of February 1940, eleven months after their first marriage and seven months after the birth of their son, the couple celebrated their second wedding in the Église de la Sainte-Trinité in Paris.

Bluebell began to worry about her girls in Italy. The Italian troupe were appearing in a show with Odoardo Sparado, the 'Italian Maurice Chevalier', who had been working with Bluebell Girls there for six years. Sparado had long been a familiar figure at the Folies Bergère, where he had appeared alongside the English actress and vocalist Jenny Golder in the revue of 1922, 'Folie sur folie'. In 1927 he had performed with Mistinguett at the Moulin Rouge. By 1940 he and the troupe of Bluebell Girls with whom he was working were huge international stars in Italy.

The head girl was a Bluebell called Kathleen. She had an Italian boyfriend who worked for American Express and she had been head girl for Bluebell in Italy on and off for three years, in order to be near him. By April 1940, when Bluebell saw how events were beginning to turn, she started to warn

Kathleen in her letters, but could not say too much because letters were now being censored. She tried to tell her the contract for the girls should be curtailed, and that probably it would be wise for the girls to return as soon as possible; Kathleen continued to assure her that everything was quiet there, the girls were safe, and that if anything happened, she would bring the girls back.

The fact was that nearly all the girls had Italian boyfriends; some were sons of eminent Italians, including cabinet ministers, well-born young Italian men-about-town with positions in society which enabled them to give the girls a wonderful time. It was not surprising that her girls were reluctant to leave. As a troupe, they were popular with the Italian people; their Italian boyfriends had told them they would be foolish to go back, since both England and France were now at war; the Germans, they argued, would blockade the seas and England would starve; France would be overrun; but here in Italy, they urged, the girls had everything they could want. Italy, they assured them, would not join the war; in any case, if anything happened, they themselves would protect the girls.

Frantically, Bluebell threw all caution to the wind and sent a wire ordering the girls to get out. She instructed them to go to Marseilles and get a boat to England from there. At the same time, Bluebell and Marcel appealed to the Italian Embassy and the Red Cross; Marcel even wrote letters to the Pope and the Italian royal family.

News began to reach her that the girls were trickling home. Some had managed to get out by boat from Marseilles and Naples. Two had come through Paris, but by this time there were no trains to England from Paris. Desperate, now, to get home, they walked from Paris to Saint-Malo. Bluebell had given them Patrick's baby carriage to wheel their luggage along the roads. It was a formidable trek, but many people were doing it. They managed to reach Saint-Malo, but by this time the Germans had reached Northern France and the girls had to often hide in the bracken to avoid being spotted by passing German convoys. At last they managed to board a boat crossing the Channel to England.

Other girls from the Italian troupe only escaped from Italy on the night of 9th June 1940, the day before Mussolini announced to huge crowds across the country his decision to join the war in support of Germany. Babs, arriving on the last train from Italy to Paris, told Bluebell of the difficulties they had encountered trying to get help from the Consulate, where no one seemed to know what was happening. She told her of other troupes of British girls in Italy, some of them former Bluebells, who had stayed on after their contracts had expired, had been arrested and thrown into work camps. It was all the more distressing that their boyfriends were now no longer able to help them. No longer were they in when the girls called, and when they tried telephoning, the young men's families had refused either to answer or to pass on messages.

By this time the Germans had steamrollered through Belgium and Holland; there seemed nothing to stop them blotting out the whole of mainland Europe. Bluebell and Marcel wanted to get away, but while there were still some of her girls in Italy, Bluebell felt she must stay and wait for them, in case they should come through Paris and need help getting home.

Denise, they knew for sure, was still in Italy. She was very much attached to an aristocratic young Italian who was an aide to Marshal Italo Balbo, Minister of Aviation and Governor of Libya, the only leading fascist who opposed Mussolini's alliance with Nazi Germany. Sadly, Balbo only lived to the end of June, when his plane was misidentified by Italian anti-aircraft guns and shot down over Tobruk in Libya.

Kathleen was also still out there, because she also wanted to stay near her boyfriend. These young women knew that to leave Italy and return to England might mean they would never see their young men again. To them it did not matter that their two countries were at war, and perhaps the war lent a dramatic aura to their romances. Bluebell found that she could no longer contact Denise's father in England, a director of a British bank; all she knew was that Denise had not boarded the boat bound for England, on which many other English girls, some recently released from prison camps, had been allowed to travel.

Sitting helplessly in Paris, Bluebell felt herself at the centre of some great big railway junction, shunting young women home in different directions, ticking their names off her list when she heard that they had taken a boat from an Italian port. But how was she to know they had arrived home? It was only by constantly persecuting embassies and the Red Cross that she was able to get any information at all. Kathleen, she heard at last, had caught a boat for Britain, which left only Denise unaccounted for.

Now there was no longer a British Embassy in Paris, British subjects were advised to go to the American Embassy for help. Twice a day, Bluebell called at the American Embassy to enquire if Denise had yet arrived in Paris but each time they had no news.

Bluebell and Marcel wanted to reach Bordeaux to try and get out via the Western sea route. They offered Georges Triel (the stage director of the Folies Bergère) and his wife seats in the car. His sole object was to get to Bordeaux and stay there, for it was his hometown and the rest of his family were there. In return, the Triels had offered hospitality to Bluebell, Marcel, Patrick and Paulette, the nanny, until they could catch a boat to England and take Patrick to safety. Marcel would have to stay behind as a member of the French army, but if France fell before Bluebell left the country, he could try to travel with her.

One by one, friends telephoned to say goodbye. They were leaving for Bordeaux, and, if they could, for freedom. Radio communiqués told of the advance of the Germans and warned that Paris might be bombarded. All sorts of rumours spread through the city, some of which seemed to be emanating from German intelligence, such was the confusing effect on the population. Finally, when they came home one day from yet another fruitless expedition to the American Embassy, Marcel gave his ultimatum: they must prepare to leave without waiting for Denise, he said. Denise was a Bluebell Girl, but Patrick was their son, and it was imperative to get the child out of Paris before the Germans started bombing the city.

They left Paris by car on 12th June. The Germans entered the city on 13th June. Bluebell and Marcel closed up their apartment in Rue Blanche. It was impossible to pack many belongings, for they were taking with them in the Citroën two friends, as well as Paulette, the nanny. They did not realise, until they reached the road to Bordeaux, how many others were doing the same. The road was wedged tight with people and cars, bumper-to-bumper, heal-to-toe, some carrying bundles and suitcases, others trundling prams; men and women carrying small children and babies; others with only brown paper parcels as luggage; some, despite the heat, wearing many layers of clothes to avoid carrying them – a pathetic river of humanity.

This was the great Exodus.

The radiator of Marcel's Citroën, packed to capacity, like all the others on the road, boiled over many times for they were dragging along at walking pace, a speed not normally suited to Marcel when he was behind the wheel. Cars broke down in front of them and sometimes they had to wait for hours before the procession began to move on again. Often, in desperation, Marcel would turn up a side lane and make a big detour, in the hope of getting further along the road, only to find they had to wait as long to get back into the stream of traffic at a point further ahead, and more often than not, after all that effort, lost their original place in the line.

Day after day went by, and although they had left Paris with a tank full of petrol plus reserve supplies, they ran out of fuel and had difficulty finding more. With six of them, including a small baby, in the car, the journey was trying and uncomfortable. Most of the luggage was strapped to the top of the car to make room inside. Each night they slept at the roadside.

All the time, German planes strafed them, and the whole journey, from Paris to Bordeaux, was made under an almost constant bombardment. Every time they heard planes approaching, they rushed out of the car and threw themselves into a ditch, or a hedge, or onto the grass at the roadside. Each time the fighters flew over the road, they could hear the rattle of machine guns, the whining of bullets and sometimes a loud explosion. It took five days and four nights to complete the 600 kilometres to Bordeaux. However, when they arrived, they found the Germans already there.

Georges' family – his brother and sister-in-law – in Bordeaux had three children, including a son of about Patrick's age. The brother had been called up into a tank regiment before his son was born, and he was still away, either a prisoner or retreating somewhere – his wife did not know.

She and the children were living in their Bordeaux apartment and made everyone feel very welcome after their five-day ordeal. Patrick was put into the nursery with the other children, and, as there were only two other bedrooms, the three women moved into one and the two men into the other. After four nights on the road without sleep, it was still impossible to rest. That night Bordeaux was bombed, one bomb falling so close, the nursery was damaged. The children, mercifully unhurt, were moved into the room with the women.

The following day, the American Consulate was swarming with refugees. A weary-looking official directed Bluebell over to the desk where an attendant was dealing with people trying to get out of the country.

'Bluebell! What are you doing here?'

Bluebell had been too tired to recognise the man behind the desk; he was an old acquaintance. When she had last seen him – it seemed years ago – it was in the offices of the Folies Bergère, where he had worked. It was good to meet someone she knew in a place and a situation like this.

'Well, like everyone else, and you too, it seems, I've come from Paris. I want to get over to England.'

'Oh, my God,' he groaned. 'You'd better get out of here as quickly as possible. Why ever didn't you come sooner?'

Then, without waiting for an answer, because there was a queue forming behind her, he went on.

'Your best bet is to go further south to Saint-Jean-de-Luz, just north of the Spanish border, and maybe you can pick up a boat there. The last British boat left two days before the Germans arrived here.'

Bluebell and Marcel walked around Bordeaux. There were not many Germans around, but those who had arrived had certainly taken command. They met British refugees everywhere. In a café, they sat down at a table with a French couple who had also hoped to get to England.

'But we have given up the idea,' the husband said.

'We've been told we might get a boat from Saint-Jean-de-Luz,' Marcel told him. 'Have you not thought of that?'

'No good,' the Frenchman said, waving his finger from side to side. 'We tried that. We went down to Saint-Jean-de-Luz ourselves, with an English couple. We found the boats would not come into harbour but stayed about half a mile out to sea. The people who wanted to board a boat had to swim out to it. The English couple did that. But my wife, she does not swim. We could not persuade anyone to row us out to the boat, because they were afraid of machine gun attack from the air. So we came back. It is not even safe now to make the journey to Saint-Jean-de-Luz . The Germans are everywhere and are cutting off the roads.'

Bluebell could not see herself swimming out to a boat carrying a baby boy only a few months old. It was out of the question. Other people expressed sympathy, but there was nothing any of them could do to help. Some suggested they might try to get into Spain, going up through the mountains on foot and hiring a guide, but they heard that a number of people had already been killed trying to do that, so it was a big risk with the baby.

They could not go anywhere by rail because all the trains had been stopped. It seemed they were stuck. Dunkirk was a thing of the past – the north of France was all taken so there was no escape that way. Now they had narrowly missed getting out via the Western sea route. There was no petrol in the town, so they could not use the car; there were no trains, and now no boats. It was all very dispiriting.

That night there was no bombing, and Bluebell fell asleep instantly. But in the middle of the night, the bedroom door was flung open and Madam Triel's husband stood there, unkempt and grotesque in a motley collection of civilian clothes, obviously borrowed. He and some others had tried to bring their tank back to Bordeaux; finding the Germans everywhere, they had abandoned it, changed into civilian clothes to avoid being captured, and walked all the way home. He embraced his delighted wife, went across the room and swept Patrick up in his arms.

'No, no!' Bluebell and Madame Triel laughed. 'Not that one, the other!'

He had never seen his son before!

Now that Monsieur Triel was home, there were far too many people trying to live in one small apartment, and Bluebell and Marcel moved into an empty villa which belonged to friends of the Triels who had fled to the south of France, asking Madame Triel to find someone to rent their villa. Marcel and Bluebell were resigned, now, to spending the rest of the war in France, however long it lasted.

Bluebell bought a bicycle, so that she could get around and do the shopping. Everything now was sold through the black market and prices were rising steeply. All British people had to register themselves at the nearest police station. This Bluebell did, but in addition to this, the French gendarmes acting now on the instructions of the Germans, had to check on all apartments and houses occupied by people who did not belong to the district. Because Bluebell had registered as a British subject in the local police station and, in addition, did not belong to the district, the Germans decided she was worth a double check, and they called at the villa to make further enquiries.

To remain in Bordeaux seemed pointless. They were living at black market rates, solely on their savings. In Bordeaux they were unable to carry on the only work they knew how to do, and now that the Germans had taken that town as well, they might just as well be in Paris. In fact, Bluebell felt far more conspicuous as a Briton in a provincial town than in the capital. But now nobody was allowed to move from one place to another without a special permit, so they went to the police station, not very hopeful, to ask for permission to travel back to Paris.

To their surprise, the police not only gave them a permit, but also a coupon for petrol, enough to get them back to the capital. Perhaps the authorities were glad to get rid of some of the refugees.

Gladly, they packed up and left right away. The road that August was now clear of all those refugees who had travelled so fruitlessly from Paris, and the stream was beginning to be reversed. Others, like themselves, were making the return journey.

The first thing they did after depositing their baggage in the flat was to go straight to the American Embassy to see if Denise had turned up. When they arrived at the embassy, there sat a red-haired girl sitting on the steps, crying: Denise!

Realising that she was not at all well, they took her home with them. She told them that once Italy had become embroiled in the war, she had remained there with her boyfriend until he had learned that he was to be sent to North Africa with his chief, Marshal Balbo. At that point, he had arranged for Denise to return to Paris, so that she would not be left alone, an alien, in Italy. After arriving in Paris, Denise had looked for Bluebell, but found she had gone. To make matters worse, she had been taken ill with appendicitis and had already been admitted to a hospital for the operation when the Germans had arrived and ordered all British patients out of the hospital. Disconsolate and unwell, Denise had returned to the American Embassy, and it had been there, on the steps, that they had found her.

Eventually, Bluebell arranged for Denise to have the operation she so desperately needed in a French clinic, but after she had recovered and was back with them, there was a rumour that there would be a check-up on all unattached British people in Paris. Denise became very nervous, but, as luck would have it, Bluebell heard that the Folies Bergère, which, like all the other theatres, was still closed, was sending a touring company to Rouen and Le Havre, and she persuaded the stage manager to take Denise with the company.

Bluebell envied her for having work to do, and each day hoped that something might come her way too. But as the weeks went by, their savings dwindled, and no work materialised. Foreigners, especially British subjects, were not allowed to have jobs, and the theatres remained closed anyway. Bluebell could no longer afford to pay Paulette's salary and, on top of this, she found she was pregnant again. Many friends advised her to have an abortion, but that was something she could never do – it was completely against her religious convictions, quite apart from any concerns regarding the safety of a termination in these conditions. She explained to Paulette that, though she would love to keep her, she was free to go. But Paulette indignantly refused to leave. She had been with Bluebell since Patrick was two weeks old, and she herself was only twenty-one, an orphan from a Catholic institute. With no other home to go to, she insisted on staying, salary or no salary, which she did, right through the war.

Denise's lucky break did not last long. One day, to their surprise, she turned up again on their doorstep, very depressed. They took her in and listened to her story. The Folies Bergère show had been a great success, first in Rouen and then Le Havre. Babs Fox and she had been the only English girls in the troupe. Rouen was very pro-British and, as a sign of freedom and resistance, the people had posted on the highest wall in town a large picture of Winston Churchill giving the V sign. Every day the Germans tore it down, and every night the people put it up again, despite a 9 pm curfew, when all were supposed to be indoors.

The company had special permits to be out late, so they were among the chief suspects for the Churchill poster escapade. It was not long before the Germans discovered there were two British girls in the company, and Denise was arrested as she was found to have no working papers. Babs was released after questioning, because, having French nationality by marriage, she had a work permit. Denise was taken off to prison and had not been allowed to take any luggage with her, except a toothbrush and her overcoat. Her fellow women prisoners took pity on her and lent her their own woollen clothing, for winter had come early and it was bitterly cold.

Eventually, Denise had been released and she had rejoined the company and travelled on to Le Havre with them. Then, while they were there, Le Havre was heavily bombed by the RAF. The Germans suspected there might be British spies in the area, and without any further ado, started to arrest all the British people in the town. The Folies Bergère stage manager had immediately put Denise on a train and sent her back to Paris, the very day after the bombing, before she could be arrested again. Now she was back again, was out of work, and did not know what to do. She could not get out of the country, so Bluebell asked her to stay with them again.

It was only after a few days that Denise remembered what her Italian boyfriend had said to her before she had left Italy: '*If you are in Paris at any time and need help*', he had advised, '*telephone …*' – here he mentioned a name and number – '*and give this password*' – he gave her a phrase – '*and he will help you*'. It all sounded very cloak and dagger, but then, that was how things were all over Europe in those days.

Denise thought it worth trying and looked alive for the first time in days. Marcel picked up the telephone and dialled the number, gave the man's name, and then the password. The man turned out to be a director of the Bank of Rome in Paris. Within half an hour, he was in their apartment. He seemed already to know all about Denise, except what had happened to her in the past few months, and he promised that he would be able to help her within a few days. Then he returned to the bank and sent a message through official sources to a friend in Rome, who in turn got in touch with Denise's boyfriend, who was in Cyrenaica at the time. In 1939, Cyrenaica was incorporated into the kingdom of Italy and became a major theatre of operations during the Second World War.

Denise's boyfriend lost no time in helping her; what he did was commendable, to say the least, and proved beyond all doubt the sincerity of his feelings for her. He asked to be relieved from his duties for a few days and obtained special permission to leave North Africa at a time when leaves were rarely being granted. With a British fleet patrolling the Mediterranean, he crossed the sea to Italy in a submarine, before travelling overland to Paris. Within a few days, he was in Bluebell's apartment and an ecstatically happy Denise was in his arms. He had brought with him two passports for her, one Italian, the other Swiss, and some money. After he had gone, he said, she was to travel down to northern Italy and stay there in a small border town he named. Then, if things became difficult there, she was to cross over the border into Switzerland, using her Swiss passport.

During his four days in Paris, he spent every evening in Bluebell's apartment. There was no doubt that he and Denise were very much in love. He had risked his job and even his life to help her. It could have gone badly for him had it been known that he had done all this for an English girl at a time when his country was at war with Britain. Yet however strong his feelings for Denise, his mind was still very much on his duties; every night he turned on the radio to listen to the latest news of the fighting in North Africa between Rommel and Montgomery, and did not try to hide his delight whenever he heard of a German and Italian advance and a British retreat.

When Bluebell saw Denise off to Italy a few days later, it was the last she ever saw of her. Later she heard that things had indeed become difficult for Denise in Italy; the people were naturally suspicious of an English woman suddenly appearing among them in wartime. Eventually, when Denise began to fear she might be interned, she crossed the border to spend the rest of the war in Switzerland. Many years later, Bluebell learnt that after the war, Denise had married the distinguished young Italian, who had risked so much for her.

The spirit of Paris is not easily crushed. Although the theatres had remained closed for nearly a year now, there were signs of a reawakening. One of the first theatres to reopen approached Bluebell with the offer of a job providing a troupe for it. It was tremendously good fortune, to be offered any work at all, for it was a decided risk to employ a British person for any work in occupied France. The theatre was the

Alhambra, and the manager a Monsieur Beauvais, who said he would like her to form a troupe to appear in the vaudeville productions he intended to put on.

'But we shall not be able to call your troupe the Bluebell Girls, you understand,' he added, apologetically. 'Much as I would like to have such a well-known name in the show, it would cause an investigation immediately. I'm afraid we shall have to be very quiet and discreet about it. Even without the name, I am sure that having you select and train the girls will make a success of the venture. Yes, yes, that will ensure the quality and standard. You will supply the troupe, train them, and choreograph the routines.'

It was decided, for security reasons, that the girls should be called the Alhambra Belles. But Bluebell was worried that she would not be able to live up to the reputation which she obviously enjoyed with Monsieur Beauvais. This was wartime; no longer could she place an advert in *The Stage* and cross the Channel to select the cream from a large audition room, full of lovely, well-trained young women in London. Yet eventually she found no difficulty in getting together a first-rate troupe.

Paris still had a large population of glamorous, but unemployed, dancing girls. There was no call-up for women in France and girls needed to work now the men were away in prison camps. The twelve Alhambra Belles were an international crowd, consisting mainly of French and Russian dancers, and they were good workers.

There was plenty of work for Bluebell to do. She had to supply the costumes for these vaudeville shows and, as the programme at the Alhambra was to be changed every fifteen days, just as at the Paramount in the mid-1930s, so she would have to provide out of her own stocks a change of costumes for the chorus line every fortnight. It would be a formidable task in wartime, but she was determined to hold down this job and was sure they could manage it with a bit of home sewing and cooperation. She was not very useful with a needle, but Paulette readily offered her assistance, and Bluebell recruited all the girls in the troupe who could sew to help with fittings and alterations and put new lace and sequins on old costumes. It would be a make-do-and-mend presentation, but she hoped that from the front, this would not show.

From time to time during her years at the Folies Bergère she had bought up stocks of costumes at the end of the yearly shows and many of them were still in very good condition. She had done the same at the Paramount and now had a large wardrobe of costumes with which she had earlier outfitted her dancers in the various Sparado shows in Italy. They had all been preserved since the outbreak of war in the two maids' rooms, now empty, on the sixth floor above her apartment. These were all brought down and examined, and it was decided that with a bit of juggling with the tops and bottoms, they could get by.

Bluebell also had to undertake a significant amount of choreography. There were to be two different shows a day, a matinee performance and an evening show, with five routines in each, and three shows on Sundays. With a change of programme every two weeks, Bluebell had to find twenty new routines each month.

Babs Fox was back in Paris after completing the tour of Rouen and Le Havre with the Folies Bergère company and was living in a Montmartre hotel. Gladly, Bluebell engaged her and made her head girl of the Alhambra Belles, for she was a reliable young lady and a proven leader. Also, being married to a Frenchman, she was safe from risk of arrest.

Babs had heard that her husband had been taken prisoner of war in Danzig. Work, she told Bluebell, would serve the double purpose of keeping her mind off things and of bringing in a regular salary.

The opening was a great success – as successful, it seemed, as any pre-war show had been. Perhaps it seemed simply so brilliant against the backdrop of wartime austerity. But there was no Champagne supper afterwards, only the verbal congratulations of Monsieur Beauvais.

'It is good, is it not, to see the theatre open once more? The people must relax, even in wartime,' he said.

Now life seemed almost back to its pre-war pattern for Bluebell, with its hectic work, morning rehearsals, afternoon matinees, evening performances and regular new programmes. As long as Bluebell was allowed to work, she reckoned that life was dealing fairly with her.

BLUEBELL'S INCARCERATION

IT WAS AT EIGHT O'CLOCK ON a cold November morning in 1941, when Bluebell was five months pregnant, that they came to arrest her.

A tall and elegant officer, wearing the uniform and flowing cloak of the Guarde Républicaine, stood at her door. Part of the National Gendarmerie, the Republican Guard reported to police headquarters at this time.

'You must be ready to leave here at 11:30 am,' he told her.

All holders of British passports, he explained, were being arrested and taken to a prison camp; he could not say where.

'But are they even arresting pregnant women?' Bluebell asked. 'I'm expecting a baby in four months!'

'That makes no difference,' he replied, though not unkindly. 'You must be ready to come with me to see the chief of police at 11:30 am.'

Bluebell's work permit

Bluebell immediately telephoned her doctor, who came right away with a certificate proving that she was five months pregnant. Then she had something to eat, telephoned the theatre to tell Monsieur Beauvais what had happened and tried to see all the people she knew nearby to say goodbye. Marcel was in tears, but Bluebell told him it would not be safe for him to accompany her to the Commissioner of Police, in case they should become interested in him as well. Better that one of them should be free to stay with Patrick.

'Don't worry,' said Paulette. 'I shall look after Patrick until you come back,' and she gave Bluebell a reassuring smile, before bursting into tears too.

The officer returned at about eleven o'clock.

'You understand that I do not like to do this,' he said gently. 'But do not take anything with you at all. It is certain that you will not be detained when they learn of your condition.'

While Bluebell got ready, she could hear the officer playing ball with little Patrick in the entrance hall, and marvelled at the ways of war, when kindly men, who one considered one's compatriots, were forced to do unpleasant things like the task now allotted to the gentle giant who had been sent to arrest her. She kissed Marcel, still in tears, Paulette, and Patrick.

'You know, I wouldn't be at all surprised if they didn't send you straight home again,' the guard said cheerfully on the way there. 'Nice little boy you've got. I have a grandson that age,' he added proudly.

As they walked to the police station, he told her that she was in the first batch of about 6,000 British men and women who had been arrested that day. They were taking them by districts. No, he still could not tell her where they would be sent, he replied when she asked him again.

'But, of course, you will not find out either, for I am sure you will not be sent,' he repeated.

And with that, he guided her into the police headquarters, where he left her. She found herself standing in a large square room, with scores of British people sitting on benches against the wall. Two German officers were seated at a table.

Bluebell went over to them.

'I'm pregnant…'

'Have you a British passport?'

'Yes.'

'Over there.'

She went over and sat down on the crowded bench. She noticed that everybody else had luggage with them. After an hour or so, they were told to go outside. Then they were all put into trucks and taken to the Gare de L'Est. They still did not know where they were heading, but they all supposed that their presence at the Gare de L'Est indicated that they were to travel east, probably to Germany. They sat in the station for twenty-four hours. It was very cold and after a while they began to feel hungry.

After some time, German Red Cross nurses brought around some black coffee and some hot water, which was supposed to be soup. One thing Bluebell could not stomach while she was pregnant was coffee. The smell of it alone made her sick and she began to reel.

'Coffee?' the German woman asked.

'I can't drink coffee because I'm expecting a baby. But could I have a cup of tea or something?'

'Coffee or nothing at all.'

'Thank you. Nothing at all.'

It made the twenty-four hours seem much longer, sitting there with nothing hot to drink. Bluebell realised that she only had what she stood up in. The clothes she was wearing were not particularly warm being town clothes and quite unsuitable for rough use.

She asked if she could use the telephone as perhaps Marcel could send Paulette to the station with a suitcase of clothes for her. However, this was refused.

Sitting next to her was an eighty-three-year-old English woman, who seemed to have reached the very depths of despair. During the cold night hours, from time to time, she spoke to Bluebell. The old lady had been a schoolteacher and had lived in France for sixty-five years.

'I'd almost forgotten I was English,' she said apologetically, 'until this.'

She was obviously ill. By dawn she seemed to be suffering from a heart attack and was having great difficulty with her breathing; shortly afterwards the Red Cross nurses came with the 'breakfast', consisting solely of more of that wretched black coffee.

'Quick! This lady is very ill,' Bluebell said to one. 'Could I have a brandy or something for her?'

'A brandy!' the nurse exclaimed. 'No, you can't have a brandy for her. Whoever heard of brandy for prisoners?'

'Then give me some coffee quickly.'

Bluebell took a cup of coffee and fed it to the old lady; after a few moments, the gasping stopped, and she revived. Then

Bluebell went into a corner to try to stop herself from being sick.

Late afternoon the next day, they were all herded on to a train. They were lucky, she kept telling herself. Although they travelled in discomfort on the wooden seats of the congested third-class compartments, in complete darkness, throughout that long winter night, she guessed that this was better than the way some prisoners were transported.

At dawn, they arrived at Besançon, close to the Jura Mountains near the Swiss border, where they were told to get out. So, they were not going to Germany after all; they were still in France. Waist-deep in snow, the city of Besançon was not a very cheerful place in November 1941. The British internees were loaded on to more trucks and driven to a big camp, which was freezing cold and soaking wet, because they had hosed it down that very morning after several thousand military prisoners had been removed and sent to camps in Germany.

The camp was in a huge citadel camp, high above Besançon. By the end of 1940, 2,400 women, mostly British, had been interned in the Vauban barracks, and another 500 old and sick prisoners in the Saint Jacques hospital nearby. The conditions were harsh; many hundreds of internees died of pneumonia, diarrhoea, food poisoning, dysentery and frostbite.

The men were separated from the women and taken to another part of the camp. Bluebell found herself with seventeen other women in a soaking wet barrack room, with bunks all around, one on top of the other. The beds were made of canvas and straw on a wooden frame, and all the bedding, from canvas to coarse blankets, was sopping wet and smelt strongly of disinfectant.

'Well,' said a lively English girl called Sally, 'they've certainly de-loused this place. But I'm not going to suffer for life with rheumatism from sleeping on this little lot.'

Some German soldiers deposited a bucket of coal outside and the women rushed out and brought it in. In the centre of the room there was a stove and they soon had a small furnace blazing in it. Then they hauled down all the mattresses and blankets and arranged them in a steaming pile around the stove.

They were each given a tin plate and ordered down to the canteen to queue up for their meal, which consisted of practically raw potatoes with some gristle.

After the first 'feast', as Sally called it, some German officers appeared in the barrack room and announced, with pleasant smiles, that they would like the women to do 'housework'.

'Now we are getting organised,' they announced, 'we want you to take it in turns to come and peel potatoes.'

When the first potato peeling party returned to the barrack room, their hands were in a bad state. They had been led to a bitterly cold kitchen, where there had been a mountain of potatoes, all completely clogged up with earth, which, being frozen on, was almost impossible to remove.

The women now had raw and bleeding hands; some already had chilblains starting.

'I'm not going to do that,' Bluebell announced.

'No, I should think not,' said another.

'No way,' declared a third.

It was generally agreed that no one would peel potatoes.

The next day, when the German Red Cross nurse put her head around the door to ask whose turn it was to peel potatoes, Bluebell answered, 'I'm not going to have a turn. I absolutely refuse to do it.'

'You do as you are told.' For a nurse, she seemed quite harsh.

'No, I won't do what I'm told. I'm not going to do this and I never shall. I'm in the theatrical profession and I intend to resume my career when you've finished with me and I will not have those kind of hands when I go back. I've never done that kind of work at home and I'm not going to do it now.'

They glared at each other. Eventually the nurse's eyes dropped. She turned to the next girl. 'You then.'

It seemed all the 'no peeling' resolutions of yesterday were gone. Meekly, the women trooped out to work and resentfully they returned with raw and bleeding hands.

'I don't mind you not doing it because you're pregnant,' said one of the women, throwing herself on her bunk. 'But it is a bit much.'

Bluebell replied, 'No, I don't think it's much at all; you should have done what I did. They couldn't carry you into the kitchen, or, if they did, they couldn't make you peel the potatoes. They may say you'll have nothing to eat – well, you don't have anything to eat. That's all there is to it. If we all did that, their schemes and plans would soon fall through.'

But the others remained docile and obedient. Perhaps they could have done with a union leader. Nevertheless, they continued to mutter and peel and moan and nurse sore hands as they swelled with chilblains and rheumatism.

Experience with dancing troupes throughout the years had already proved to Bluebell that when you have a crowd of British women together, the atmosphere is generally a cheerful one. On the whole, they were not downhearted and, despite the conditions, they passed the time as happily as possible in that camp. Frequently there were sing-songs in the hut, and someone had brought a pack of cards which was so much in demand that they rarely found their way back into their case. People were incessantly joking.

'Dead quick on the repartee, you are,' said Kitty Dent, a Cockney, after she and Bluebell had a verbal match together. Kitty was engaged to a Frenchman.

'Wish I'd married him already,' she said. 'Then I wouldn't be in this ruddy hole.'

It was true: all the girls, like Babs, who had French nationality by marriage, were exempt from arrest whereas those with boyfriends or fiancés, who had remained in France to be with them, had been arrested. Indeed, Bluebell discovered that there were two other girls in the hut who had worked in other dancing troupes in Paris and had remained in France because they had boyfriends or fiancés.

Outside it was terribly cold. The camp overlooked the old quarter of Besançon. Bluebell watched the twinkling lights glistening up through the snowy night and imagined it would be very pretty in peacetime. Often, she would daydream about the future and wonder whether life would ever return sufficiently to normal so that people might be able enjoy a winter sports holiday in a place like this. It all seemed very unlikely.

Years earlier, when she had first arrived in France as a Jackson girl, it was a regular joke among the girls to say, '*Next time I return from a holiday in England, I'm bringing my own lavatory back with me!*' But if public conveniences in continental towns were uncivilised, those at this camp were beyond the pale. To get to them, one had to go out into the snow, climb up some steps on to a wooden scaffold like a hut on stilts, an erection which obviated the necessity of digging latrines. There was no roof, which made it rather more than uncomfortable in that sub-zero weather, and especially so when it was snowing. The floor consisted of a long plank of wood with holes in it, and bins underneath on the ground. That was all. Two men came each day to empty the bins.

Perhaps as the camp had originally been built as a men's military prison, the communal privy had not been found too trying to male prisoners who, after all, were at a mechanical advantage over women when negotiating such public inconveniences. It was hard to imagine the indignities and difficulties suffered by five elderly Irish Sisters of Mercy nuns, who occupied the hut next to Bluebell's and who, with their flowing and heavy habits, found it an almost Herculean task to cope with these primitive privies, and became quite frightened of them. Bluebell and the other women had to hold them up to stop them falling backwards through the holes. It was Sally, predictably, who came back with a privy story to beat them all.

'There was I,' she said, her eyes still round with surprise, 'in our elegant toilet. I had just settled down to sharpen my skates, when I heard someone say, "Eh, une seconde, tu vois?[26]" And I looked between my legs, and there were two men looking up... those two Frenchmen who change the bins. It gave me such a surprise, I nearly fell through the hole!'

'Huh!' said Kitty. 'If it had been me and they'd been Germans, I'd have done it all over them!'

---

[26] French: Hang on a second, can you see?

After a few weeks, whereas the others seem to be bearing up with the diet and cold conditions quite well, Bluebell began to feel the effects of camp life. She realised she hadn't had a medical check-up for two months, and she should have had one of her regular prenatal examinations weeks earlier. She went to one of the German Red Cross nurses.

'I'd like to see a doctor,' she said.

'Well, there is a doctor in the camp. Go and see him,' she replied.

'No. He's a military man. I want to see a female doctor, because I'm pregnant.'

The nurse sighed. Bluebell had already established herself as one of the more recalcitrant prisoners in the camp. Then she shrugged.

'We haven't got anybody like that here,' she said flatly.

But it was clear that the nurse reported the case because the next day all the pregnant women were rounded up by the nurses. There were twelve in all, and Bluebell's pregnancy was the most advanced. They were put in a truck and driven down to the hospital in Besançon, where they were examined by a doctor.

Bluebell had never seen so many truly sick people. Many were tubercular; other patients were obviously advanced in various diseases and seemed depressed in the extreme.

After the examination, the doctor asked, 'Would you like to come in and stay here instead of staying at the camp? I might be able to arrange it.'

Bluebell looked around her at all the sick people and the misery and disease.

'Not for the time being, thank you,' she said. 'I think I'd be better off at the camp.'

One day there was great excitement in the camp. The nuns, it was learned, were going home.

'And so they should! What wrong have they done anybody?' said one motherly woman in the canteen, illogically enough, for what wrong had any of the inmates done? The nuns were to be released, they were told, because they were Irish, and therefore not British at all, but neutral.

Count Gerald O'Kelly de Gallagh, the former Irish minister in Paris, had called at the camp. When the official Irish legation followed the French government to Vichy, he returned to Paris in his capacity as 'special plenipotentiary'. He ran consular services out of the premises of his wine company, Vendôme Wines, in Paris. In collaboration with the legation staff in Vichy, he was able to provide some relief to Irish people in distress. He also ensured that anyone who had been detained was quickly released and offered temporary Irish passports to many.

He had come all the way to the camp specifically to obtain releases for the Irish nuns, and, whilst there, had heard that there was a woman in the camp who was not only Irish-born, but pregnant as well.

Bluebell had met him once. Some years before, she had called at the Irish Legation in Paris to register there because of her Irish birth, proof of which she always carried around with her in the form of the birth certificate Mary had given her when she had first left for the Continent.

It was here that she had first met Count O'Kelly. Now that Irish birth certificate was to serve her well.

Count O'Kelly immediately requested her release from the prison camp too. Bluebell did not see him in the camp, and the first she heard about his visit was after he had left, when she was sent for by the camp's Commandant, whom she had not yet met.

The Commandant, quite tall, correct, and upright, struck her as typically German. *Put a German in uniform*, she thought bitterly, *and he could not help standing to attention and becoming the perfect heel-clicking, saluting soldier. So different from the relaxed, often willowy, yet equally efficient British officer.*

'You're Madame Leibovici, are you?' he asked in crisp, perfect English.

'Yes.'

He looked at her for a moment, then said, 'Why do you use make-up?'

Bluebell stared at him, stunned at the irrelevant question. Apart from stage make-up in her dancing days, she had never worn much make-up except lipstick. She had lipstick in her handbag when she had been arrested, so that was the only make-up she was wearing now.

'I've always worn make-up. Why?'

'You know that Hitler doesn't like women wearing make-up?' he asked.

Bluebell's eyes flashed. 'Look, I'm married. And my husband has never said anything to me about my wearing make-up, so I don't know why I should worry about what Hitler likes.'

The Commandant glared at her and turned away. Bluebell felt like kicking herself. Now, surely, she would not get out; she did not want her child to be born either in the camp or at that depressing hospital down in the town. In any case, the diet they were living on was hardly suitable for any human being, let alone a pregnant woman. If the Irish nuns were leaving, then she ought to be doing her best to leave too. How silly of her to cheek this man, when she should have stood there, cap in hand, meekly accepting anything he wished to say about Hitler's diktats to women.

But she was lucky. Count O'Kelly must have performed quite a miracle to get her this far, or maybe he had used a bit of blarney, for she had only an Irish birth qualification, a birth which had occurred when the whole of Ireland was still part of Britain, which made her British-born as well, quite apart from the fact that she had been brought up in England, which made her position far from clear. Nevertheless, the Commandant bent over his desk and signed her release; then he handed her the paper. She was free!

Although the Germans could not and would not do anything for British people, they seemed to be all for the Irish Republic, Bluebell noticed. Even the severe German Red Cross nurses changed their tone completely and became quite pleasant when they heard she was Irish. When she returned to her hut, she was exuberantly congratulated by the others and they all settled down to write letters to their relatives and friends in Paris for her to post when she arrived back in the capital.

One of the nurses came to the door. With a pleasant smile she said, 'You'll be leaving tomorrow. Will you please make yourself ready and pack your things in good time?'

'Thanks, but I have nothing to pack!' Bluebell said.

She still had only the clothes she was wearing when she was arrested; anything extra she needed, she had borrowed from the other women.

The following day, six of them left the camp together: the five Irish Sisters of Mercy and herself. They were driven in a truck down to Besançon station just before midnight. The train was due to leave on the hour. As they helped each other down from the truck and walked on to the platform, the German soldier with them said, 'Now you must go to the booking office and buy your tickets.'

The nuns all looked at each other. One of them burst into tears.

'Don't be silly,' Bluebell exploded. 'Buy a ticket? What with? Do you think we've got money? Anyway, you brought us here, so why should we have to pay for tickets to get back? You didn't ask us to pay our fare when you forced us to come here. Now you can get us home.'

'This has nothing to do with us,' the soldier said. 'It's to do with the French railways.'

'It *is* to do with you. *You* brought us here and now *you've* got to get us back,' she fumed.

'What shall we do? We'll never get away now. The train will be here in a minute,' one of the sisters moaned.

Bluebell turned to her. 'Of course you'll get away,' she said impatiently.

The train was almost due in. Abruptly the soldier turned away and went to the telephone booth. A few moments later, he came out again. The train was coming in to the station.

'All right. Get on the train,' he said, and spoke to the guard and the ticket collector. The women were put in a third-class compartment.

The Sisters of Mercy settled down and made themselves comfortable for the night journey. It was strange to Bluebell, having spent some of her childhood in a convent, to see, for the first time, nuns taking off their veil, but the great winged headgear the sisters wore was hardly suitable for a long night's train journey, and in the camp, they had soon learnt to relax before strangers. She noticed that underneath their wimples they wore little cloth caps, and she marvelled at the way they had managed to keep the habits so starched and white in the camp. It was only when they removed the veils that she noticed they were much older than she had thought they were. The Mother Superior was at least seventy-five, and the youngest could not have been much more than ten years younger. Camp life, even for nuns whose whole lives had been dedicated to stringency, must have been hard for them. But now they were laughing and joking, and they all behaved as though they were going on holiday.

It was, in fact, holiday time. They left Besançon on the night of 23rd December, and it was on Christmas Eve that Bluebell stood on the doorstep and knocked on her own front door. She had been unable to contact Marcel all the time she had been away, so he did not know she was coming home or where she had been.

She arrived just in time for Christmas dinner, although until the moment her amazed family had opened the door and seen her standing there, they had planned nothing in particular.

Now they went out to a little bistro in Rue Blanche, the proprietors of which were such old friends of theirs by now that they seemed just as delighted as the family at seeing Bluebell out of prison. There was only room in the bistro for eight or ten diners in all, and the friendly couple put the whole establishment at their disposal for what was, for them, the big evening of the year.

They had travelled right out into the country to buy black market turkey and Madame, through dint of carefully saving ingredients during the war months, had baked a Christmas cake. It was their first and last good meal of the war.

Marcel also had a Christmas present for her. But it was not a material one, though tangible enough. It was the news that, in a rather underground way, he was working once more. Neither he, nor Bluebell, being aliens, was allowed to work. But Marcel had met a wholesale tobacconist whose ambition it had always been to break into the musical side of show business. Marcel was writing and arranging music that the tobacconist put his name to and sold, for records, radio and live performances, and for which the tobacconist received good money. In return he gave Marcel cigarettes which he was able to exchange for food. In addition to this, Marcel and Bluebell's head girl, Babs Fox, had kept the girls at the Alhambra going, and had worked out the new numbers during Bluebell's absence.

Bluebell was now anxious to get back to her work, but first she needed a check-up with her doctor, who tut-tutted and fussed over her as if she were an underfed Christmas turkey. He announced that she was suffering from malnutrition, was underweight for her condition, was thoroughly run-down and, 'in no fit state to have a baby, mon Dieu!'

He gave her a tonic and told her to see him every few days for a few weeks. On her way home she called at the Place Vendôme to thank Count O'Kelly for getting her out of the prison camp and was told that it was 'no trouble at all, at all.'

To Bluebell, right then, he was a saint. He told her that within a few weeks, all the other pregnant women at the camp would be returned home, even though they were English. Furthermore, a complaint had been received from the British

Red Cross who had heard about the terrible conditions at the Besançon camp. They had sent an official message through the Red Cross that Germans interned in Britain were living in far better conditions than those of the British interned on the Continent and were protesting strongly. As a result, he said, the Germans were planning to transfer the Brits at Besançon to the more comfortable climate of Vichy.

Bluebell was very glad to learn later that this had in fact happened. She hated the idea of Sally and Kitty and other friends she had made in that bitterly cold camp staying there for the rest of the war.

MARCEL'S FLIGHT

ONE DAY, WHILE BLUEBELL was clearing out a drawer, she came across a yellow badge among Marcel's clothes. She asked him what it meant. What he told her froze her with horror, and made her realise that, far from being a united happy family once more, what happiness they now had might be temporary.

The year 1942 saw the second phase of the Nazi's Final Solution, following upon the operation of mobile killing units in eastern territories of Europe, which had begun the previous year. The second phase of mass murder, including concentration camps, stretched across all the German-occupied territories of Europe, including France. In May that year, while Bluebell had been away, an order had been given that all Jews report to their local police stations within forty-eight hours.

Marcel had recalled that as a boy he had never been fully aware that he was Jewish – he had only become conscious of the fact the day that his music professor at the Conservatory of Music and Drama had mentioned it. Now he was proud of his Jewish heritage. Without hesitation he had reported to the police station and registered. From then on, all Jewish adults had to sew yellow stars on to their clothing. They were not allowed to go into theatres, cinemas, or any place of entertainment; and they had a twelve-hour curfew every night lasting from 8 pm to 8 am. The Germans stuck notices outside theatres and cinemas stating: 'Forbidden to Jews and dogs.'

Like everyone else, Jews had to carry passes, but the word 'Jew' was stamped on theirs in yellow.

It was perhaps this kind of oppression which was beginning to rouse Frenchmen and women all over the country from passive resistance to the active Résistance movement. France had gone through a period of apathetic defeatism, and for months the country had seemed stunned by their defeat for it had happened so quickly. Now the population was recovering from its first shock and the Résistance movement was gathering in force. Because of one or two incidents, the Germans had put up notices in Paris stating that for every German soldier killed by the Résistance, fifty Jews and fifty communists would be executed. For every second German killed, 500 of each would be killed, then a thousand…

Already Marcel had several friends in the movement, and from time to time they informed him of Jewish friends who had disappeared and were able to tell him which concentration camp they had been sent to. Because things were becoming too risky for all Jews, Marcel no longer wore his garish yellow star for fear of being summarily arrested in the street and sent to Auschwitz or Dachau, the two camps to which many Jews in Paris were being sent.

Already his family doctor, Dr Benedict Vecsler, a socialist and a Romanian Jew, had lost his wife. She had been taken away and later they learned that she was gassed at Auschwitz.

Bluebell realised how difficult it was for Marcel to work at all. The composing and arranging he was doing in secret was bringing in some food; in addition he was now writing and arranging music for a well-known man in show business, who was putting his name to Marcel's work and thereby collecting half the fees. Paulette was still with them, and very soon there would be another baby, another responsibility.

Bluebell considered herself very lucky she had her work at the Alhambra to return to, and she quickly choreographed new routines and polished up the girls' performances with a spate of rehearsals.

Her costumes, too, needed augmenting. One day Marcel heard that the Jewish owner of a big store in the Marche Saint-Pierre, known to all Parisians as the 'Land of Fabric', had been arrested, and a relative of his was endeavouring to sell all his stock on his behalf before the Germans could confiscate it. Bluebell took out all her savings, hurried to the warehouse containing most of the stock, where she bought up 50,000 francs worth of silks and satins. They were to last her the rest of the war.

Bluebell was amused to see that Madame Derval, Paul Derval's wife, was also there, buying up material. She had not heard from them since the war had started, nor was she to hear of them again until the end of hostilities. But she learned that the Dervals had also left Paris for a while, as she had done, and, in their absence, the Germans had taken over the Folies Bergère. Derval had hurried back to find the Germans planning their own show there and had protested. Consequently, Derval was back in his old work in the Folies

Bergère, putting on mainly French shows; of course, now there was a liberal sprinkling of grey German uniforms in the audience, where evening dress had once been seen. Bluebell wondered who was running troupes for them now. It was only later that she heard that one of her former girls, Mabel, the one who had taken over Josephine Baker's lover, had now also taken over Bluebell's job of running a troupe at the Folies Bergère.

By now, her own Alhambra Belles were becoming quite famous, and the shows they appeared in were first class. Stars like Édith Piaf and Yves Montand played in them to packed houses every night. Piaf performed in various nightclubs and brothels which flourished during the war. Various top Paris brothels, including Le Chabanais, Le Sphinx and Chez Marguerite, were reserved for German officers and collaborating Frenchmen. However, being popular with German soldiers did not necessarily mean collaboration: Le Chabanais doubled as a place of safety for downed British airmen on their way to the Free Zone because 'the Madam and her daughter are ardent supporters of de Gaulle'.

Along with a number of others, including Piaf, Bluebell was invited by Colonel Feldman to take part in a concert tour to Berlin. She refused on the grounds that as she had a British passport and had relatives who were fighting against the Germans, she could not *for a moment contemplate entertaining your troops*.

Opening night every fortnight was as important to Bluebell as any annual opening at the Folies Bergère. Throughout her professional life, Bluebell was never to miss an opening night, except one. Due to the curfew, even doctors had to be indoors by 11 pm, and thus, on a Saturday night in April, Dr Lamaze had to give a protesting Bluebell an injection to precipitate the arrival of her second son, Francis. His opening night coincided with the only opening night Bluebell ever missed, a particularly successful one.

Over the course of 16th and 17th July 1942, 13,152 Jews in Paris were rounded up, including more than 4,000 children. The majority were held at the Vélodrome d'Hiver stadium for five days, with virtually no food or water, before being deported to concentration camps.

On 17th July, a friend in the Résistance telephoned to say that Marcel would be arrested the following day. Marcel had only a few hours to get away; his friend urged him to leave immediately, giving him directions to follow. In order to avoid attracting attention, he packed nothing and that evening he said goodbye to Bluebell and walked out into the summer evening to the nearest Metro.

What happened to him later came to Bluebell in regular bulletins through the Résistance. There were a great number of Jews in the Parisian theatrical world. Now they were being persecuted, there were many Jews who had formerly been in show business, who were actively supporting the Résistance. It was therefore through old friends in the business that Bluebell heard of Marcel's movements, and it was former colleagues who sped him on his escape.

By then the railway network was working normally again, and Marcel caught the 8 pm train that evening from Paris to Bordeaux, arriving at seven o'clock the following morning.

The French demarcation line was the boundary line marking the division of France into the territory occupied and administered by Germany (le Zone Occupée) in the northern and western part of France and the Free Zone (le Zone Libre) in the south created by the Armistice of 22nd June once France had fallen in May 1940. The Free Zone was nominally unoccupied and known as 'Free France', although the people there still lived under strict military control, like the rest of the country.

Pierre Larrieu, the pianist they had known at the Folies Bergère, was now living permanently at his family home in Bordeaux, and he met Marcel at the station. It was not safe, Pierre told him, to stay in Bordeaux; he would have to go on to a small town twenty miles further south. He gave Marcel the name of a contact in this town, and within an hour had found a bicycle for him to make the journey. Marcel cycled on to his next rendezvous, where he was met by another member of the Résistance, who specialised in passing people to safety. He took Marcel to the door of a jeweller's shop, made a sign through the door, went in, gave a password and then left without saying any more.

The old watchmaker behind the counter looked at Marcel and said, 'You can pass in one hour's time, or perhaps two hours.'

Then he gave him a book of watches to look at so that if anyone came in, he would look like a customer choosing a watch. After two hours, someone arrived and took Marcel to a small house on the banks of La Gironde river and handed him over to another man, who rowed him across the river. There he was left, once more alone.

On this side of the river was a large wood, patrolled on one side by French gendarmes and on the other by German police. The idea was for Marcel to pass through the wood while both the gendarmes and police and their search dogs were eating. It would be a difficult part of the journey, crossing the wood, but providence was to play a big part in what happened to him during his flight. Marcel met a young girl who lived in the small town on the far side of the wood which he was trying to reach, and the child accompanied him to the outskirts of the town. To anyone looking, they would have seemed like father and daughter. He then reported to a small hotel which he had been told about.

Meanwhile, the police came to Bluebell's apartment to arrest Marcel, and she had to explain why he was not there. He had gone, she said, long before; they had quarrelled and parted months ago. The police left but no doubt they formed their own conclusions.

Hundreds of miles away to the south, Marcel sat self-consciously at an hotel bar and ordered himself a drink, not daring to talk to anyone, but listening carefully to everybody else's conversations. Before long he heard that the previous night the gendarmes had found three Jews whom they had been seeking, and the three had been shot that day.

He felt even more apprehensive when two gendarmes walked in and sat down at the bar next to him discussing with three men who had been shot. The proprietor of the hotel, a member of the Résistance, took Marcel aside later that evening and told him the situation was too dangerous at present for him to stay there, and that he must leave early the next day.

Feeling rather like a hot potato that everybody was trying to pass to someone else, Marcel left by train at six o'clock the following morning for the next big town, Marmande, and reported again at an hotel, the proprietor of which was yet another member of the Résistance. Here, once more, he was told things were getting so difficult he would have to move on the following day.

He spent a wakeful night in one of the hotel rooms between two others occupied by German officers, and the next morning the proprietor gave him false identity papers and sent him on his way to Montpellier. Here he was met by a former colleague and this time he was able to remain in one place for fifteen days, staying with the musician and his family. But at the end of this time, his friend told him he was terribly afraid of keeping him any longer. He had a wife and two children and all their lives might be in danger if they were found harbouring someone wanted by the Germans.

Marcel knew there was a Résistance safe house in the mountains where he could hide until the situation eased, if it ever did. But he did not want to do that. He needed to earn his living, and he felt that perhaps he could do that on the Riviera, where many musicians in the same position as himself were now living. His old friend Jacques Charles, whom he had known since 1928, was now living in Cannes. Marcel decided to try to join him, travelling via Marseilles, where he could meet his old friend, Dr Vecsler, who had been in flight since his wife had been murdered at Auschwitz.

When Marcel got off the train at Marseilles, he was delighted to see Vecsler on the other side of the platform barrier, waiting for him. But his friend made a discrete signal to him not to approach and Marcel saw the reason why. He had to pass three rows of policeman before he could get through the barrier: one of French gendarmes, all in navy blue; one of French police; and the third, an immaculate line of pearl grey, the German police, all wearing glittering chains and insignia. Marcel knew that to walk on might mean questioning and arrest, but to halt might cause suspicion.

Providence worked again. A chattering crocodile of schoolgirls passed by, walking towards the barrier. Marcel hastily attached himself closely to the group of teachers at the rear, and passed through, unquestioned. Once out of the station he dived into a taxi in which Vecsler was waiting for him.

The news was bad. He had landed in Marseilles right in the middle of a terrible three-day purge. The Germans had forced the government in Vichy to do the same as in Paris, and in three days, 8,000 Jews were arrested and deported. Now trains were too dangerous to travel on; inspectors could come through them and examine travellers' papers in transit.

Instead, Marcel went on to Cannes by car. Jacques Charles met him there, but during his three days in that city, Marcel had to change hotels each night to avoid being caught. The morning after his arrival in the town, he reported to the office of the Résistance, and was introduced to the Chief of Résistance. He told Marcel that thenceforth he must call himself 'Marcel Lebeau – Youth Control Officer.' He was asked to leave all his real papers there, and the following day they would give him a full set of false ones.

But the next day, when he turned up at the Résistance offices, he saw police cars outside. At the time of the raid nobody had been in the office except a secretary, who had rushed out of the back door when the cars drove up, leaving all the papers, including Marcel's, for the police to find. He had no choice now but to get to his mountain retreat, Saint-Geniez d'Olt, as quickly as possible. He arrived there on 9th August 1942.

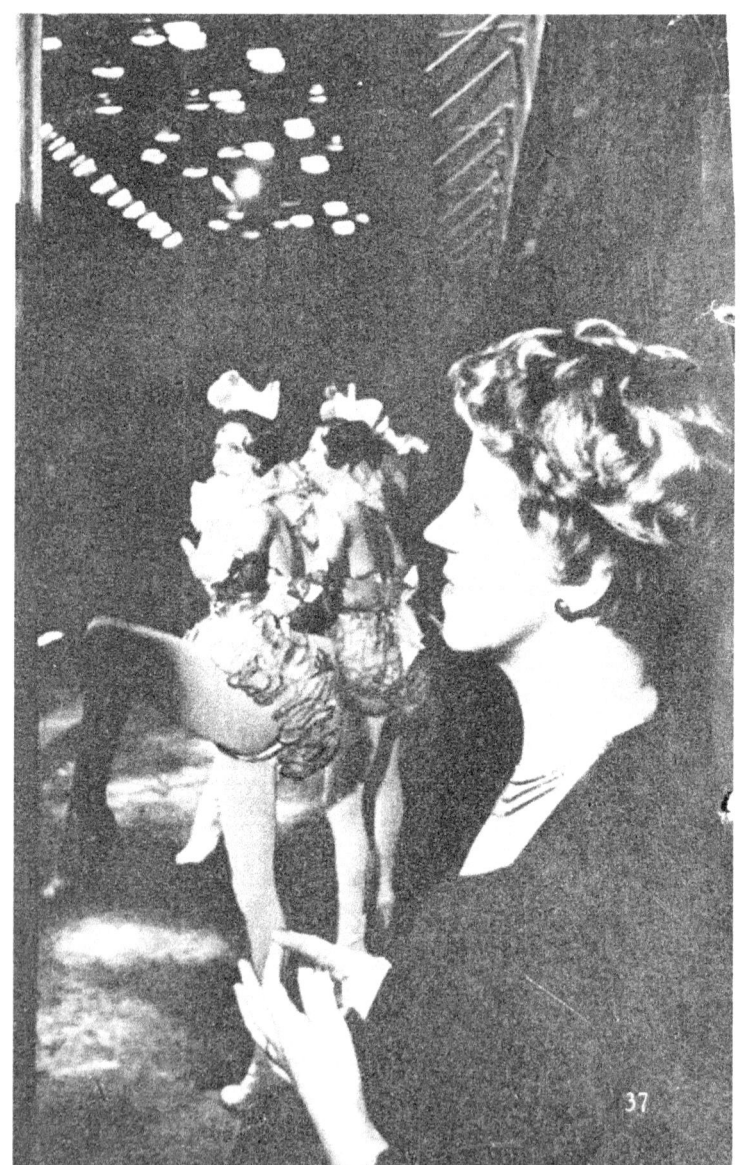

BLUEBELL ALONE

IT WAS AT THIS TIME THAT it was announced that the revues at the Alhambra would come to an end within two or three months. Now Bluebell had to quickly find more work. She had two babies and the invaluable Paulette, as well as herself to feed. Furthermore, she was in the precarious position of harbouring someone the Germans were looking for – Marcel's cousin, Anita, who had lived for some time in Paris with her mother. Bluebell had hardly known them before the war, but one day, soon after Marcel had left, the Germans raided their ghetto and, while her mother was being arrested, the girl had escaped through the staircase window at the back of the building, shinned down a drainpipe and made straight for Bluebell's apartment. Anita never saw her mother again.

It had been announced often enough that you risked death if you sheltered a Jew who was being sought. Bluebell's problem was that, being British, she was far more likely to be raided by the police than most people, and she asked Anita not to go out of her apartment unless it was absolutely necessary.

But regularly Bluebell would find that Anita had slipped out to go shopping, or to visit friends. Many times she had quarrels with her about it, but nothing would stop the girl. She would doll herself up and go out as if it were peacetime. It was decidedly risky for her, and not at all good for Bluebell, if only because it was always suspicious if various people were seen coming and going from the same door.

Bluebell was faced with the bleak prospect of searching for a job, when her very nationality prevented people from being able to employ her. But she had to work; there were five of them to keep, and God only knew what might happen to Marcel, wherever he was. He could not help the family now; all she could do was pray for him.

Her old theory that one door opened when another closed seemed to have given out on her, and she was ready, like someone drowning, to clutch at any straw when, in fact, a straw and nothing more was thrown her way.

Another door was beginning to open, but only a chink of light showed through. She was helping to bath the children at home one day when the telephone rang. She did not know who it was speaking, but the voice told her there was a small troupe of eight girls who were to appear in a short run in a Paris theatre before going on a tour of military camps. It was a French ballet company, and they had nobody to arrange their work. *Would Miss Bluebell be willing to choreograph a couple of numbers for them?* She kept her voice calm and business-like as she accepted it. After all, it was only one small job, and when the troupe left for the tour, that would be the end of it.

The French girls were a very pleasant group, and the weeks of rehearsals helped to take Bluebell's mind off her domestic worries. Every week she had a bulletin about Marcel, but he did not know that his aunt had been arrested, nor that his cousin Anita was sheltering with Bluebell. Throughout his flight he heard very little about his family.

Eventually the French troupe was ready to leave. Their two-week run in Paris was a success and Bluebell was paid off. From time to time her girls at the Alhambra asked her what their chances of work were after the Alhambra shows came to an end. Bluebell had nothing to offer them. She could not approach anyone for a job, as it would be dangerous for anyone to employ her. She could only hope that the telephone would ring again.

It did, but, as before, Bluebell did not recognise the voice at the other end.

'Miss Bluebell? You do not know me, but I am telephoning on behalf of a Monsieur Antoine Peretti. You have just finished choreographing for a troupe of girls who have recently left Paris? Yes? One of them worked for Monsieur Peretti and he came to watch a rehearsal and was very impressed. He would like you to come to see him. Would this afternoon at three o'clock be suitable?'

Bluebell felt like shouting for joy. *Yes, of course she would come. Yes, yes, tell Monsieur Peretti she would be there. Thank you, thank you.*

Monsieur Peretti was Corsican and very charming. He owned a small club called the Chantilly in Rue Fontaine, Montmartre. He admitted that he had crept in to watch one of Bluebell's rehearsals with the French girls in a practice room in Rue Blanche, near her apartment. One of the girls had formerly worked for him at the Chantilly, and she had told him about Bluebell. He had heard, of course, about her work in Paris before the war and he would be very honoured if she would assemble and manage a troupe to perform in a cabaret at his club every night from midnight till 3 am.

Bluebell agreed right away but could not be sure what sort of person he was, nor what kind of club was the Chantilly. She told him she could only do the work on one condition – that the girls would not be allowed in front of house. In spite of the war, she intended to keep up her usual standards. Monsieur Peretti agreed, a contract was signed and Bluebell was back in business. He wanted her to start as soon as possible, which meant asking her Alhambra Belles if they were willing to 'double', meaning to work for the remainder of the Alhambra contract in addition to going on to perform at the Chantilly afterwards each night. In this way they would be assured of continuous work when the Alhambra revues ended. Without hesitation, the girls agreed.

Babs was head girl once again. The eight dancers consisted of Babs, four French girls and two Greeks, and one excellent Russian dancer, Irina Borowsky, a former beauty queen who had once been described as 'Miss Russia'. They were a glamorous troupe, and in addition there were twelve showgirls, who were no less good-looking. There would be a change of show every two weeks and Bluebell had to supply the costumes. Once more the maid's rooms upstairs were ransacked and costumes dragged down while the young women all worked together in busy sewing parties.

Due to the curfew, Bluebell had to stay overnight at the club at the beginning of the show, because, being British, she had no late pass. But eventually she took the nightly risk of cycling home in the middle of the night. Her bicycle had now become essential to her, for her car had been confiscated by the Germans after she and Marcel had returned from Bordeaux. Nearly all Paris now either walked or cycled. Ironically, before the war, Parisian designers had been constantly looking for ways to make cycling appear elegant, though divided skirts had to be disguised once the occupying forces placed a prohibition on women wearing trousers. Inevitably, Bluebell became an expert cyclist. Every two weeks she somehow had to balance a bag containing about 60 kg of costumes on her handlebars to take to the club. The materials she had bought earlier during the war were now coming in very useful.

By opening night they had managed to produce a cabaret show that looked from the front as sumptuous as any pre-war show. No one would have guessed that it was a make-do-and-mend presentation, and although, without Marcel's help, Bluebell had used old music scores, it came over well. The music, if not new, was tried and tested. Some of it was American, despite the prohibition on playing 'enemy music'. All the old Folies Bergère lavishness was on display; girls wore daring little costumes and straw boaters, or floor-sweeping sequinned evening dresses with the huge white ostrich feather fans Bluebell had bought so many years ago after *The Great Ziegfeld* production. It was the kind of elegance that Parisians had grown to hunger and thirst after in these days of bleak austerity.

Now Bluebell was earning a regular salary, she was able to send Paulette and the children away to live in the country, while she continued to inhabit the apartment with Anita, who had now been with her for three months. It was difficult providing for her without a ration book, though things were easier now Bluebell was earning money, and extra food could be bought through the black market.

With Paulette and the children away, however, Anita was still more restless alone at home and it was increasingly difficult to keep her indoors. One day, when Bluebell was preparing to go out shopping at the Galeries Lafayette, Anita asked if she could come with her. Bluebell had almost given up trying to dissuade her from going out, and she agreed, knowing that Anita would go out on her own anyway if she said no. It was a lovely summer's day and it seemed harsh to insist that she stay indoors in such weather.

As they walked along the sunlit street, Anita was telling Bluebell about some silk scarves she had seen in a shop window the day before. She would rather like to have one. Bluebell was looking about her to make sure there were no uniforms about and was prepared to walk Anita down the nearest Metro if she saw any.

Suddenly, two youths, wearing open-necked shirts and sports jackets, wandered over to them.

'*Vos papiers, s'il vous plait.*[27]'

Bluebell gaped at the two boys, with their curly blonde hair and civilian clothes. They looked like students.

'Why?' she asked.

'Because we want to see them.'

'What about yours?' she said tartly. 'Who are you?'

'Police.'

'Can you prove that?'

They showed their cards. They were police alright; French collaborators. Bluebell gave them her papers first, including her British identity card.

'How is it you are a British subject and are not in a camp?'

'I've been in a camp, and was released by the Germans.' She gave him her release paper which she always carried about with her.

---

[27] French: Your papers, please.

'Alright.' They handed back the papers.

'Now you,' they said to Anita.

Anita produced her false French identity card, issued in some northern province. She had been born in Romania but had lived in France since she was a child and had been educated in Paris.

'How is it,' began the youth, 'that you have a French identity card when you have a Romanian accent?'

Now Bluebell had no doubt they were police, juvenile though they looked, for it was obvious they had been trained for this kind of work. In all the months Bluebell had lived with Anita, she had never noticed a trace of accent in what she regarded as her perfect French tongue.

Anita could not answer them.

'You must come with us to the police station,' they said to her. Turning to Bluebell, they said, 'You can go.'

They took Anita by the arm. Twisting round as she was led away, she burst into tears and shouted to Bluebell, 'Please do something!'

It was the last Bluebell ever saw of her.

Bluebell went straight home and telephoned her friends in the Résistance, but nobody could do anything for Anita now. The Résistance could do little once a person had been taken. At the same time friends in the Résistance urged Bluebell not to let herself be incriminated as a result of this incident.

Peretti was particularly upset when he heard what had happened. It was bad enough, he said, to be a British citizen in occupied France, but to be married to a missing Jew and harbouring another one...

One morning at six o'clock, Bluebell was sleeping soundly in her apartment, when there was a loud banging at the door. Dead with sleep, for after coming home from the Chantilly club at 3 am she had been asleep for less than three hours, she got up and stood behind the door.

'Who is it?'

'Police.'

'Wait a minute.'

She had never been one for facing strangers decked out in all her night-time glory. She stumbled back to her room, took her hair out of curlers, put on a dressing gown, washed her face and cleaned her teeth. She must have left them about ten minutes standing at the door but was still too dazed with sleep to realise that the delay itself would make them think she was hiding something. She opened the door and found three men standing there: two Germans and a French interpreter. She invited them into the dining room.

'Your name?' the Frenchman asked. She told him.

'You have been hiding Mademoiselle Zelermu.'

During all the months Anita had stayed with her, Bluebell had never bothered to make a note of her surname. It was another example of her absent-mindedness and anyway she had other things on her mind.

Now the fact that the name meant nothing to her, especially in her sleepy early morning state, gave her a heaven-sent breathing space.

With genuine surprise she said, 'Hiding a Mademoiselle Zelermu? I don't even know who you're talking about.'

'You must know. She has been living with you for three months. She was arrested while walking with you in the street.'

It was only then that Bluebell snapped awake. Of course. Anita.

'Ah yes, I remember. She was a girl I had met a couple of times before. We had been introduced somewhere. I met her in the street that day and was talking to her when these two men stopped us.'

He looked at her reflectively for a while, then said, 'Well, she says she's been living with you for three months.'

'Look, you've only got her word against mine. You've got to believe either her, or me.'

'We would like to look around.'

'You're perfectly at liberty to do so.'

They searched the whole apartment, under the beds and in the wardrobe, even in the dirty linen bin in the kitchen. At length they left, saying, 'We'll speak to her again and we'll contact you.'

Anita had also given away the Frenchwoman in the Résistance who had issued her with her false identity card. The woman was more unfortunate than Bluebell, for she was called up to the Prefecture of Police and confronted with Anita. She knew Anita was lost and could see no reason why she, who could still help those who were free, should be taken too. She swore that she had not given the girl the card, and Anita swore that she had. Eventually they let the Résistance worker go.

There is no doubt that Anita went through a punishing grilling, but what vexed Bluebell more than anything was the thought that had she remained in hiding, she need never have been arrested. So often when people were caught after finding a safe retreat, it was their own fault. They were responsible because they did not only involve themselves, but also the people who were shielding them. So often the core of the Résistance movement was endangered by the careless practices of a few of the very people whom it was trying to help.

For days the policeman's words *We'll speak to her again and we'll contact you* rang in Bluebell's ears. She knew now why so many people took fright and disappeared, thus convicting themselves and ultimately leading to their own capture and arrest. But somehow, she had no fear of the Germans, and it was possibly this impassive attitude which saved her in the various interviews she was to have with the Germans and the police later. By being stoical and quite genuinely unafraid, she behaved as only an innocent person would, though as far as her knowledge of Résistance work was concerned, she was far from innocent.

Her only fear was of the consequences of her possible imprisonment. The last time it had not been so serious, because she was able to leave Marcel with the child. Now there were two children, and no Marcel to provide for them in her absence, and Marcel himself might need her help.

Bluebell realised how deeply involved she was. Her husband was a Jew in hiding. She had been harbouring a Jew. Her family doctor was another Jew in hiding and she was even employing, through the Résistance, a well-known Jewish theatrical designer who was in hiding in Paris.

After this, her apartment became a regular calling place for police searching for suspects, and they always came in threes: two Germans and a French interpreter. They were not necessarily looking for Jews each time; sometimes they were searching for British military personnel whom they thought might be there because she was British. Nearly always the police called early in the morning, at about six o'clock. In all they called about seven or eight times, usually looking for people she had never heard of. They did not always search the place, but when they did, they invariably, to her chagrin, searched her dirty linen bin.

While people in England and America were singing the nostalgic war-time song, 'The Last Time I Saw Paris' and dreaming about the gay, feminine city they had known before the war, renowned for its bright lights, nightlife, excitement and beautiful girls, and looking forward to the time when once again they could enjoy Paris and all that it meant, they were unaware that the flame of Paris cabaret life was being kept alive by a British woman.

The Chantilly prided itself that its clientele was largely French, and that the Germans who came to see the show were in the minority. It seemed to be established right from the start that certain theatres were 'German' and others 'non-German'. This, however, did not prevent Germans going into whatever theatres or cabarets they pleased, and sometimes they came into the Chantilly.

By now Bluebell wasted no love on the Germans. They had broken up her family, deprived her of her husband, dispossessed him of his job, hounded him into hiding and made it difficult for her to work.

When she was out with Babs, she always made a point of talking in a loud, English voice whenever there were Germans about. One time they were walking along the street together when a car full of German officers stopped by them, and when one of them asked in French the way to the Opéra,

Bluebell replied in English, 'I know where it is, but I'm not telling you.'

They just laughed and drove off.

All the time she tried to frequent places not normally used by Germans. The little café near the Chantilly was one such place. It was owned by a Frenchman they called Gérard, who was a real patriot, and Germans were rarely seen there.

One day, when Bluebell and Babs were sitting drinking coffee in the bistro after a rehearsal, a German soldier came in and paused when he heard the girls talking in English. With a rather pronounced swagger, he came over to them. In English, he said, 'We've conquered France. Britain will be a breakfast for us.'

Bluebell looked at him coldly over her cup.

'Often breakfast gives you indigestion,' she retorted, and he stomped out.

But the German occupational forces were not all the same. One evening Babs and Bluebell went into the café between shows. A young and rather inebriated German soldier was there when they arrived.

'Really, Gérard, why do you have to…,' Bluebell began to ask the proprietor, who was by now an old friend of theirs.

'Shhh!' Gérard hissed. 'This boy has just learned that his father and two brothers have been killed on the Eastern Front and now he, too, must leave for Russia tomorrow.'

But the boy had overheard. Slowly he pulled himself to his feet, came over to their table, gave the girls a drunken salute and staggered out.

Those Germans who spoke English – and there were many of them – always seemed rather proud of the fact. One elderly officer, who came into the Chantilly and was having rather too much to drink, asked the band to play 'Roses of Picardy'.

During the war no music written by the 'enemy' or by Jews was supposed to be played, especially such a well-known British tune as 'Roses of Picardy'. For about ten minutes, the orchestra tried to ignore the officer's repeated requests for the song, but he was persistent and eventually the band struck up the first few bars, whereupon the German rose and, standing unsteadily to attention, sang the whole of the song to the accompaniment of the band, in perfect English!

Bluebell now had sixteen girls in the troupe at Chantilly, dancing in a revue that lasted until 1 am, followed, after half an hour's break, by a cabaret. She was happy in the thought that she was well established in work again, Marcel was sensibly hiding out at the mountain retreat, and the children safely established in the country with Paulette.

And then, one day towards the end of 1942, her brittle castle of contentment was shattered again. Gui Delamaniere, the local Résistance chief, called on her to tell her that Marcel had been taken away to a concentration camp.

MARCEL INTERNED

MARCEL'S DISCOVERY WAS the result of the most dreadful misfortune. After Marcel had been safely in hiding for some months, he had decided that it would be a good idea if his old Romanian Jewish friend Dr Benedict Vecsler, whom he had last seen in Marseilles, could join him and hide out with him. The big house Marcel was hiding in belonged to a good friend who was quite willing to take in another refugee. Vecsler, who had been living in fear of arrest in Marseilles, readily agreed to come, and arrived by train. From the station he had to take a bus to the house. He did not know the district at all, and when he gave his fare to the driver, he asked to be put down at the house. Sitting near him, however, was a French gendarme in plain clothes. It must have seemed suspicious for a man with a foreign accent to be asking his way in a small town.

Within one hour of Vecsler's arrival at the house, gendarmes arrived and demanded that both Marcel and Vecsler should go with them to the police station to be interviewed by the French chief of police. They had the choice of two courses of action: to produce their false papers and make up a story, or to tell the truth and hope for leniency. They told the truth and after their interview they were both allowed to return to the house.

It was a harrowing night for both of them. Any moment they expected the police to call and arrest them. In the middle of the night Vecsler, who had already lost his wife the same way, could bear it no longer and made his escape.

The following day Marcel was arrested. He travelled for two days and nights by train first to Marseilles and then to the Rivesaltes internment camp near Perpignan in the Pyrannes-Orientales, near the French border with Spain. This notorious camp was used to house more than 60,000 'undesirables' before and during the war. From January 1941, the Vichy regime used it as a transit camp, where Jews, gypsies and communists were held prior to being sent to Nazi death camps in Eastern Europe. Later that year it housed an estimated 8,000 prisoners, 3,000 of whom were children. During one three-month period in 1942, nine convoys carried 2,313 Jews to Auschwitz.

There were two sections in the camp, one for Spanish people (men, women and children, some of whom had been born in the camp), all refugees from as long ago as the Spanish Civil War; the other section was for Jews. The two sections could see each other across the barbed wire. It was the sight of the Spaniards that horrified Marcel more than the Jews. The Spanish refugees, who had been suffering from severe malnutrition in the camp for nearly eight years, walked around the camp, staring vacantly.

Some had no clothes and they lived on what even the other camp inhabitants described as 'dirt' – potato peelings and rotting vegetables. They were far worse off than the Jews there. Every night the Spaniards would crawl under the barbed wire which separated the two sections of the camp, at the risk of their lives, to collect the garbage from the Jewish sector.

For a long time, Bluebell heard nothing, and she passed numbly through the weeks in a state of fearful tension. Then bulletins began to come in more regularly. Marcel remained at the camp near the Spanish border through the bitterly cold winter. Every three days the German officers would march round to all the barracks, each containing twenty-five prisoners. The officers would give the prisoners five minutes to pack all their belongings together as if to move. Then they would make them stand to attention by the wooden plank 'beds' on the earthen floor, sometimes for six or seven hours, until a number would be called away and taken to Dachau and Auschwitz, where many were executed.

During the time Marcel was there, about 2,000 were taken away from the camp, 1,800 of them from the non-Spanish sector. However, three Jewish prisoners were always passed over as they were married to Catholics. It was the first time that, quite unknowingly, Bluebell saved Marcel's life. Presumably the Germans felt that someone who was married to a Catholic could not possibly be a fully practising Jew.

In March 1943, a prison commission was sent from the Vichy government to Rivesaltes and the cases of the three prisoners married to Catholics were examined. It was decided to send them on to labour camps. They were taken first 150km up the coast to Montpellier, which had become a huge sorting post, from which prisoners were sent out to neighbouring labour camps. Thousands of prisoners were collected there that day, and they were all ignominiously herded into a field, where they had to sit on the ground under the surveillance of a German soldier carrying a sub-machine gun.

As they sat there, a man cycled past on the road. Marcel glanced at him idly, then looked harder, and realised that the man on the bicycle was an old friend, a lawyer, who lived in Montpellier. Marcel could not cry out to attract his attention, and yet strangely it was as if he had, for suddenly the man turned and looked into the field of prisoners, and his eyes rested almost immediately on Marcel. Almost falling off his bike, he walked into the field and asked the officer in charge for permission to speak to one of the prisoners, explaining that he was an old friend.

Then he came across to Marcel. He had to be brief, for the officer had allowed him only half a minute, but he said, 'I can't do anything for you right now, but when you know where you are going, please get a message to me somehow.' And he gave Marcel his address.

Marcel felt that any labour camp must surely be an improvement on the one he had left, but when he arrived at the labour camp in Gignac, he found that the only improvement was that the prisoners housed there were not condemned to be sent to concentration camps in Germany. If anything, the conditions at Gignac were far worse. The internees were subjected to incredibly hard work and a near-starvation diet, conditions under which they could not expect to survive for very long. The prisoners slept on the frozen earth floor of a decrepit old church, which had neither windows nor doors and was running with rats.

Prisoners had to get up at 5 am before leaving in trucks to travel the seven miles to the fields where they worked. This area had been a rich flower, fruit and wine growing district before the war, but now the grapevines were to be torn down and vegetables planted in their place by the prisoners. They started work at 6 am and all they had to eat throughout the day was a cup of lukewarm black liquid called 'coffee' at 10 am and later a dish of clear, tasteless soup containing two or three potatoes, bread and cheese, and more 'coffee'. On Sundays, each prisoner would be given one small piece of dry meat. On this diet they had to work hard; if they did not, they would have to walk the seven miles back to base at the end of the day as a punishment. Marcel lost no time in getting a message to his lawyer friend in Montpellier.

His friend quickly found a way to help him. Twelve miles away from the camp was a Spanish labour camp where conditions were better than at Gignac. The prisoners there managed to organise a weekly concert, to which the German officers in charge were always invited. During the rest of the week the performers worked as hard as the prisoners in Gignac, though the work differed because their area was still a wine-producing one.

One day, about a month after Marcel had been at Gignac, the pianist in the Spanish camp, whose job it was to heave the wine barrels about, had his fingers crushed by a barrel and could no longer play the piano. Marcel's friend immediately informed the commandant at the Spanish camp that there was an excellent professional pianist – from the Folies Bergère, no less – at the Gignac camp.

Marcel was bundled into a truck and taken to the other camp to find that he had to arrange a concert for the very next day. He could not go back to Gignac that night and had to sleep, without covering, on the floor at the Spanish camp before getting up early to prepare for that night's concert.

The following day after the performance, he was sent for by the commandant, a German colonel, who informed him that it had been the best concert they had ever had and told Marcel that he wanted him to stay permanently at the Spanish camp.

Now that he had something to sell, Marcel realised that he was in a position to bargain: he said that if his living conditions were going to be as bad as they were at Gignac, he would rather return there, where at least he could speak the same language as most of the other prisoners. The colonel agreed to strike a deal: there was no one to do the clerical work in the office, and if Marcel could undertake this work, as well as the weekly concerts, he would see to it that his living conditions would be improved. Marcel agreed, walked the twelve miles back to Gignac, rolled up his few belongings in a blanket and walked back.

Marcel threw himself into the task of reorganising the office at the Spanish camp. The bureaucracy resulting from the paperwork associated with the 6,000 Spaniards imprisoned there required a great deal of organisation. All the records and reports were in a chaotic state, as hitherto there had been no one to deal with them.

Within three days Marcel achieved an orderliness in the camp office which had eluded the camp officers for three years. The work also gave him ideas. Although his standard of living was now significantly improved, he still wanted to get back to Paris. In the office there were identity papers for every prisoner in the camp; there were also permits issued to prisoners to leave the camp – day or half-day passes. With all these at his disposal, Marcel planned his escape.

Whenever anyone escaped from the camp, 20,000 copies of their pass and their photograph would be made and circulated to all police stations in France. Before acting, however, the authorities would wait three days while the neighbourhood was searched. The Colonel signed hundreds of blank passes for Marcel to issue, and now Marcel signed one for himself, then systematically destroyed all his own papers.

Every week his friend in Montpellier contacted him and then sent Bluebell a message to let her know how Marcel was getting on. Learning by this means of Marcel's escape, she relayed a message to Gui Delamiere, asking him to help her find a hiding place in Paris for him. Gui, who had been at music school with Marcel, travelled down from Paris across to the 'other side' – so-called 'Free France' – to escort her husband back. He took with him a set of false papers for Marcel, who once again had to change his name, this time to Marcel Lenoir.

After they had spent the night in Montpellier, they travelled back to Paris. Bluebell did not dare to meet Marcel at the station, for it would have been too dangerous. With tremendous bravado, Gui operated his Résistance service from his studio in Place Saint-Michel, right opposite the Préfecture de Police on the Left Bank, facing the Île de la Cité, and here Marcel stayed hidden, not going out once, for six months.

Bluebell and her principal girls backstage at the Lido, Sunday Times, 1961. Photographer: David Montgomery

PARIS AGAIN

BLUEBELL CYCLED THE four kilometres from their apartment to Place Saint-Michel as soon as he had moved in. It was difficult to believe that this was Marcel, for he had changed greatly, and was very thin. But he was back, something for which she had hardly dared to hope, and that was all that mattered. There was a telephone in his room and through this she was able to keep in daily contact with him. Even so, they had to be careful and they used a telephone pass system. She would let the telephone ring four times, then ring off. She would repeat this twice more, and then Marcel would know that it was her and answer.

As soon as Marcel arrived back in Paris, Bluebell was able to give him work to do. They were still changing numbers at the Chantilly regularly, and finding fresh music without a resident composer had proved very challenging. Now at last they had a composer, though someone else had to sign the music which Marcel wrote and arranged and for which the signatory received half Marcel's payment. At the same time, Marcel resumed writing music for the wholesale tobacconist for whom he had previously worked at the beginning of the war. Bluebell went to his room on the Left Bank and described the new show she was putting on – one that was to run for three months and she wanted everything to be absolutely fresh for it.

Without a piano, Marcel went to work on the scores. He had returned to Paris spilling over with new ideas; perhaps he was simply glad to be back at work again – or maybe it was a mixture of both – but the music for this show was as good as anything he had ever done before. It was exciting and Anglo-American in tone – the kind of music no one was producing in Paris at that time.

When the opening night came and the first bars of Marcel's music crashed out, Bluebell could have cried to think of him sitting alone in the silence of his small room. She stole into the theatre office and telephoned him, then carried the telephone across the room and left the receiver on a table by the open door so that he could hear his music being played. And in his room at Place Saint-Michel, Marcel sat and wept as he listened to it.

In the theatrical world it was well known that Bluebell was working at the Chantilly. Friends in the profession knew where she was, but apart from her duties at the club, she did not do much work for other people; they did not dare to ask her too often because of her nationality. However, about this time a woman whom she knew, Jeanne Sonale, opened a small theatre called Les Optimistes, where she put on revues. She asked Bluebell to choreograph and rehearse three shows for her. Bluebell agreed.

It was during a morning rehearsal at Les Optimistes that the office clerk there approached her and said, 'Mademoiselle Bluebell, someone wants to speak to you.'

She walked up the auditorium wondering who it could be, for she had kept it very dark that she was working there.

A pleasant-looking Frenchman, in civilian clothes, was waiting.

'Could I speak to you, please?' he asked.

'Yes, of course.'

'Where?' He looked about him. Clearly this was to be a private interview.

'In Mme Sonale's office,' she suggested and led the way.

The Frenchman seemed very discreet and well mannered, if not a little embarrassed. When the door was securely closed, he explained, 'I've had a letter from the German authorities regarding you.'

'Well, what would you like to know?'

'They have had a letter from someone saying that you are a British Jew and that you are still practising your business in Paris.'

This was a new approach.

'Well I'm certainly British,' she said. 'But do you think I look Jewish?'

'No, I can't say you do. What are your particulars?'

She told him she had been born in Dublin, and had been baptised in the Catholic cathedral there, and that she was on her own in Paris.

'Could I see your papers?' he asked.

'Certainly, but I'm afraid they're at home.'

Bluebell excused herself from the rehearsal and they went to her apartment in Rue Blanche, where she showed him her baptism certificate, her birth certificate, and her Christian marriage book.

After he had examined them all, the Frenchman turned to her. 'Thank you very much. I'm sorry, very sorry. You understand I do not do this of my own free will, but when the occupying authorities contact us about anybody, we have to check up on them.'

'Of course,' Bluebell responded. 'I quite understand that. If they want any more particulars, tell them to come to see me themselves.'

It seemed a shame that this polite young Frenchman had to do someone else's dirty work.

At the door he stopped.

'This is not the first denunciation you have had. You have been denounced before. I think that is why they made me make a formal check on you this time.'

She stopped him. 'How many times have I been denounced?'

He hesitated. 'Five times,' he said and left.

Bluebell walked back into the apartment with a slow smouldering rage gathering strength inside her. Who could have denounced her five times? Who could have harboured such a vendetta against her that they had gone so far as to denounce her? Certainly she could not think of anyone in the business who could be guilty of such a degree of professional jealousy – and yet, was it possible? She knew that information leading to the arrest of a Jew was often rewarded in cash. Were people getting so desperate for money that they were creating Jews where they did not exist? It made her feel sick.

She sat down and buried her face in her hands. If it wasn't enough that her husband's life was in constant danger, now people were denouncing her. And on top of this, she was going to have another baby.

Throughout those war years, when Bluebell was living alone, she had three good friends on whom she could always rely: Babs, her English head girl at the Chantilly, and a dancing double act called Florence and Frederick, who had been friends of hers since the Folies Bergère days. Close though these friends were, Bluebell did not dare to tell even them of Marcel's whereabouts. As far as everyone else was concerned, Marcel was away, probably in a concentration camp or perhaps worse. Bluebell always kept her private affairs to herself and never talked of them, a habit which probably stemmed from those very tender and proud teenage days, when she was too ashamed to invite anyone home.

At the Chantilly everyone knew her as Mademoiselle Bluebell and some did not even know she was married. No one at the Chantilly knew that at least twice a week, sometimes daily, Bluebell cycled across Paris to the Left Bank to take loads of food to Marcel, it being imperative that he should not leave his hiding place. She had a box on the carrier at the back of the bicycle to put food in, and a big bag on the front for his washing which she always did in her apartment.

She was becoming quite a strong cyclist, for the box and bag were used on other days to transport loads of costumes, which she carried down from the sixth floor above her apartment and took to the Chantilly. The bicycle, in fact, was doing the work of a small van. In the end, as her pregnancy progressed, Marcel grew increasingly anxious; he finally telephoned Dr Lamaze to inform him about her strenuous pre-natal activities. *Let her do exactly what she has always done,* was the doctor's advice, and Bluebell pedalled on.

She was seven months pregnant when two Frenchmen arrived at her apartment and told her she must report immediately for an interview with German intelligence. They waited while she put on a jacket and fetched her handbag and then escorted her to Avenue Friedland, where many of the Gestapo authorities were situated. It was one of several beautiful avenues in Paris, which doubtless many people all over the world throughout the war were recalling with nostalgia. But in the minds of many Frenchmen, for decades thereafter, their very names evoked fearful memories.

She was shown into a spacious, beautiful room and was left alone for an interminable wait, wondering what they wanted this time. With a sudden cold fear, it struck her that they might have caught Marcel.

A voice said in French, 'Will you come this way?'

She followed someone into a large elegant office. Her guide silently withdrew and closed the door. At the far corner of the comfortably carpeted room an enormous German officer with a great bull-like head sat behind a king-size desk. Flanking him were two outsized, good-looking German officers. They looked a formidable trio, and Bluebell could only assume that the two young officers were there to protect this Titan from her, a woman 5'4½' in height and seven months pregnant!

'Sit down, will you please?' the seated German said in French. 'Which language would you like to speak in?'

'In my own language, of course.'

He turned to one of the officers. 'Will you bring in Frau Kleiner?' he said in German.

A little white-haired German woman came in. She looked frail and must have been about sixty-five years old. The German inquisitor barked at her and she turned to Bluebell.

'We would like to know where your papers are,' she said.

Bluebell produced a British identity card, which she handed over to Bull-Neck.

Another bark. 'We would like to know where your husband is,' she said.

Bluebell tried not to show any emotion, but this must surely mean that they had not caught him after all.

'I think he is in Germany. I believe he's been deported,' Bluebell answered.

'Where was he before?'

Bluebell named the work camp where he had last been.

'We want to know where he is now. You must tell us.'

'How should I know? You ought to know. You took him away.'

It was obvious to the Germans that Bluebell understood German, just as it was clear to her that Bull-Neck could both understand and speak English. The poor old lady's presence was superfluous, but neither Bull-Neck nor Bluebell would speak the other's tongue; occasionally Bluebell accidentally jumped the gun and answered before the woman could translate, and so did he. The translator grew more and more embarrassed and was softening in her translation of some of the questions he was firing at Bluebell. Now he blazed the questions directly at Bluebell in German and only momentarily waited for the translations. Bluebell fired her answers back at him in English.

'When did you last see your husband?'

'Eighteen months ago.'

There was a momentary silence. It was hardly the answer to be expected from a heavily pregnant woman, but surprisingly enough the next obvious question never came.

'Wouldn't he like to see his children?'

Bluebell waited for Frau Kleiner to translate. Then she turned to the little woman.

'Will you ask him if *he* has any children and would *he* not like to see them? I presume many men want to see their families, but tell him that because of his country, they can't.'

Frau Kleiner turned to Bull-Neck. 'This lady would like to know if you have any children, and if so, would you not like to see them?'

But she did not translate the rest. She was clearly upset, and Bluebell decided that she was the only pleasant German to whom she had spoken during the war.

Frau Kleiner turned to Bluebell and said in as comforting a tone as possible, 'It is not because they want to harm you that they are asking these questions. They just want to find out the names of those in the Résistance movement.'

The Colonel exploded. 'Are you here for us or for this woman, Frau Kleiner?'

'I'm here for you, sir,' she said, shakily.

'I don't know anything about the Résistance. I don't know where any Jews are, nor where my husband is,' Bluebell repeated stolidly.

The interview went on and on. Questions were repeated and so were the answers. The Colonel became more and more threatening.

At last the inquisition came to an end. She had come through it only by answering the questions as belligerently as the Colonel had put them. But she felt exhausted as she was escorted home by a French official. It seemed clear to Bluebell that he was a collaborator.

As she went in to the apartment he stood in the doorway. He looked across to the bathroom door which was open, at the line over the bath with Marcel's clothes hanging to dry. Then he looked her up and down with a slight sneer. Bluebell shut the door on him.

She did not dare to telephone Gui, nor Marcel, that afternoon to warn them. It was more than likely her telephone would be tapped. In the end she cycled over to the Left Bank to see Marcel at four o'clock the following morning after the Chantilly show had ended.

The only time that Marcel stirred out of his hiding place in Place Saint-Michèle was when Bluebell gave birth to her third child on 22nd October 1943. She went to the same clinic that she had always attended, the Bologna, a beautiful building which had once been the castle of Napoleon III. Marcel had been present at both previous births and because Dr Lemaze was not entirely happy about Bluebell's condition, Marcel wanted to be with her now, whatever the risk. This time there were complications. After what seemed a very long time, she heard Marcel's voice begging the doctor not to perform a Caesarean because he did not want her to be scarred, but Bluebell had given up caring one way or the other.

Bluebell's gentle-natured daughter Florence, named after Bluebell's dancing friend, was to have a slight tremor in one hand ever after, possibly, the doctor said, as a result of the birth. Bluebell believed that the complications were not the result of cycling or carrying heavy weights during the previous months; rather they were due to the nervous strain she had been under during her husband's ordeals – the result of months of fear, the most stressful months of her life.

Babs' time as a Bluebell Girl was soon to end. Her husband, who had been a musician in private life and a non-combatant during his service in the French army, was released from his prison of war camp. The first thing he did on arriving in Paris was to telephone the Chantilly; but Babs, who knew nothing of his release, was dancing on stage at the time and was unable to come to the telephone. Her surprise and delight when he arrived there that night was such that the whole of the company, being both theatrical and Gallic, a combination of humanity and emotion, dissolved into tears of happiness for the young couple. Of course, she stayed on at the Chantilly, for, like Bluebell, Babs had kept the family finances on an even keel while her husband had been away, and it was still necessary to continue to do so for a while. But it was not long before she, too, was expecting a baby and within a few months she left.

Bluebell envied her. Other husbands were coming home from prisoner of war camps, but hers had to remain in hiding, it seemed indefinitely. Bluebell had taken a great risk three weeks after Florence's birth when she had taken all her children to see their father for the first time since he had fled Paris; but when they had arrived home, Patrick had yelled out, 'On a vu Papa!'[28] to someone before she could clap her hands over his mouth, and she knew that it was too much of a risk to let the children see their father again.

Soon after this, Gui Delamaniere's secretary was denounced, and the Germans raided her apartment, which she also used

---

[28] French: We saw Daddy!

as an office and meeting place for members of the Résistance. She was in the apartment at the time but escaped via a back door. In her hurry, she had to leave behind the papers, records, names and addresses, literature and documents connected with Gui's Résistance work, including his own address, where Marcel was in hiding.

All this fell into the Germans' hands, and the secretary rushed to the nearest telephone box to call Gui and all the other Résistance workers likely to be affected. Gui did not dare to return to his own apartment, but telephoned Marcel and told him to get out within ten minutes, giving him the name of a hotel in which it would be safe for him to seek refuge. The proprietor of the hotel, a Madame Easer, was working in league with the Résistance, and she gave Marcel a small, secret cupboard-like room facing on to the courtyard. It would have been a pleasant enough spot for him to stay permanently, but she was afraid to keep him and told him he must find another place within a week.

Bluebell could not visit him in the hotel because one could never tell when an hotel might be raided. The police would only have to look at a name on the guest list and go straight up to the room. If Bluebell were with him, they could both have been caught. For the sake of the children, at least one of them must remain free. So they met each day under a bridge nearby, for all the world like a couple of clandestine lovers. Gui was not able to go back to his home for two or three weeks. Even then it was out of the question for Marcel to return there.

After a week, a tiny apartment on the Left Bank was found for him, consisting of a diminutive room, a small kitchen and a bathroom. It sat within a large, old house in the Latin quarter and belonged to a frail, white-haired lady of about eighty, one Madame Steadmann, who also acted as concierge.

Once more, Bluebell resumed her practice of taking loads of food and washing across to Marcel twice a week. The tide of the war had changed and she felt that she would not have to keep Marcel in hiding very much longer. He had not been able to do any regular work after the Folies Bergère had temporarily closed down in 1939 and when work did come his way, he seized upon it eagerly. But by the time others had received their cuts for appending their names to his music, there was little money left for him.

Bluebell felt sorry for Madame Steadmann, who looked such a weak, old lady. Every time Bluebell went to see Marcel, she gave her two or three thousand francs – the equivalent of about $40 at the time, which was quite a large amount of money and considerably more than was paid to the landlady by other refugees whom Bluebell noticed coming and going at her address – presumably all with their own tales to tell of their struggle to survive. Bluebell also gave the old lady food and her rations of tins of Nestlé milk, which she had stored up for Marcel instead of consuming during her pregnancy.

Gui kept in contact with Bluebell, and it was not long before they heard that yet another key Résistance worker had been arrested. This one knew of Marcel's hideaway, and Bluebell was worried sick as to whether the Germans would be able to get the information out of their prisoner. She was due to call at Marcel's apartment the following day but decided she must cycle across Paris that night, before, perhaps, the Germans themselves called. A friend had recently sold Bluebell an almost new racing-style bicycle, with narrow wheels and dropped handlebars, and Bluebell could get up quite a speed on it. Although it had been a boon throughout the war years, her old bicycle had become very worn. It had borne many a burden, from skips full of cabaret costumes to anything up to 15kg of food for Marcel and also his washing, quite apart from herself in varying stages of pregnancy. Now she would fairly bound along on this latest machine and she estimated that she could shave several minutes off her previous best time across Paris from Rue Blanche to Marcel's hideout.

That night she wheeled her bicycle away from the Chantilly at 3 am and pedalled off, with a load of potatoes and other vegetables on the front and various tins of food and clean laundry on the back. It was quite a long way from the Chantilly to Marcel's place on the Left Bank but she knew that if she went fast enough, she would not be stopped by anyone. But as she turned into the tree-lined Boulevard Saint-Michel, heading towards the Pont Saint-Michel and the Place Saint-Michel, her narrow racing wheel slipped into the junction of a tramline.

Before she knew what had caused it, she was flying over the handlebars and found herself lying on her face in the road, blood pouring from her nose and mouth, and potatoes, carrots, tins and laundry lying all over the road around her. She was so winded that at first, she could not get up, and then, as she raised her head, she saw four boots right in front of her eyes. Looking up, she saw two policemen standing above her with their bicycles.

'What are you doing here? What happened?' one of them asked.

He had every right to ask the first question. She was breaking all the rules being out during curfew.

'It's alright, please. It's nothing. I'm not doing anything. *C'est rien, c'est rien.*[29]'

---

[29] French: It's nothing, it's nothing.

Bluebell had never managed to speak French with anything but a very plain British accent, and in times of stress it became even more pronounced. There was no doubt now that the gendarmes thought she was an Englishwoman trying to escape from somewhere. They would want to know where she had come from, and where she was going, with all that food and laundry. She could feel herself beginning to sob. The shock and the taste of blood and her teeth all loose in her gums combined to destroy all the confidence she normally exhibited in the face of officialdom. Her ribs were stinging and she still had not got her breath back.

Huge numbers had been recruited into the gendarmerie during the war and it was difficult to know where their sympathies lay from one individual to another. What kind of gendarmes would these turn out to be? She was fortunate on this occasion.

'You'd better hurry off. You know you shouldn't be out here. Get on your bike and go away quickly, and if you meet anyone else on your way, don't say anyone has seen you.'

Frantically she fumbled around on the cobbled street hurriedly gathering together the scattered vegetables and tins and the now-soiled laundry. Mounting her bicycle, she pedalled away as fast as she could.

By the time she reached Marcel's door she was in a bad state; she could not stop crying, her two front teeth were very loose and her nose was still pouring with blood. Marcel thought it was the police pounding on the door, because she had not been able to let him know she was coming at that time of night, and at first, he would not open it, until Bluebell cried out who it was.

The bleeding would not abate, but Marcel could not call a doctor – medical assistance was out of the question for hidden refugees. She stayed most of the remainder of the night lying on his narrow bed while he put a cold wet cloth on her nose, and she tried to explain why she had made this unexpected call. She was afraid that even at that moment, the Germans might come. But Marcel decided to stay and bank on the Résistance worker not giving him away. He was right. In any case, he told her, Madame Steadmann was very good to him. He was sure he would be safe where he was until the end.

The months went by and winter turned into spring and summer. On 6th June 1944 the long-awaited Allied invasion of northern France, codenamed Operation Overlord, began. Fighting was intense and the advance slow and costly. In many of the towns they reached, the Allied soldiers encountered ecstatic demonstrations of support from the local people. Marcel remained in hiding, for Jews were still being rounded up.

News of the Allied advance became erratic and although the battle for Paris itself began on 15th August, Bluebell did not realise how close the Allies were until the evening of 18th August, when the proprietor of the garage down the road telephoned to say her car had gone. The Germans had left a receipt for her, which she could exchange for compensation the next day at the Head Transport Office.

So this is how the Germans are going to make their glorious exodus, she thought, *in French cars. Well, they'd find her battery flat.* But she realised that this meant the Germans would be off within the next twenty-four hours, with her car, and everyone else's, it seemed, leaving Paris immobile.

At the transport office the next morning the Germans would not pay her the 4,500 francs they owed her unless she produced her grey motorist's card, which she had not carried around for years. There was nothing for it but to cycle all the way back across Paris from the Transport Office near the Arc de Triomphe and return again before 11:30 am, when the Germans were moving out of the city.

As she cycled away, she wondered whether to go home through the back streets to Montmartre, which was certainly the quickest route. Then she thought, *No. It's a beautiful day and I've got time. I'll go down the Champs Élysées.* Bluebell had always loved the Avenue des Champs Élysées, the most beautiful street in Paris.

On this particular morning the sun was shining from a cloudless sky and birds were singing in the trees flanking the handsome avenue as she cycled along with about twenty other people, all on bicycles; somebody was whistling 'The Continental' from the Fred Astaire and Ginger Rogers movie of 1934, *The Gay Divorce*. The Arc de Triomphe was behind her and the Elysium fields swept like a broad silver ribbon down towards the Place de la Concorde which she could see shimmering in the heat haze way ahead.

As she approached it, she noticed two big black police vans, full of young men and boys, while men, who looked like officials of some sort, put yet more boys inside. She thought to herself, *Oh, those poor kids. Fancy getting taken just now, at the end of it all.* It had been a dismal, regular sight – people being bundled into police vans throughout the Occupation. Before she reached the Place de la Concorde they had gone, and she began to pedal across.

It was only then that she became aware of the explosions. Cars backfiring, she thought, for all sorts of fuel was being used other than petrol, and cars struggled with what they were expected to run on.

Then she noticed that all those other cyclists who had been with her in the Champs Élysées had disappeared. There were no cars, no cyclists, no pedestrians, nothing, in a great city square, 500 paces across, in the middle of the day.

Then, just as she was circling the Egyptian Obelisque in the centre of the Place, BOOM, BOOM, BOOM, RAT-TAT-TAT-TAT, and all at once she knew what was happening. This was no car backfiring; it was machine-gun fire and mortar shells, and it was all going on right there in the square. She had cycled in solitary splendour across no-man's-land with a battle raging around her and machine gun bullets whistling across her handlebars.

Christ! she thought, falling to the ground with one leg sticking up in the air, the bicycle still between her legs. Those boys being put into the police van, she realised, were being gathered up by the Résistance to help with the battle. This indeed was the case. The patriotic French – 'all men from 18 to 50 able to carry a weapon' – were being roped in to join the struggle against the escaping occupying forces. The Résistance, with their mortars and machine guns, were massed to Bluebell's right, on the banks of the Seine beyond and below the low stone balustrade. To her left was the Ministry of Marines.

Bluebell had fallen down near the Obelisque, right in the middle of the square, facing the Ministry. She could see the German machine guns on the Ministry window ledges, pointing, it seemed, straight at her. The whistles of mortar shells mingled with the whine of machine gun bullets, and Bluebell remained frozen in the same ungainly position.

After a quarter of an hour there was a lull, and Bluebell began to pray. *Now let it stop, let me live, please God let me live. Don't let me die after I've got through so far. Let it stop.*

Her head crunched down again on the gritty road as the battle recommenced. Dust flew up into her face and she could see nothing now; she could hear distant groans and hideous gasps of pain – people who had tried to run for it, she supposed, the other civilians who had been less absent-minded than she. Her fellow cyclists, who had either dispersed into the woods of the Champs Élysées near the Place de la Concorde, or thrown themselves down by the stone barricades near the Ministry, could by now all be injured or dead.

The noise was shattering. Suddenly, all that the war had meant for her welled up inside her to a roaring crescendo. The persecution and the denunciations, the death of friends, the imprisonment, the constant inquisitions, the fight to get work and the dread secrecy she had maintained all the time; the fears and worries about Marcel; not knowing, when he was in concentration camps, whether he was dead or alive; hiding and keeping him in Paris; never talking about herself to anybody, so that she could hold the family together somehow and work to keep them fed. She had been both man and woman in business, father and mother to her family, breadwinner and comforter. But now all her woman's instincts screamed out against this mad, unnecessary fighting and the life that had been put upon her.

Just as suddenly as it had begun, the battle ended, at exactly a quarter past eleven. It had only lasted thirty minutes, but it had seemed like hours. Bluebell lay there, shaking with sobs, a solitary woman in the centre of the square. All the firing had gone over her head in that first battle of Paris. Now the silence was as nerve-wracking as the firing had been.

A German, who was by the Ministry and carrying his submachine gun, walked towards her. She watched his approach with horror, *What a fool!* Suppose one of those fight-starved Résistance boys had one more bullet left and tried to get the German and shot her as well.

Still lying on the ground, she yelled at him, 'Get away! Clear off! Leave me alone!'

Another German was coming up behind him, and the first stopped abruptly when he heard her shrieking at him in English. He shrugged his shoulders at his comrades.

'She is English,' he said; and then an attempt at a joke: 'They are already here, it seems!'

Bluebell was crying hysterically, her face covered with stinging mascara and road grit, her white summer's dress ruined, torn and dirty. She stumbled to her feet and unsteadily began to walk away, still weeping and cursing.

After about thirty yards, she remembered her bicycle. It was no use leaving that behind; she shrugged her shoulders and walked back to fetch it. She had no chance now of getting any compensation for her car anyway, and she did not care anymore. Too shaken to get on her bike, she pushed it away from the battle scene and started to walk towards the pavement on the far side of the Place.

As if by magic, a number of people materialised out of hiding places and came rushing up to see if she was alright, and she could only keep on repeating that *I thought I was – yes, I thought so*. But she could not stop shaking and sobbing.

By the time she reached home, her mind was made up. She could not live alone under these conditions anymore. She needed Marcel back. Soon after her arrival home, he telephoned and, still snuffling, she blurted out what had happened. The Germans were leaving anyway, and there would be no more persecution of Jews. Marcel left his hiding place for the last time, walked across Paris and arrived at the apartment in Rue Blanche at last, a free man. It was the first he had seen of his home for more than three years.

From this moment onwards, Paris seemed to be embroiled in the worst turmoil she had experienced during the war. The eleven days of fighting were bloody and chaotic; almost 1,500 Parisians died in the struggle to expel 20,000 occupying German soldiers as well as collaborationist snipers, who fired from rooftops throughout the city. Theatres and nightclubs closed and during the six days between the first day of the German retreat and the arrival of the Allies, battles raged throughout the city. They had begun on 19th August with the battle of the Place de la Concorde, of which Bluebell had been such a close observer, and from then on it had not been safe to cycle anywhere in the city.

Even if the Chantilly had remained open, Bluebell could not have reached it, for it was not even safe for her to go out of her own front door, as the Rue Blanche was on the Germans' exit route. There was a constant stream of German tanks, lorries and cars containing German officers rolling past her building. Résistance fighters were installed in windows all around her flat, and were shooting at the escaping Germans, while up on the roofs, members of the 'Darlan', French collaborators, shot at the Résistance fighters in the windows below, Frenchmen shooting Germans and Frenchman shooting Frenchman.

A few days after Marcel's homecoming, he and Bluebell heard that Madame Steadmann, the little white-haired old lady who had harboured Marcel, had been arrested by the Free French forces and accused of denouncing Jews and Communists. Confounded, they left the safety of their apartment and cycled all over the Latin quarter until they found the police station where she was being held. By convincing the superintendent that the old lady had protected Marcel for six months, they secured her release.

However, a few days later she was re-arrested. This time the superintendent was obdurate when they went back. Grimly, he produced Madame Steadmann's file. It gave detailed and conclusive evidence of nine denunciations of Jews and Communists by the old lady, some of whom had been sheltered by her, just as Marcel had been, right up to the time of their arrest. She had received 2,000 francs from the Germans for each denunciation.

'It was for money, no less, that she sent those people to their deaths,' he told them.

Bluebell and Marcel cycled home in silence, each knowing what the other thought. The frail-looking but treacherous old woman must have carefully weighed up whether or not to denounce Marcel. Only because Bluebell had regularly given her an additional two or three thousand francs and some extra food had Madame Steadmann decided, rationally enough, that she was better off keeping him than denouncing him for a mere one-off payment of 2,000 francs. Bluebell's old habit of over-tipping and her pity for the elderly lady had saved Marcel's life, yet again. Madame Steadmann was shot that night.

An estimated 76,000 Jews were sent to extermination camps built by the Vichy government. Official estimates are that only 2,500 of them survived the war. Marcel was one of them. It is, perhaps, unsurprising that there was a wave of retributions. Grievous crimes committed by domestic traitors – such as Mme Steadmann – had swift trials and were often followed by swift executions.

On 26th August, only eight days after Bluebell's terrifying ordeal in the Place de la Concorde, the Champs-Elysées witnessed a very different scene. General de Gaulle, having spent the war sheltering in England, made his triumphant walk alongside the Allied Forces down the tree-lined boulevard, with thousands of people shouting 'Vive de Gaulle!'[30] as he did so.

If the Allies expected to see gay Paris awaiting them, they were disappointed. It was a bruised, if not battle-scarred city, with all its theatres and cabarets closed which greeted the liberators. The Chantilly had closed down completely, without any immediate signs of reopening. Bluebell, though now free to work openly, was out of work once more.

It was the Alhambra, as at the beginning of the war, which came to her rescue. It was one of the first to return to business as usual, this time under different management. The impresario, Bruno Coquatrix and the band leader, Ray Ventura, put on a series of operettas starring the singers Yves Montand, the ballet dancer Ludmilla Tchérina and the French comedian, André Bourvil. The Alhambra operators struck just the right note for the rather bleak post-war period. While film companies were already busy making war movies and other theatres continued to put across 'the sort of stuff to give the troops' – of which troops and civilians alike were already tiring – the Alhambra plunged into a world of fantasy. The sight of Bourvil dancing underwater with a crowd of Bluebell mermaids was precisely the sort of ridiculous nonsense that jaded post-war Paris audiences needed.

When the operettas finished, the Chantilly reopened, and Bluebell willingly went back to her wartime refuge. Then, to her surprise, she heard from Paul Derval for the first time since the outbreak of war. Derval had managed to keep the Folies Bergère open throughout most of the war – it being a favourite venue of the Wehrmacht occupiers, along with the Gaieté Parisienne. Derval now wanted Bluebell to form

---

[30] French: Long Live de Gaulle!

a troupe for his new peacetime presentation, to be called 'La Revue de la Libération'.

Bluebell gathered together a large troupe of French girls. She was in no hurry to bring English girls over to Paris yet. Everything was still stringently rationed – far worse than in Britain. The black market was rampant everywhere and hotels were difficult to book.

But rationing or no rationing, one person who just had to come to Paris was Aunt Mary, looking exactly the same as she had looked eight years before, or twenty-eight years before that. It was typical of Mary Murphy that, without knowing it, she had to arrive for her first visit to Paris on Bastille Day. When the family met her at the Gare du Nord there were flags out everywhere, bands playing and people dancing in the streets.

Mary stared at them, entranced. 'Oh, I love Paris! What a wonderful city, and what happy people!'

And she wanted to go and join in the dancing. She refused to believe that Paris was not like that every day of the year. Aunt Mary was as eccentric as ever – and looked it too. Bluebell's children loved her and her outré dress sense, and she adored them instantly, though she had never met any of them before.

Returning to an old and favourite haunt is not always a good idea. So often it does not live up to one's memories; perhaps it has changed, or possibly one's own standards have changed in the meantime. Or maybe it was, for Bluebell and Marcel, still haunted by the memory of German soldiers who spent so many of their leisure hours there. Paul Derval had provisionally offered Bluebell two year-long contracts at the Folies Bergère, but well before the end of the first year she asked him to release her from the second. Derval seemed surprised, even a little annoyed, because very few people tried to leave the Folies Bergère, but he agreed. Neither did Marcel return to the Folies. From now on he devoted his whole time to the management of the Bluebell Girls.

As soon as the war ended, Charlie Chaplin's 1940 film *The Great Dictator* came to France. It had appeared throughout all the unoccupied Allied countries during the war, and such had been its success that it was scheduled to run in Paris for eight months at the Paramount, where the Bluebells had danced before the war. Now a contract was signed for twenty-five Bluebells to dance in the programme presenting the film. But after only six weeks, one million French prisoners of war were brought back to France and many of them had to be housed somewhere in Paris. Several buildings were appropriated for this purpose and the Paramount was one of them. The film's run ended abruptly and the girls' contracts were cut short. The union – Le Syndicat de la Danse[31] – could only claim that it was due to force majeure. One cannot do anything about a chance occurrence or an act of God – but Marcel did, and the girls were recompensed for the rest of their eight-month contract.

Pre-war Bluebells began arriving in Paris again, including Bessie Bird from England with her little boy, to be reunited with his French father. Some Bluebells even arrived in uniform with the liberating army. One, a former Bluebell head girl, had returned to England when her French husband had been taken prisoner of war, had joined the French army in Britain, and had once even driven General Eisenhower's car in Normandy. Others had thrown themselves into quite unaccustomed war work. Nearly all of them had married.

Then one day Bluebell's former head girl, Dodo Felton, turned up in Paris with her husband. She telephoned Bluebell,

---

[31] French: The Dancers Union

who invited her to dinner. They had a pleasant evening talking of old times. Two days later Bluebell heard that Dodo had signed a contract with the management of the Lido – an up-and-coming nightclub in the Champs Élysées – to supply a troupe of British girls who were to be named the Mears-Felton Troupe, after Dodo and her husband. Although Bluebell waited for Dodo to ring to tell her more about the exciting new contract she had landed, there was no doubt that Dodo now considered herself a business rival. Bluebell never heard from her again, although Dodo remained in Paris for a whole year.

Bluebell's own work increased, and very soon she was expecting her fourth and last child. Hotels throughout Paris were opening up cabarets and Bluebells were dancing in them. In the first peacetime summer, Bluebells danced again on the Riviera and in Italy, and Bluebell and Marcel took the children on the only complete family holiday they were ever to have, in Monte Carlo.

Back in Paris, Bluebell acquired her first post-war English Bluebell girl, a pretty girl called Penny, who came to Bluebell and asked her for work. Bluebell engaged her, but shortly afterwards she received a stern note from Pierre Louis Guerin, the managing director of the Lido. Guerin had already made a name for himself in show business as a man of big ideas. He had been in the profession since 1933 and had been the owner of the '60' Club until the end of the war.

In 1946, he had been invited by two building contractors, the brothers Joseph and Louis Clerico, who had just bought the Lido with a view to making it a lucrative show venue, to take it over as general manager and partner. Guerin informed Bluebell that she had taken a girl who was still under contract to them. Without any fuss, Bluebell declared she knew nothing of any existing contract, but instantly offered

Leader Magazine, 1949

the girl back. Guerin was surprised and impressed by such straightforwardness and invited Bluebell and Marcel to see a Lido show.

When they went, they were intrigued. In size, the Lido was not very large, and yet it had enormous possibilities. It had a very good orchestra, but it was a fairly simple, straightforward and unpretentious cabaret. As Bluebell had to go on to the Chantilly that evening, she and Marcel only stood at the back, by the bar.

She almost jumped when she heard a voice in her ear ask, 'What do you think of the show?'

It was Monsieur Guerin himself, tall, good-looking, and about the same build as Paul Derval of the Folies Bergère.

Guerin remained leaning against the bar chatting for about half an hour. Then suddenly he turned to Bluebell and said, 'Why don't you work with us?'

While he had been talking, Bluebell had been watching the show and thinking of a thousand different ways a full-sized troupe of tall, long-legged British girls could be used on the stage. She turned and looked at him.

'Why not indeed?'

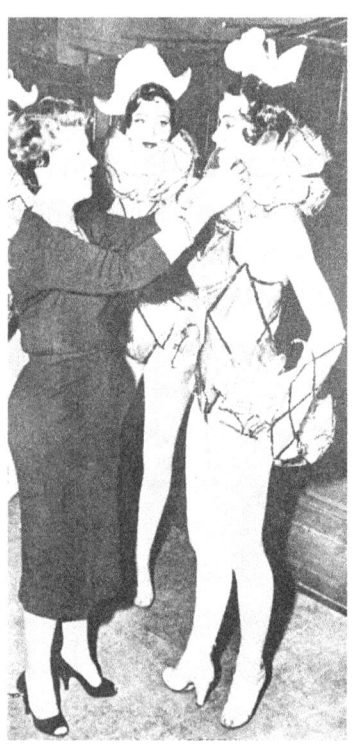

(Top) Bluebell perfecting a Bluebell Girls' costume before a performance, with the author's sister Eleanor Landreau in the middle

All photos from Illustrated Magazine, 1956

Donn Arden, creator of the famously provocative dance routines performed by the Bluebell Girls

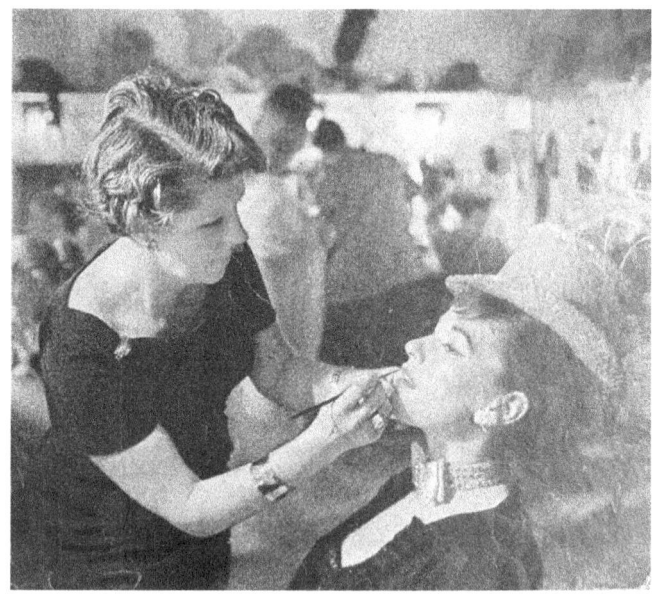

Miss Kelly helps 17-year-old Jose Downe

Bluebell dancers having tea at Miss Bluebell's Paris apartment

The Bluebells perform a vigorous Charleston to the music of 'Yes, We Have No Bananas' and 'Ain't She Sweet?' in the production number called 'How Beautiful You Were in 1925, Ladies'.

Photographs from Life Magazine, 1958

Elaina Stephen and Paula Colchester adjusting their hats and hair at the Moulin Rouge. Photographs from Life Magazine, 1958

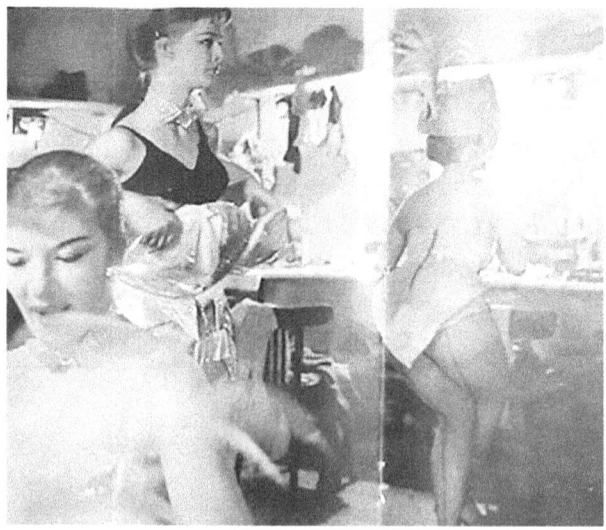

Miss Bluebell, London Daily Express

*Bluebell Girls backstage, Time Magazine, 1963.
Photographer: Loomis Dean*

Pierre-Louis Guérin, the director of the Lido

Bluebell's flat, March 1982

EPILOGUE

AND SO IT WAS TO BE through the Lido that the post-war resurgence of the Bluebell Girls was to come, leading to Bluebell Girls being invited to dance in as far-flung venues as India, Japan and the USA, and to the never-ending work without which Bluebell knew she would have been lost.

It was only when Marcel died in a car crash in 1961 that Bluebell knew that there was one door which was closed for ever.

In past struggles she often had doors closed on her and had to wait for another door to open before she could go on. Now every door seemed open and her path was strewn with successes. Future triumphs would include honours from both Britain and France; she was made an Officer of the Order of the British Empire, a Chevalier of the Légion d'Honneur, a Chevalier des Arts et Lettres, and a Chevalier de l'Ordre National du Merité. She even had an audience with Pope John Paul II.

Patrick emigrated to the USA and has been a realtor in the Las Vegas Valley since 1981. Florence also emigrated to the USA and became a top realtor in Las Vegas; she died in August 2016. Francois is a tutor and academic in France. Jean-Paul pre-deceased his mother in 1996 at forty-eight years old.

Bluebell died after a long illness, aged ninety-four, in Paris on 11th September 2004. On that night, two shows were danced in her honour at the Lido nightclub.

She is buried in Montmartre Cemetery. Jean-Paul is interred alongside her.

As to the world famous Lido, on 30th July 2022, it closed its doors for good after seventy years. Bluebell had been the driving force and choreographer at the Lido for over three decades. Her talent, resilience and hard work ensured her Bluebells were the best cabaret dance troupe in the world.

In a career spanning over six decades, more than 14,000 Bluebell Girls were to pass through her hands, their whole lives to be temporarily and sometimes permanently altered by their contact with her.

Fourteen thousand women, for many of whom their Bluebell career was the high point of their lives.

Many more Bluebell Girls continued to join the troupes across the world following Bluebell's death and continued to bring joy to many thousands of people for years to come.

POSTSCRIPT

WHEN I HEARD THAT Marcel's death had been announced in the *London Evening News*, I knew instinctively that it must have been due to a car crash. Of course, in those days, cars were not fitted with safety belts. Patrick was travelling on a business trip with his father at the time of the accident, and he told me his version of the event. He had been driving for some hours while Marcel slept. When Marcel awoke, he said that he would take over the wheel. The car engine was warm and responded to Marcel's acceleration while Marcel was not yet fully awake. The car crashed into a bridge at which point Patrick was knocked out as he tore through the roof of the Citroën.

When he woke up he found he was lying in the road. When he tried to get up, he fainted again from the pain of a broken ankle. When he came to the second time, he saw his father being carried on a stretcher to an ambulance. The sound of his father's laboured breathing through lungs punctured by broken ribs was enough to cause Patrick to pass out for a third time.

Bluebell was devastated and many thought that Marcel's death would signal the end of the Bluebells.

But with her habitual hard graft and resilience, Miss Bluebell decided to carry on.

For as they say in showbiz, the show must go on.

ABOUT THE AUTHOR

SYLVIA DISLEY (née Cheeseman) became an international athlete at the age of seventeen whilst still at school. She went on to compete in the Olympic Games in London in 1948 and in Helsinki in 1952, winning a bronze medal in the sprint relay. She also won two medals at the 1950 British Empire Games, as well as winning seven AAA British National Championships in seven years.

Sylvia entered Fleet Street as a journalist in 1950 and began working for a sports paper called *The Sporting Record*. She went on to write her own column in *The Sunday Graphic*, by which time she had managed to move away from sport and become a general reporter. She freelanced writing features for *The Daily Express* and *The Star* before being invited to join the staff of the latter. In 1960, she left *The Star* in order to write *The Bluebell Story*.

Sylvia's late husband was John Disley, the Olympic steeplechase medallist, and they had two daughters, Kate and Emma. Sylvia lives close to her daughter Kate in Leamington Spa, Warwickshire.

ACKNOWLEDGEMENTS

I send my deepest thanks and gratitude to everyone who has helped with this project, including the following.

Miss Bluebell, without whom there would be no story

Marcel Leibovici, who was able to give me so much comprehensive detail

Alfred Jackson, for introducing me to many Jackson Girls

Eleanor Landreau, my sister

The Bluebell Girls

The Jackson Girls

Paul Derval of the Folies Bergère and Pierre Louie Guerin of the Lido, who both gave Bluebell her biggest opportunities

My daughter Kate Disley, whose help with final edits and introduction to Book Brilliance Publishing, has been invaluable

Brenda, Olivia and Zara at Book Brilliance Publishing, for bringing it to fruition.